Derek A. Bardowell is the author ~~Race~~, a Sunday Times and Finan 2019. He is the CEO of Ten Yea and a Thirty Percy and Mission

'A rich and complex mix of impressive personal testimony, expansive cultural knowledge and analysis of systemic inequality ... Intellectual and passionate, brave and radical, it offers us new and improved routes forward.' Bernardine Evaristo

'A game changer in terms of how we need to look differently at how we approach philanthropy ... Derek provides a framework and mantra for policy makers, funders and the wider voluntary and community sector.' Patrick Vernon

'The book you didn't realise you wanted but desperately need! I will never think about charities in the same way again ... Bardowell shows how we can reimagine our idea of charities and giving without entrenching the very inequality that is inherent in the idea of the "rich" giving to the "poor".' Marcus Ryder

'An indictment of the world of philanthropy and charity through an unapologetic Black lens ... A book that is as much about class, race and music as it is about giving, by a writer who has been at the heart of Black Britain for decades.' Symeon Brown

'Bardowell delivers a delicious yet essential rallying call of a read that will do an enormous amount to help us all understand how we can enhance society.' Nels Abbey

'A thoroughly argued case for how charitable giving can be redesigned to make the difference it should be making. Raw, honest and beautifully written ... essential reading for anyone who wants to make the world a better place.' Angela Saini

'Equal parts poetic, heart-wrenching and actionable; Bardowell provides the system-level framework needed to change our world.' Charlotte Cramer

Also by Derek A. Bardowell

No Win Race: A Story of Belonging,
Britishness and Sport

GIVING BACK

How To Do Good, Better

DEREK A. BARDOWELL

dialogue
books

DIALOGUE BOOKS

First published in Great Britain in 2022 by Dialogue Books
This paperback edition published in 2023 by Dialogue Books

10 9 8 7 6 5 4 3 2 1

A CIP catalogue record for this book
is available from the British Library.

Paperback ISBN 978-0-349-70198-1

Typeset in Berling by M Rules
Printed and bound in Great Britain by
Clays Ltd, Elcograf S.p.A

Papers used by Dialogue Books are from well-managed forests
and other responsible sources.

Dialogue Books
Carmelite House
50 Victoria Embankment
London EC4Y 0DZ

www.dialoguebooks.co.uk

Dialogue Books, part of Little Brown, Book Group Limited,
an Hachette UK company.

To the Bardowells

To the social artists and outsiders within

'Reparations is what love looks like in public.'[1]

'I want for my people to want to live, not just exist waiting to die. There is a type of suicide that we don't speak about that isn't about actively attempting to die but not actively attempting to live.'[2]

—WHITNEY ILES
(Founder and CEO, Project 507), 2022

Contents

Part 3: Stand for something

Part 4: Just cause

Preface

GIVING BACK is a book about radically changing our approach to giving to good causes.

It is a book about the things we should consider before we donate money, time, resources, activism or ideas to contribute to a fairer society for all.

This is a book about what it means to embrace our hearts and reject our fears.

It is about looking beyond what we think is attainable and working towards making the unimaginable possible.

Introduction

Beyond the reserve's line

When my parents moved from Manor Park, east London to Chigwell, Essex in 1987, I discovered for the first time a place where I could walk in a straight line without my senses being disturbed. No more would sleeping bikes on the pavement, sirens, car beeps, soulless buildings with sharp edges, or the haunted, hollow sounds of the inner city disturb me. Chigwell did not move incessantly like Manor Park. Little to hear. Clear air. Country smells. Even when a violent wind blew, you didn't feel as if a blunt knife was scraping every inch of your face. It was quiet, peaceful, but sterile. A place for older folks, not young people. There was no colour. I missed the rattling chime of kids playing out in the streets, the aroma of creamed coconut and cumin wafting out of houses. I missed the warmth of the neighbours, a neighbourhood that didn't necessarily understand me but was familiar enough with my culture, my cultural presence, to embrace me. In Chigwell, I felt like a stranger in a recognisable land.

I quickly decided that I wanted to continue going to my school in East Ham, situated between Barking and Plaistow, not too far from West Ham football club. I didn't mind the journey: nearly a mile-long walk to the nearest bus stop, a twenty-minute bus ride to Ilford, a ten-minute bus ride to Barking and then a ten-minute walk to school. I needed familiarity more than I needed extra sleep, more than I needed light on the way home during winter.

Two weeks into the first term of school (I was in the fourth year/ Year 10 at the time), I was strolling home via Manford Way, the main stretch between my house and my nearest bus stop. Manford Way offered little in the way of engagement: an unwelcoming pub, a health centre, a large primary school, a rarely occupied park and a mix of multi-coloured flat-roof houses (their gardens backing on to the street, protected by five-feet-high brick walls) and bland semis with driveways and sloping patches of green space separating the houses from the pavement. The stretch was about as colourful as a damp paving stone.

As I wandered down the street, I encountered an older white woman walking fifteen yards or so ahead of me. She wore a grey or beige overcoat. Can't quite remember the colour. But the coat was light in tone and stiff, like rigor mortis had set in. She had a complete head of grey hair, and while not exactly frail, she shuffled awkwardly, like someone trying to overtake a parent with a double buggy down a narrow path. I attributed the stammering nature of her walk to age. I felt her turn to gaze at me, but our eyes didn't meet.

She looked again. Felt it, but I was in a daze; often was during this stretch. I was probably thinking about Eric B. & Rakim's 'I Know You Got Soul', a no-look Magic Johnson pass, a Sugar Ray Leonard bolo punch, or why my parents had moved to the sticks. I understood why. They had been in Manor Park since '68. Manor Park had provided affordable housing, a Caribbean community, and a willing seller to a Black* family. Yet after nineteen years, they'd had enough. Our house and car were broken into; the local post office became a casualty of an armed robbery. Our local secondary school, Little Ilford, had a mobile police unit permanently stationed within its grounds due to persistent racially motivated attacks on Black and Asian pupils.

The racist 'political' group, the National Front, brazenly recruited and leafleted outside my primary school gates. My parents craved a safer neighbourhood, a house with off-street parking, a semi, a quiet life. They traded bigger (home) for safer (area), chaos for calm, brownness for whiteness.

As I continued my walk home from school, my thoughts were interrupted. The old lady turned again. I noticed that she had started to walk even faster. Despite this, I had still been gaining on her. She turned and looked at me again. Our eyes briefly met this time. I smiled. She grimaced. Her looks were starting to unnerve me. I was only a few yards behind her now. Her shuffle transformed into a kind of hop. Tried to ignore her. Told myself it wasn't me. It couldn't be me. Didn't want my head to drift too far into what she may have been thinking.

I approached cautiously. Five yards. Four yards. Three

---

* To capitalise or not to capitalise, that is the question. I capitalise Black throughout the book to acknowledge its importance as a political term, meaning people who suffer racial discrimination based on the colour of their skin. Black is how I self-identify, the term I remain most comfortable with. But I also appreciate the limitations associated with capitalising Black and the use of this term to define people of African and Caribbean heritage. My use of capitals and this term is not to denigrate other expressions, such as minoritised racial people, people of colour, people minoritised due to race, Global Majority people, etc.

yards. Maybe this older woman needed help? If so, I'd offer. If not, I'd stroll past. She turned again. This time she looked directly at me. Alarmed. Fraught. I became paranoid. Couldn't figure out what was wrong with her. Well, I knew. I just didn't want to believe it.

I started to slow down. *That'll help.* Not slow enough. Then I decided to walk closer to the roadside, so when I'd overtake, there would be enough distance between the two of us for her to feel safe. I'm two yards behind her now. She did not appear to be in any physical pain; I had been her pain. No doubt, she feared being mugged. I feared that she might accuse me of mugging her.

I started to look around. Felt like a criminal. Maybe I had been blowing this out of proportion. Perhaps I would pass her, and this farce would end. By the time she'd crossed a road, I was by her side, about to overtake. Freedom. Free-doom. As she stepped onto the pavement, she collapsed to the floor. Her crashing body sounded like a leather overcoat flung violently onto concrete. She rolled onto her back. I approached to help her up. 'Are you all right?' I asked. She lifted her hands in front of her face as if trying to protect herself from a punch. 'I'm not gonna hurt you, are you all right?' I held my arm out to help her up. She flinched, her arms protecting her face, eyes startled like a child confronted by a hostile dog. I withdrew my hand. 'Do you want me to help you?' I asked. She did not say a word.

Here I was, a near six-foot-tall Black boy in ill-fitting school clothes standing over a frail white woman crumpled on the pavement. I saw this scene before I realised I was a part of it. Should I stay or should I go? I was confused. My head and my heart were at odds – how would anyone passing by perceive me? How would you have perceived me?

Hold that thought.

Maybe she. Maybe you.

Hold it. What do you think would have been the first thing you thought had you witnessed this scene? Whatever that thought was, hold on to it.

This story, a true one, is not about victim versus villain, right versus wrong, good versus evil, Black versus white. Not that. Not about her or me. It's about the lens through which you have just witnessed this scene. A scene where – on the surface – an old woman felt so threatened by a Black boy, a perception of blackness, that she panicked herself into falling. I'll never know what she really thought or felt. You'll never know.

Go back to your lens for a second. What shaped your lens? What shaped how you view life or how you view 'race'*? How do you view immigration, nationalism, Brexit and some of the many issues Britain struggles to discuss without pre-judging? Were your opinions shaped more by your parents? The media? Your friends? Your environment? Your schooling? No doubt all the above, to varying degrees.

Do you hold the same political beliefs as your parents? Do you believe everything you see in the media, particularly

---

* I have put race in inverted commas, only in the first instance, because it is a social construct. There is no scientific basis for the racial hierarchies created from this construct. As Ta-Nehisi Coates said, 'race is the child of racism' (Ta-Nehisi Coates, *Between the World and Me*, New York: Random House, 2015, p.7). Despite this, race and its father continue to dictate the life and death chances of people of colour across the globe.

concerning things you know little about and people with whom you have little contact? When you see your old school friends, would you say that your politics still align? Consciously? Unconsciously? Fundamentally? What was your conception of race and immigration, of national identity, growing up? How diverse are your nearest and dearest friends, you know, the ones you confide in, the ones you frequently invite round for dinner? What did you learn about race, religion, immigration, colonialism, and Britain's historical relationship to these things at school? How did you experience difference? How do you experience difference?

I could have picked many more stories, from the blatant: being persistently stopped and searched by police for no reason or having to hide out in the back of a car while being caught in the middle of a National Front rally. To the subtle: bus drivers refusing to let me on the bus, security guards following me around stores,* or the many taxi drivers refusing to pick me up. To everyday issues: the uncomfortable stares, being ignored or bypassed at the shop counter, the micro-aggressions. To the unseen: being overlooked for promotion at work, white folks 'picking my brain' and misappropriating

---

* A security guard followed me round a Co-op recently. Big, grown-up-ass forty-seven-year-old me. This was pre-lockdown and I was wearing a hoodie. So, I thought I'd have a little fun and I ended up moving around from aisle to aisle to see if he'd follow me, which he did. It was liberating. I always feel tense entering shops. I never like to stay long, I never bring in items purchased in other shops, I never pick up anything unless I am going to buy it. I avoid doing anything where I might be accused of something. Been accused too often of stealing things. It may have been the first time that I'd had such a comical response. To think, that it has taken me almost forty years to get to a point where I can find humour in this situation. To think that almost forty years on, the same sort of thing that used to happen to me as a primary school kid would still be happening to me as a middle-aged man.

my knowledge, decisions made when I am not in the room. Blurred lines. Blatant, subtle, the everyday, the unseen merge into one. Not perpetrated by skinheads in Doc Martens with tats, a scowl and a glare. I am talking about bus stops, shops, trains, school, work. My livelihood. My future. I am talking about actions and body language and feeling 'othered'. Emotional, everyday violence.

Giving Back is not about this elderly woman and me. It's about change. It's about transformation. It's about challenging our perceptions. It's about history, how we behave and how we relate to one another. It's not about individual incidents. It's not about, for example, how she felt but *why* she might have felt the way she did. The impact of the way she felt, on herself, on me. Her lens. Your lens. Us.

I want you to confront your lens for a moment. Put aside some of the things you think are the truth and explore ideas about how we can contribute to a better world. *Giving Back* is a call to radically alter our approach to 'giving'* to good causes, be it volunteering or donating money, time, resources or ideas. I call for a change rooted in justice, not charity, a change from giving as a top-down, bureaucratic, institutional approach to an everyday practice rooted in the experiences and expertise of the acutely marginalised and

---

* I am uncomfortable with the word giving, which is why I have, in this first use of the term, put it in inverted commas. For many, giving is commonly viewed through a charitable lens, which often locates problems within the people being helped, not systems and structures. It can also be more about how the person giving feels than the real needs of the people they are supposedly helping which, in turn, can be misguided, condescending and, for recipients of aid, undignified. I explore the functionality of this term later in the book.

most impacted communities, a change that must start from within us.

* * * * *

I adapted the passage above from a report I wrote for my Churchill Fellowship, titled 'They Just Don't Know'.[1] The title referred to what I perceived as Britain's ignorance of how different groups experience society and how everything, from our education system to our media, reinforces the fear of the 'other', the 'foreigner'. How these institutions and the people who govern them strive to keep the public ill-informed and divided to retain power to a point where, despite my near fifty years as a Londoner, my everyday experiences and feelings as a Black man remain something most people just don't know.

I was wrong. The COVID-19 outbreak early in 2020 taught us many things about race in Britain. Primarily, that Black and racially minoritised people are systematically disadvantaged, and no amount of blame on individuals' actions or choices supersedes structural racism in society. We were twice as likely as white people to catch the coronavirus. Precarious jobs, inadequate housing and poor environments were among the factors that increased the risk for Black people. By August 2020, ethnic minorities made up 34 per cent of critically ill COVID-19 patients despite comprising 14 per cent of the population.[2] The pandemic exacerbated existing racial disparities. There was no hiding place for people in Britain. And, for the first time in my adult life, white folks en masse did not appear to be in complete denial about it.

*

I entered the charitable sector, which I will refer to as the social sector throughout the book,* full-time in 2003, after many years as a journalist. While writing, I had always volunteered at youth centres, prisons, schools and for mentoring schemes. I had seen how inequality played out in the lives of young people. I could see Britain's relationship with us – my family, Black people – had not advanced suitably. The social sector struck me as a place where invention and activism could thrive, a space that would challenge the prevailing norms within our society.

Civil Society Futures: The Independent Inquiry's report, 'Civil Society in England: Its current state and future opportunity' probably has the best definition of what I call the social sector. The report, which defines the sector as civil society, states:

> Civil society involves all of us. When we act not for profit nor because the law requires us to, but out of love or anger or creativity, or principle, we are civil society. When we bring together our friends or colleagues or neighbours to have fun or to defend our rights or to look after each other, we are civil society. Whether we organise through informal friendship networks, Facebook groups, community events and protests; or formal committees, charities, faiths and trade unions, whether we block runways or co-ordinate

---

* OK, this is where it gets a little complicated. I use the term social sector, in part, because it is the simplest way of describing what may better be known to many as the charitable sector, civil society, third sector or the voluntary sector. None of these terms are as universal as the private or public sectors. But there really is no consensus about what the social sector should be called, which, as I will explore later in the book, is one of its problems, a lack of identity.

coffee mornings, sweat round charity runs or make music for fun; when we organise ourselves outside the market and the state, we are all civil society.[3]

However you want to term or describe the social sector, this space felt like a middle ground for me as I was neither a grass-roots activist nor a civil servant. It felt like the middle ground between the private and public sectors. But the longer I spent in it, the more I found out how ill-equipped it was to tackle long-term social issues.

Segregation is rife in the social sector. There is the mainstream or institutional part of the industry: the 'super-major' charities (income over £100 million), the 'major' ones (between £10 million and £100 million), and the large ones (between £1 million and £10 million), as defined by National Council for Voluntary Organisation (NCVO).* These are generally well-established organisations with fundraisers and a solid track record of attracting income from various sources, be it from independent trusts and foundations, the government, high-net-worth individuals, corporates, events and appeals, the general public or from their own enterprises (shops, selling training packages, etc.). However, the vast majority of the UK's 166,000+ charities are micro or small organisations.[4] These figures do not take into consideration

---

* NCVO defines the size of voluntary organisations by the following income bands: less than £10k (micro), between £10k and £100k (small), between £100k and £1m (medium), between £1m and £10m (large), between £10m and £100m (major) and over £100m (super-major). The majority of the 166,000+ charities in the UK are in the micro (47 per cent) and small categories (35 per cent).

the many individuals and unregistered groups also delivering charitable activities.

The super-major charities will be familiar to us, like Cancer Research UK, the Salvation Army, the Royal British Legion, the National Society for the Prevention of Cruelty to Children (NSPCC), the Royal National Theatre, St. John Ambulance and the Royal Opera House. Many of these organisations have been around for a long time. You can also include the large trusts and foundations that fund charitable activities nationally and internationally, independent of the government. Overall, these organisations (those delivering services and resources) tend to add value to or fill gaps in the state's social services but rarely will they challenge structural barriers. Some of these organisations, particularly the large arts institutions, only serve a small section of our society, mainly the elite.

While *Giving Back* concerns itself only with institutions and organisations outside of our core public services and the public sector, many universities, private schools, think tanks, and corporate foundations are also charitable entities. They, too, often only serve a small and privileged few and with questionable charitable objectives. But that's another book.

Another problem lies in the corporatisation of the social sector,* which has led to a flood of well-meaning but soft-celled graduates and business types entering social purpose work with no genuine desire to change the status quo significantly. Leadership in the social sector looks like a Lloyds Banking

---

* Amrit Wilson's article in the *Guardian* in 2019 brilliantly summarises the corporatisation of the charitable sector: https://www.theguardian.com/commentisfree/2019/feb/07/womens-aid-ceo-ukip-katie-ghose.

Group board meeting. Beyond the lack of diversity, you have frequent government meddling and policies such as the Cohesion Guidance for Funders Consultation in May 2008 and the Lobbying Act in 2014, restricting the voice, advocacy activities and funding to campaign groups, particularly those serving marginalised communities. We will probably never know the extent to which divestment from specialist services aimed at specific communities has fundamentally ruptured community relations or inadvertently driven social problems underground.

Similarly, we will likely never discover how divestment from these services has fed large, generalist charities, many of whom replicate public sector harm by ignoring communities of colour, disabled people or domestic-abuse survivors. One of the social sector's critical roles, representing public opinion, has been fundamentally undermined by the government. Its voice has become weaker in recent years as the gaps between the major charities and smaller ones have increasingly grown as a result of the social sector's greater intimacy with the government. This is a sector that should be challenging the ills of our society, not replicating it.

We exist in a world where the twenty-six richest billionaires own as much capital as the poorest 50 per cent (3.8 billion people) of the world's population.[5] A world where it is estimated that the Global North drains $2.2 trillion from the Global South every year. This sum could end extreme poverty across the globe fifteen times over.[6] A world where a tiny fraction of wealth from the world's richest men could do a great deal to alleviate starvation across the globe. For example, in 2021, David Beasley, Director of United Nations' World Food

Program, pointed out that $6 billion from Tesla and SpaceX founder Elon Musk – an estimated 2 per cent of his wealth at the time – could help save 42 million people from hunger.[7] A world where, at its core, the wealthy are beneficiaries of an economic system that exploits Black, indigenous and people of colour and our natural resources. A world where the rich are beneficiaries of a system that is widening income inequality while increasingly closing the borders to those most vulnerable to the damage that capitalism has caused. A world where these billionaires control our behaviour and voting patterns and enhance our fears through social media platforms. The social sector should be a place we turn to when we want to challenge the root of such blatant disparities.

The problem was that you just couldn't reveal these issues to anyone outside of the social sector. I liken it to being one of the 'clean' athletes in a professional sports event. You knew that some of your competitors were probably taking performance-enhancing drugs. You may have also suspected that the authorities were complicit but may not do anything about it for the sake of reputation preservation or profit. You knew that by taking part in the event and not saying anything, you were also complicit. You also knew that most of the lesser competitors were probably clean. You knew of the financial value of this event and the damage it would cause if you snitched. You knew that you could ruin it for everyone, including yourself and the cleaner athletes. The difference is that whereas elite athletes' success can enable money to trickle down to lesser athletes, that is not the case in the social sector, where the major charities tend to soak up the wealth and control.

The general public may not have known many of the details outlined above, but the mainstream social sector's veil fooled no one. Grassroots football fans probably felt this way in the early nineties, during the Premier League's onset. The gap between the fans and the players widened. Given football's importance in our everyday lives as a form of escape and belonging, charity's as a place we may turn to in times of crisis, guilt or generosity, we endure, even if we complain about it as much as we revere it (a definite British trait). While public trust in charities improved in 2020[8] from the Charity Commission's last survey in 2018, it remains lower than in 2014. From the ambiguity over where our donations go and the high salaries of major charity heads to 'poverty porn',* which exploits vulnerable people's condition for profit and sexual abuse in international aid, social sector organisations remain maligned and misunderstood.

But this is a space that matters.

The social sector employs over 900,000 people,† contributing £18.2 billion to the UK economy.[9] Every year, close to 12 million people formally volunteer (with an estimated value in 2016 of £23.9 billion), while British people

---

* Poverty porn 'is any type of media, be it written, photographed or filmed, which exploits the poor's condition in order to generate the necessary sympathy for selling newspapers or increasing charitable donations or support for a given cause. Poverty porn is typically associated with black, poverty-stricken Africans, but can be found elsewhere. The subjects are overwhelmingly children, with the material usually characterized by images or descriptions of suffering, malnourished or otherwise helpless persons.' Collin, Matt (1 July 2009). 'What is "poverty porn" and why does it matter for development?'
† To put this into some context, the NHS is the largest employer in the UK with close to 1.5 million staff.

donate over £10 billion to good causes.[10] These figures do not consider the vast social value of the sector, for example, informal volunteering or savings to the economy by reducing homelessness, health problems, crime and other significant issues.

We are a nation that gives, but also a nation where the most generous are often those who have the least. Back in 2011, Professor Yaojun Li from Manchester University found that the poorest 20 per cent of the British public gave 3.2 per cent of their wages to charitable causes while the richest 20 per cent gave 1.3 per cent.[11]

Through corporatisation, we have however lost genuine ambition, imagination and grassroots communities' voices. Direct action and tech are achieving more immediate results, leaving social sector institutions, much like the British education system, woefully outdated and ill-prepared to meet everyday and modern needs. In response to the climate crisis, the COVID-19 outbreak, the police's lynching of George Floyd and state violence against women and girls, it was climate justice campaign group Wretched of the Earth, Black Lives Matter UK, Extinction Rebellion, Sisters Uncut and other system-changers and grassroots collectives that mobilised people to protest.

While the approaches of some, such as Extinction Rebellion, were not necessarily inclusive, these groups succeeded where so many charities had failed, by stimulating interest, involvement and action among ordinary folks. The power of the 'unregistered' social sector worldwide, from Black Lives Matter US to the #MeToo campaigns, from the

Stansted 15 to Occupy Goldsmiths, has shown that the social sector, as an institution, is increasingly struggling to reflect the needs of the public.

During the COVID-19 outbreak and the Black Lives Matter protests sparked by George Floyd's death in 2020, we did not see many immediate bold ideas from the large charities, funders, or the mainstream social sector. Worse still, as I attended numerous Zoom calls talking about social change, I didn't know where the mainstream social sector stood on issues such as racism, climate or unethical AI. I wasn't even sure of the degree to which they cared beyond their own financial reserve's line.

I had witnessed over the years how central the white saviour complex was to the culture of charities and how corporatisation had created an even greater gap between the charitable sector and general public. The PowerPoint presentations looked better. The language was more commercial. The dissemination of ideas appeared to be more credible. But when the crisis hit, the social sector appeared further from challenging the norm than ever before. It merely reinforced the government's 'few rotten apples' theory that they applied to the police. The sector pats itself on the back and its institutions corral around each other when under attack. At no point did it hold a mirror in front of itself long enough to acknowledge its complicities in weakening the voice of marginalised people. In all likelihood, it could not afford to do so.

For me, the bold and transformational ideas emerging before and during the COVID-19 crisis came from the outsiders within. These were ideas with the potential to shift the paradigm without leaving any community behind. I first encountered the term in Barbara Ransby's epic biography *Ella Baker & the Black Freedom Movement*, in which she used the phrase to describe Ella Baker, the civil rights activist. I would later find out that American academic Patricia Hill Collins coined the expression. 'Collins asserts that black women cannot fully be a member of feminist thought nor black social thought because the former assumes whiteness while the latter assumes maleness. The makeup of their identity and consequently their experiences as black women maintain their position as outsiders within spaces of oppression.'[12]

The term 'outsider within' seemed so relevant to me during my years in the social sector for two reasons. First, it reflects the lived experiences of the many organisers, youth workers, activists, cultural producers, social entrepreneurs, lawyers and writers I've met who are applying those experiences to create some of the most imaginative, radical and ethical ways of establishing a fairer future. Second, their positionality offers a unique outlook, with an ever-evolving understanding of what needs to change in our society based on continued experiences. Their lens is often anti-racist and intersectional, embraces the most marginalised, does not undermine or harm other communities, and has the potential to create a just future for all. If the social sector was centred in this way, the potential for transformational changes in our society would be less a dream and more a reality.

I have been lucky to observe many changemakers over the years, many of whom, to me, are outsiders within. They are curious, imaginative, questioning, unwilling to accept the conventions of society. Rarely do they receive a fair share of funding. Some may call them rebellious, brave, radical, unconventional or fearless. However, they are perceived, they appear to accept this position, as difficult as it may be – something many of us struggle to embrace through fear of being considered interlopers – and harness this to try and change the world for the better.

While *Giving Back* primarily features the innovations and activism of women of colour, they are not exclusively Black or African American. So, in using the term in this book, I am not always staying true to Hill Collins's original definition. But this position, this foundation and those that seem to embrace it and use it to do good, offer – I believe – the greatest hope for our future.

There is likely an element of the outsider in many of us, to varying degrees; something about us that doesn't quite fit in, something we try to ignore, something often too painful to acknowledge. There are layers to this. Some communities are more oppressed than others. Less visible minorities can pass. But we are unquestionably living in a system of oppression that benefits a small percentage of our world at the expense of the majority, particularly the Global Majority. We are increasingly a world that is acknowledging our multiple identities, far more than what government policies and services choose to recognise. We are also in a world where economic divides continue to increase and those with the power to design the policies and services we consume, the minority, keeps a good portion of us on the margins. We are not all in the same boat. But we are also not as far apart as those in power would make it seem.

*

I remember listening to Azeem Azhar's *Exponential View* podcast, where one of his guests said that we needed goals that are better than our world. It struck me that those I had worked with who were challenging the system were those with visions that were better than our current world. That is why I have written this book. I didn't want to focus on the ills of how the institutional social sector responds to need. There are plenty of problems. Too many. And they come up throughout the book. But why look back? By doing so, I'd be guilty of doing the very thing that appears to get politicians elected – looking back, promoting fear, keeping marginalised folks to the rear.

I, of course, set the context of what philanthropy looks like now, in the first section of the book, 'Band-Aid', and look at how the COVID-19 outbreak exacerbated existing disparities. I also explore, in Part Two, 'That's why I'm giving', what motivates us to donate time, money or resources to good causes. Part Three, 'Stand for something', looks at nine characteristics we need if we truly want to transform our world through our giving. The final section, 'A common project', is a call to re-evaluate the way we give and how, by adopting these characteristics, we may contribute to a society that benefits the well-being of us all, not just the wealthy.

A focus of the book is on those 'clean' athletes, the ones who should oversee the country, those we rarely see on *Newsnight*, those who should be on or hosting *Sunday with Laura Kuenssberg*. I focus on those we should invest in, their ideas, visions and innovations, those who want Britain to be great in all its multi-racial and multi-ethnic glory, and not because of some outdated conception of Empire. Those who embrace difference.

For funders, investors, the public, high-net-worth individuals, commissioners, anyone who gives, particularly those reinvigorated to contribute after the events in 2020, this is a time to think about how we give, to whom, and to what end. Where should we go to capture our energy to give? How can we be more effective in our giving? How can we balance both the satisfaction we feel when we give with our desire for our efforts to have a tangible impact? If you are inspired to give, *Giving Back* offers a guide to helping you take the first steps to enable your donations to go further.

In two decades of working in the social sector, I shifted from the front line – as a youth and community worker supporting people on estates, in schools, in young offenders' institutions, youth clubs and prisons – to directing the distribution of tens of millions of pounds to good causes across thirty-four countries. Over the years, I designed, led or delivered creative education programmes that served around three thousand people. I read thousands of funding applications during this time. My work took me from Nairobi to New Orleans and Shanghai to Cape Town, supporting initiatives tackling issues from gender inequality and racial injustice to climate change and disability discrimination.

I received a Churchill Fellowship in 2014, which enabled me to travel to the United States to spend time with organisations like Color of Change, Race Forward, Peace First, Harlem Children's Zone and The People's Institute for Survival and Beyond. I also became an inaugural Knowledge Equity Fellow at the Skoll Centre for Social Entrepreneurship, Saïd Business School, University of Oxford and host the podcast *Just Cause*, exploring the intersection of race, culture and philanthropy. I am currently the chief executive of Ten Years' Time, aiming to inject ambition, imagination, justice and equity into philanthropy by reducing the proximity between financial wealth and community wealth [knowledge]. Our core purpose is to mobilise more money and resources into ideas and initiatives led by individuals from the most impacted communities, particularly people of colour.

Over the years, the people with the most to say embodied an activist and imaginative position, not career-driven but life-driven. This included Professor Carlene Firmin – pioneer of contextual safeguarding, Farzana Khan – co-founder of Healing Justice London and Resourcing Racial Justice, Marai Larasi – former executive director of Imkaan, and Yvonne Field – founder of The Ubele Initiative. This also included Baljeet Sandhu – founder of the Centre for Knowledge Equity, Immy Kaur – co-founder of CIVIC SQUARE, Ruth Ibegbuna – founder of RECLAIM, The Roots Programme and Rekindle, Amahra Spence – co-founder of Yard, and Whitney Iles – founder of Project 507, among many others.

To the social sector's detriment, these voices are often missing at the highest levels of governance in this field. Their absence in such positions means that we are left with a hierarchy that, institutionally, replicates government power dynamics and appears less interested in a pluralistic society. Professor Leslie Lenkowsky once emphasised the importance of philanthropy to minority groups, innovators and those advocating for changes that may be considered unpopular.[13] The social sector has enough resources to challenge and transform our society. So, who holds power in this space, who governs it, how it mediates our giving, and how it operates matters to all of us.

While there are some wins in the social sector, too often it operates like a non-waterproof plaster in a swimming pool. It tries to soothe the cut instead of treating the cause of the abrasion. It doesn't have enough money to resource sufficient waterproof applications, so the efficacy of this treatment will likely be limited. While dishing out plasters, like contributing to food banks, may appear to be doing something worthy, it would be better off investing in the places where the 'cuts' initially occur. In the example of food banks, tackling the root causes of food insecurity such as low wages, support for people during challenging circumstances or ill health, tackling job precarity or inadequate benefits. It would also be better to listen to the voices of those most vulnerable to these cuts because they will have greater experience and understanding of the problems and ideas on eradicating them.

* * * * *

When I think of our society at its abundant best, I remember opening the new Black Cultural Archives (BCA) building in Brixton on 24 July 2014. They opened with a private view, a few speeches and a concert in Windrush Square. Felt like a national holiday to me. Never before had I seen so many of my favourite public figures in one place.

The launch featured Linton Kwesi Johnson, a man whose poetry eloquently encapsulated the Black experience in Britain. Orange Prize winner Zadie Smith was there; *Time* magazine included her debut novel *White Teeth* (Penguin,

2000) in its list of the 100 Best English-language novels from 1923–2005. Also present at the launch were activist and educator Professor Gus John, the former Director of Education in Hackney and the former coordinator of the Black Parents Movement; and Stella Dadzie – founder member of the Organisation of Women of Asian and African Descent (OWAAD) and co-author of the seminal book *The Heart of the Race* (Virago, 1985), which won the 1985 Martin Luther King Memorial Prize.

My former boss, Baroness (Doreen) Lawrence of Clarendon, was also present. After the murder of her son, Stephen Lawrence, her tireless campaigning led to the Macpherson Inquiry, which concluded that the Metropolitan Police was institutionally racist. The spectre of the Supplementary School movement* was also present. This movement educated thousands of Black children where the state had failed them through often unlawful school exclusions or low expectations. The poet Benjamin Zephaniah, named one of Britain's top 50 post-war writers by *The Times*, attended. I also saw rapper, activist and author Akala, Baroness (Ros) Howells of St Davids, and actor-playwright Kwame Kwei-Armah, the second Black Briton to have a play staged in the West End (*Elmina's Kitchen*, 2005).

What I witnessed that day – the people, the culture, the history – was unique because it reflected a broad conception

---

* Here is another issue: funding for supplementary schools has been pulled in recent years, according to people I've spoken to, through fear that they had become places where young Muslim children were being radicalised. However, there wasn't much evidence to suggest that this was the case. Supplementary schools, for many communities, have played a huge role in educating young people when mainstream education had failed.

of Black-Britishness, the depth of which is rarely taught in schools or told in the media. Mainstream concepts of Black-Britishness remain scandalously narrow. Beyond music and sport, the media reduces us to slavery and colonialism (presented as a distant memory, a mistake the nation would rather forget), Windrush (a bittersweet part of British history), gangs (problematising Black youth) and October (our 'reward'). Limited narrative. A claustrophobic feeling if you're Black. Many marginalised folks in the UK will feel the same way about how they are perceived and represented in society.

The BCA's opening represented a broad conception of the social sector I had grown up with, even if I had not been aware of the term. The legacies of New Beacon Books and the Race Today Collective were present that day – places where activists distributed books from their living rooms, transformed local activities into systemic change that saved lives, changed laws and created awareness around racial injustice. Like many major social change initiatives, the Stephen Lawrence campaign didn't have a formal charitable route and likely would not have achieved as much had it had one. But Baroness Lawrence's campaign changed race relations law.

The labour of those present at the BCA launch enabled a younger me to discover the books not in WH Smith or on the school curriculum – books that spoke to my experience, existence, history, and relevance. Their activism made it harder for employers and landlords to reject me; it enabled me to see faces on television that resembled me; their work held the police to account for trying to kill people like me. We laud the laws that symbolise change yet somehow forget the activism that sat behind them. We praise the politicians who signed key documents but forget that they wouldn't have made such a change without a demand.

We celebrate the privileged few who may shove social change over the finish line of a relay race, but we forget about those who ran the first three legs. We forget that significant change often goes against public opinion and rarely occurs due to politicians' goodwill, but mainly because generations of activists have demanded transformation, altered beliefs, and forced governments to act. The law is not the only landmark of change. At its best, the people, the movements and the social sector are the landmarks, often without statues or peerages. And that's where we should be investing.

This is historic. They challenge orthodoxy. Slavery. Voting rights. Apartheid. All legal at one point. Abolitionists and reformers were enemies of the state (some still are). People could not envision a society where Black people were free(r), where women could vote. Many people featured in this book are improving our public services, speaking truth to power, and cherishing and celebrating ordinary people's voices. They are imagining and building a world that many of us just cannot conceive. They envision a world where there's a more even distribution of wealth, where success does not necessarily mean growth, where difference is not something to fear. They envision a world where sharing is more valuable than just winning.

Philanthropy is not just about the wealthy giving money to the 'needy'. A philanthropist is anyone who gives money, ideas, time, power, services, connections, anything that makes the world a better place. The majority of us are philanthropists. The majority of us are contributing to a better world.

With this book, I am calling on you to embrace a new way of contributing to a better world. I am not calling for you to stop donating to your favourite charities. Philanthropy should be personal, it should be about the heart, and for many, the element of self-interest or instant gratification will always be a factor. This book is not about whether we are generous or not; we are. It is more of a call to rethink the nature of our giving, to question who controls how we give, and to understand how changing the way we contribute can help us have a greater voice in our society.

Giving Back is for anyone who gives, from wealthy donors and foundations to the public. This book is about creating a new culture of giving to alter everyone's life chances radically. More than anything, it's about listening to those on the margins. It's about learning from those achieving change. It's also about you, your lens, your power, and the things you need to know.

It's a book with potential solutions to Britain's and the world's problems and how we all can contribute to these ideas for change. We need something more than what charities can offer. I don't think that capital can defeat capitalism. I don't think that giving is the answer to all our problems. I know that the revolution will not be funded. But I think it could be better resourced.

Part 1

Band-Aid

1

Smirks and fever

> 'Historically, pandemics have forced humans to break with the past and imagine their world anew. This one is no different. It is a portal, a gateway between one world and the next. We can choose to walk through it, dragging the carcasses of our prejudice and hatred, our avarice, our data banks and dead ideas, our dead rivers, and smoky skies behind us. Or we can walk through lightly, with little luggage, ready to imagine another world. And ready to fight for it.'[1]
>
> —ARUNDHATI ROY, author and activist, 2020

In his book *The Mavericks*, Rob Steen said that former England football team managers Alf Ramsey and Don Revie 'were either unable or unwilling to recognise their own shortcomings and prejudices, let alone eradicate them. Their egos were even grander than those selections.' You could say the same about the Conservative government and how they handled the coronavirus outbreak. You could excuse Ramsey and Revie because they were *only* picking players for a football team. They were not running a country. They were not responsible for people's lives.

Are we talking about a revolution? Not in Britain. We may dislike our government and distrust our leaders, but we are still more likely to blame other countries and each other than the people who govern the nation. The British government's management of the outbreak was a microcosm of all that was wrong with Britain's leadership. Over 155,000 dead.

More people than most of us can ever imagine meeting in a lifetime. Mothers, fathers, grandparents, children. Not enough said. Had our leaders been pilots before a flight, doctors giving a prognosis, head teachers convincing children to attend their school, we would have booked another flight, sought a second opinion or gone to another school.

If you were judging Prime Minister Boris Johnson's cabinet on performance, ministers would have been sacked, struck off or given an inadequate Ofsted rating. The government and all it represented – the preservation of Empire, wealth and power; financial growth by any means, colonialism, eugenic thinking, patriarchy, elitism, individualism – failed to prioritise the health and well-being of its citizens while arrogantly smirking its way through the whole crisis.

Through unclear instructions on how the public should contribute to curbing this outbreak, the government weaponised ambiguity to mask its inability to take decisive action, including mass testing, mandatory mask-wearing, quarantining arrivals from abroad, an early and sustained lockdown, appropriately timed school closures, an effective test and trace system, and sufficient supply of personal protective equipment (PPE).

The British government should have been better prepared.

After the crisis unfolded in China, we watched in horror as Italy and Spain recorded daily death counts of over 700.[2] Britain had time to respond. On 17 March 2020, the government's chief scientific adviser, Sir Patrick Vallance, declared that containing the death toll to 20,000 would be a 'good outcome'.[3] The national medical director, Professor Stephen Powis, would later say that 'we will have done very well' to keep the death toll to 20,000.[4] Before long, however, Britain had passed Italy and Spain in the total number of deaths related to the coronavirus. The conservative estimate of deaths in the United Kingdom by 13 November 2020 was close to 51,000, fifth only to the United States (over 248,000 deaths), Brazil (over 164,000), India (over 128,000), and Mexico (over 97,000). The population in Britain in 2020 was approximately 67 million, in comparison to approximately 330 million in the United States, 212 million in Brazil, 1.38 billion in India and 128 million in Mexico. Britain had missed its target by over 30,000 deaths. This was before the new variants started emerging in December 2020. Yet we had almost become anesthetised to the government's failures.

To add to this, by the end of March 2020, civil liberties had changed. Our very nature and way of life – contact with family, friends, touch, access to food – was severely compromised. We were locked up, locked down by a government that did not appear to know what it was doing, further adding to the nation's anxiety.

Two things struck me early. Firstly, when the country needed clear direction and action, Johnson maintained that personal responsibility and our collective choices and sacrifices as a society would be essential to us getting through the pandemic with as few deaths as possible. Conveniently, he reversed Thatcher's lamentable 'self over society' philosophy, a stance he steadfastly advocated for, and now claimed that he did not want to impose draconian laws on the British public.[5]

It was his way of creating a level of trust in the public while shifting blame and responsibility away from the government (true to Thatcherism) and onto ordinary citizens. Our actions and not government rule would primarily dictate how well the country got through this crisis. In Britain, people in positions of power love a framework. Frameworks provide a template, a structure from which to build often without a clear roadmap or sufficient transparency levels to make them accountable.

Of course, any plan needs to be flexible, iterative and responsive to need. But, if there's ambiguity from the outset, it is tough to hold anyone in authority responsible. The government's haziness made it easier for them to place most of the blame on us and our actions and to deflect our focus away from itself. We were told to wash our hands for twenty seconds and social distance long before we were told to wear masks.

Failure to adhere would be our responsibility. However, confusion and uncertainty reigned over wearing masks, how we could effectively socially distance in public spaces and the risks associated with re-opening pubs and schools. The delay in the government's decision-making around when and how to lock Britain down or ease lockdown measures created opacity when it came to determining who was primarily responsible for the 50,000 deaths by mid-November 2020.

Despite a relentless Conservative narrative of self-interest since Thatcher came into power in 1979, the Tory government was now prophesising 'society over self' in a moment of crisis. Thatcher had told us that there was no society, just the market, just individuals. So, it stood to reason that many people, during the early days of lockdown, would put themselves first before thinking of others during this impending crisis. These actions manifested in panic buying of toilet paper, pasta, flour, anti-bacterial wipes and hand sanitisers.

For many, the first instinct was to hoard rather than to think of each other. The majority right-wing national press needed little excuse to highlight how the public had been selfish by flouting the rules. There were headlines about stockpiling triggering shortages in goods or people going to the park when they shouldn't. This created a narrative that we were increasing the potential for a spike in the virus and reducing the NHS's capacity to respond to our needs. Even though there were also many people actively serving the needs of their communities.

Through it all, we endured the daily briefings designed to provide clarity and to show us that the government cared. The scenario became familiar – Johnson bumbling, Matt Hancock confused. Dominic Raab distracted. Priti Patel sneering. And Rishi Sunak, sounding every bit like Tony Blair, announcing every financial bailout as if revealing the winner on a game show. Through it all, one clear fact remained. The people governing this crisis did not represent or understand the needs of those most at risk of catching the virus.

Had this been a parent–child relationship, the government being the parent, it would be abuse in the form of wilful neglect. The violence may not be physical, but it occurs in the government's policies, behaviours, practices, and the narratives it creates. Smirks and fever. In this case, the government's failure to act swiftly enough to prevent harm led to more deaths than were predicted and deemed tolerable. The behaviours of some of its officials – the unelected Dominic Cummings driving 260 miles from London to Durham during lockdown while suspected of having the coronavirus, Secretary of State for Health and Social Care Matt Hancock breaching social distancing rules while kissing aide Gina Coladangelo in Whitehall, and the alleged Downing Street parties in 2020 and 2021 that breached lockdown rules – completely undermined the government's authority and reinforced the feeling that there was one rule for them and another rule for the rest of us. Then there were the state's practices such as policing, which saw over 20,000 stops of Black men aged 15–24 years during the first lockdown, with fewer than 20 per cent resulting in further action.[6]

During the early stages of lockdown, we saw the best and the worst of Britain. In some cases, our first instinct was to take, not to share or trust. Imagine if we only ever took what we needed? What if we always considered others in our actions? Indeed, such change would likely only occur if we fundamentally trusted our government or felt we had a voice in this society. A society where those with greater wealth couldn't dodge taxes, where transparency and accountability were core to decision-making, where we hadn't been fed *self, self, self* narratives by successive governments, where we knew more about each other and our histories, where we had equal access to decent housing and health provision. A society that didn't neglect the elderly or ignore the young. And a government geared towards reviving the NHS, not selling it.

More than anything, we would have a regime that modelled the behaviours it expects from its constituents. Had that been the case, perhaps people may not have felt as if they needed to get supplies before their neighbours in some morbid pandemic 'keeping up with the Joneses' game show. This is not to excuse the behaviour of all British citizens. Many misbehaved, by not wearing masks, gathering illegally, hosting and attending parties, assembling in confined spaces. But the leadership of the country inspired no confidence and continued to blame individuals while causing anxiety through uncertainty.

Through it all, the British government failed to provide sufficient information or support to people. I remember social and civil activist Immy Kaur saying to me, 'At a very crass level, every time there is a massive change in society, we need new tools. If those tools are kept away from everyday people, then they're not able [to have] what they need to deal with the transition. When they don't have the tools, they turn on each other while the 1 per cent keep everything that they need to themselves.'

Divide and rule is a common tactic to prevent people from working collectively to spotlight the root of the problem, our structures, not our neighbours. Marginalised folks collaborating is the greatest threat to power and what the government fears the most. So, the government will always do enough, economically, to level up, to give us a little too much to lose to act in the interests of the common good.

*

Britain is an island that will declare that it is not as bad as other countries before it scrutinises its own government. Self-interest, capitalism, individualism and the Empire State of Mind, which automatically looks upon Britain as superior, runs through the country's veins. There will always be excuses for why the UK perpetrated acts of violence historically to gain wealth. The country will forever condemn others for committing acts that it has done to others.

But the route to Britain's wealth was violence. I haven't lived abroad long enough to know how other societies respond to their governments. However, the Brits are subservient to their leaders partly because of the way they dictate – through algorithms, the media, bureaucracy, freedom without power, education, science, policing, competition – to preserve wealth and white supremacy for a few by creating fear of the other, of each other. The response to a perpetually failing government should be to change it. Or indeed to change the parliamentary system.

But the UK does not tend to think this way. Britain is wealthy, but its wealth does not reach all communities, and people are less satisfied with life.[7] The government will gladly use its wealth to repel the threat of civil disturbance to prevent insurrection, but it will always blame its inadequacies on others, including you and me. It will always revert to self over society.

The second thing that struck me during lockdown was how little Britain has progressed in tackling racism. In 1900, at the First Pan-African Conference in London, African American scholar, civil rights activist and writer W. E. B. Du Bois said that 'the problem of the twentieth century is the problem of the color line.'[8] He could have been referring to the twenty-first century too. Britain still greets racism with disbelief. While some will completely deny its existence, many will treat it with suspicion, while others remain shocked and offended that it remains.

Either way, it is difficult to move forward when every major racist incident is treated like a 'daily epiphany'[9] and not a historical, structural and everyday problem. When we speak of the damage of capitalism – like climate change, the wealth gap, poverty – people of colour usually bear the brunt. COVID-19 illustrated that when bad shit happens, it tends to strike Black and other minoritised racial communities first.

And this has nothing to do with genes and everything to do with society, circumstance and economic systems. We remain the 'canaries in the mine'. A warning to the rest of the world. Yet it felt as if, for many people in power, we as Black people are predisposed to misfortune because of some fault lines in our blood and that our bodies do not hold the same value as white bodies.

During the early stages of the outbreak, COVID-19 had a disproportionately negative impact on Black people in Britain. The statistics told us that 35 per cent of those critically ill with the coronavirus were from BAME backgrounds.[10] Minoritised racial groups comprise about 14 per cent of Britain's population. It was clear that people of colour were overrepresented in frontline or key-worker roles, with many working in hospitals, care homes and other settings with an increased risk of infection.

We were more likely to be suffering from respiratory

illnesses and to live in overcrowded accommodation and more run-down neighbourhoods. Given the variances in the background of communities within the BAME category, which the government used to define us, it was also clear that not even the most blatant eugenicists could cloak everyone within a broad and flawed colour-coded genetic lens as a reason for our vulnerability. The impact on racially minoritised communities had everything to do with poverty, racial discrimination and human-made conditions.

Poor social conditions did not only impact people of colour. As Alastair Parvin, co-founder of Open Systems Lab said at the Department of Dreams Festival on 19 June 2020:

> It [COVID-19] exposed an underlying epidemic of loneliness, depression and stress. Thousands of people stuck in abusive or toxic relationships. Domestic abuse has gone up by 49 per cent[11] during lockdown. It exposed 280,000 people living homeless. 1 in 5 households — and 1 in every 3 *children* living in poverty. Millions of parents going without meals to feed their children during lockdown. In one of the wealthiest, most technologically advanced societies in the world.[12]

Historical injustices aside, one need only look at the impact of the Tory government's austerity measures through the 2010s to uncover more recent disparities. From 2010 to 2020, the Tory government (first as part of a coalition with the Liberal Democrats from 2010 to 2015) destroyed public services. According to the Runnymede Trust's report, 'Intersecting Inequalities: the impact of austerity on Black and Minority

Ethnic women in the UK', the poorest families will have had an average drop in living standards of 17 per cent by 2020 while lone mothers will have experienced a decline of 18 per cent. The report also found that 'Black and Asian households in the lowest fifth of incomes will experience the biggest average drop in living standards of 19.2 per cent and 20.1 per cent respectively.'[13]

When the then Home Secretary Theresa May created a Hostile Environment for immigrants,[14] the government discriminated against Black people, particularly the Windrush generation. This state-led 'ambiguous apartheid' saw Black people lose their jobs, homes, health care and citizenship; be deported; and in some cases face an increased likelihood of death due to stress.

The most marginalised communities suffered the most. People in socio-economically deprived areas, those in precarious work situations, cleaners and other frontline staff, women and children at risk of domestic violence, individuals with poor health, disabled people were among the most vulnerable to catching COVID-19 or facing hardship due to lockdown. Yet, the government did not appear to understand or acknowledge the plight of those living on the margins. The infrastructure that could have enabled communities to be more resilient during the early stages of the outbreak, the things that make us a 'safe and just society', barely existed. 'The community was deleted,' says Immy Kaur. The system had been killing us.

Through the COVID-19 crisis, Black and brown people were also key to crisis response efforts, doing their utmost to heal the nation, often with little to no protection from the state, often while receiving abuse for their service. In an article on 5 April 2020, *Observer* chief leader-writer Sonia Sodha pointed out that the four doctors who had lost their lives to COVID-19 to that point were from BAME backgrounds.[15] She illustrated that the NHS, the darling of Britain, constructed in part through the labour of Caribbean nurses and migrants, had almost 20 per cent BAME medical staff. Sodha had to deal with a torrent of abuse after tweeting a comment about how reliant the NHS is on BAME and migrant nurses and doctors.[16]

The government continued to ignore, deny and maintain a stance that COVID-19 did not discriminate, that we were all in this together. Author and activist Afua Hirsch pointed out, in an article for the *Guardian* on 8 April 2020, that the government's ignorance of social conditions – such as cramped housing, potential contact with the police with their 'new social control powers' and those that cannot work from home – would be detrimental to the most vulnerable in our society.[17]

The social conditions and deaths of Black folks during the COVID-19 outbreak would have gone largely ignored had it not been for George Floyd. A film emerged of police officer Derek Chauvin kneeling on a distressed Floyd's neck for over seven minutes. This took place in broad daylight, with Chauvin's colleagues looking on and his victim shouting that he could not breathe. It sparked the most extensive anti-racism protests globally in my adult life and the biggest civil rights protests for a generation. Where the COVID-19 stats had seemingly done little to raise the public's consciousness of structural racism, Floyd's death and its blatant nature spoke in a language that people could understand. Loss. Unlike austerity or the outbreak, there was no ambiguity about the state's role in a Black person's death. Had it not been for a

Black female teenager, Darnella Frazier, endangering her life to film the incident, the public likely wouldn't have believed it.

There were allegedly protests in 260 towns and cities in Britain alone, with over 200,000[18] people participating in demonstrations. During the demonstrations, protesters toppled the statue of slaver Edward Colston in Bristol. Over five million people in the UK supported racial justice movements since May 2020 by signing over 1,500 petitions on Change.org. 'Until this year, the biggest anti-racism movement in the UK happened in 1833 during the monumental anti-slavery movement, when 1.3 million people across the UK put their names to petitions,' said Kajal Odedra, UK Director of Change.org in the Huffington Post on 13 November 2020.[19] Floyd's murder had become symbolic of a disease far broader, more embedded than individual acts of racism, something that stretched beyond America's borders.

The chief execs and directors of many charities and businesses quickly proclaimed that they believed that Black lives matter. Still, they swiftly found that they were ill-equipped to address the issue, mainly because it had never been a serious consideration within their work. It became clear that this nation had no understanding of racism – its everyday impacts and how denial and fear reinforce one of the biggest lies in history. Successive British governments had deliberately supported this ignorance. Even through COVID-19, Grenfell, Windrush and George Floyd, and Brexit, numerous BBC slip-ups, and inhumane border controls, our institutions remained in shock and without much of a clue about how to respond.

It also became clear that the government would continue

to deny the reality of institutional, systemic and structural racism at any cost. They would not concede that it was a reality or a problem, choosing to ignore data for an ideology that places everyone's fate solely in their own hands, with no reference to history or social circumstance. Among the many events that reinforced the notion that the government was not willing to acknowledge the presence of racism in British society:

- In practically every negative statistic related to COVID-19, from deaths to the critically ill, from job losses to pupils most likely to receive lower predicted grades to those most likely to be stopped by police, Black and other groups minoritised due to race were disadvantaged. Yet the government's response was not proportionate to the level of need in these communities.

- A government review launched in May 2020, *Beyond the Data: Understanding the Impact of COVID-19 on BAME Groups*, omitted or compressed evidence from community groups that explicitly linked the disproportionate effects of COVID-19 on people of colour to structural racism.

- When the government decided to commission an inquiry on race disparities once more, it rolled out Black and brown faces who would likely reinforce a Tory world-view, where ideology, not evidence, drives policy. The government selected Munira Mirza to oversee the commission, a woman who believes institutional racism is a myth.[20] They also brought in former *The Voice* columnist and founder of education charity Generating Genius, Dr Tony Sewell, to chair the commission. Sewell once told *Prospect* magazine that 'much of the supposed evidence of institutional racism is flimsy'.[21]

- Dame Cressida Dick, the then Commissioner of the Metropolitan Police Service, denied that the police are institutionally racist, stating that she 'did not find it a very helpful label' and adding that 'We are not collectively failing in all the ways described in Sir William's definition. There is no collective failure. It is not a massive systemic problem. It is not institutionalised. More to the point, we have come such a very long way.'[22] She said this despite all of the stops and searches of young Black men in London. Dick later closed the Stephen Lawrence case, even though three accused assailants remain free due to the Met's incompetence.

- Then Prime Minister Boris Johnson continued to enforce 'ambiguous apartheid'. First, he created thirty-six new life peers, many of whom were his Brexit supporters. Then, he allegedly pushed for the appointment of former *Telegraph* editor Charles Moore (whose comments on race, minority groups, climate change and gay marriage have attracted criticism) to be the BBC's chairman, and former *Daily Mail* editor Paul Dacre (who supposedly does not believe in statutory regulation) to run the UK's communications regulator Ofcom. Soon after, the Department of Education issued guidance to school leaders that using anti-capitalist materials in schools would be an act of illegal activity, deeming it an 'extreme political stance'.[23]

- In December 2020, Liz Truss, the International Trade Secretary and Minister for Women and Equalities, set out her vision for fairness and created a framework for social division. In her speech, she said: 'It will be about individual dignity and humanity ... not quotas and targets, or equality of outcome.' She also said, 'It will reject the approach taken by the Left ... captured as they are by identity politics, loud lobby groups and the idea of "lived experience".'[24] It was a divide and rule speech. Truss suggested that anti-racist, disability justice and LGBTQ+ rights groups were fanatics swimming in victimhood. She devalued lived experiences, almost treating the inequality faced by those with protected characteristics as a fad. The speech also indicated a further dilution of equalities data and monitoring, and pitted the 'white working class' and white liberal women against 'woke' human rights groups. We knew it was coming. As Faiza Shaheen, then a Labour candidate for Chingford and Woodford Green and director of think tank CLASS, said on my Just Cause podcast released in December 2019: 'The white working-class narrative is going to be key to how Boris Johnson's government divides us further in the years ahead. We need to wake up and start organising at the grassroots, building solidarity across working-class communities.'*

---

* The podcast, which also featured the then Director of the Runnymede Trust, Omar Khan, was recorded on 25 October 2019, but released on 19 December 2019.

- In another attempt to suppress the voices of anti-racist and climate activists, the government tried to introduce the Police, Crime, Sentencing and Courts Bill (the PCSC Bill), giving the police new powers to silence protesting and exact stricter measures on demonstrators. These new controls would include up to 10 years' imprisonment for damaging memorials, greater stop and search powers and the authority to impose substantial fines on activists and conditions on demonstrations they deem to be disruptive. In short, the police would have the ability to decide whether a protest is acceptable or not. They would then have the policy muscle to ban or restrict rallies or marches, taking the right to protest out of the public's hands. The proposed bill led to demonstrations across England in March and April 2021. During one rally, protestors allegedly chanted, 'ten years for protest, five years for rape'.

- The Commission on Race and Ethnic Disparities, led by Tony Sewell, was widely condemned by social sector leaders and Black and brown communities because it suggested that institutional racism does not exist. Indeed, housing and homelessness charity Shelter deemed the report 'an example of institutional racism'.[25] Among the strongest retorts came from race-equality think tank Runnymede Trust, which stated:

  > The very suggestion that government evidence confirms that institutional racism does not exist

is frankly disturbing. A young Black mother is four times more likely to die in childbirth than her white friend. A young Black man is nineteen times more likely to be stopped and searched by the Metropolitan Police than his young white neighbour and those with Black or Asian "sounding surnames" have to send in twice as many CVs as their white counterparts, with the same qualifications, to receive the same jobs ... As we saw in the early days of the pandemic, 60 per cent of the first NHS doctors and nurses to die were from our BME communities, despite the NHS comprising only 20 per cent BME staff in total. For Boris Johnson to look the grieving families of those brave dead in the eye and say there is no evidence of institutional racism in the UK is nothing short of a gross offence. Tell those 60 per cent BME NHS doctors and nurses who died from COVID that institutional racism doesn't exist.[26] Runnymede concluded the statement by saying, 'Frankly, by denying the evidence of institutional racism and tinkering with issues like unconscious bias training and the use of the term "BAME", the government have insulted not only every ethnic minority in this country – the very people who continue to experience racism on a daily basis – but also the vast majority of the UK population that recognise racism is a problem and expect their government to contribute to eradicating it. All on Derek Chauvin's trial day, no less.'[27] Twenty Tory MPs would later urge the Charity Commission to launch an inquiry into Runnymede's work, claiming that the Trust is pursuing a political agenda.[28] The Charity Commission opened a case on Runnymede Trust in April 2021. The Commission found the Trust to be compliant with the charities and political activity regulations.

Author Toni Morrison's 'Racism and Fascism' speech at Howard University in 1995 kept flashing into my head while I was observing the government's response to COVID-19. She said, 'In 1995 racism may wear a new dress, buy a new pair of boots, but neither it nor its succubus twin, fascism, is new or can make anything new. It can only reproduce the environment that supports its own health: fear and denial, and an atmosphere in which its victims have lost the will to fight.' Morrison warned that such behaviours are not limited to one political party. 'We must not be blindsided by these Pepsi-Cola, Coca-Cola labels because the genius of fascism is that any political structure can host the virus and virtually any developed country can become a suitable home.'[29]

The Labour Party's response to the British government's actions lacked promise, never clearly stating what the party stood for. This, too, was true of the mainstream social sector. Opposition came from the public. While they may not have been consistently forceful in protest against the management of COVID-19, many dissented through their giving.

Black Lives Matter UK raised over £1 million through its crowdfunding appeal. There were over 4,000 Mutual

Aid groups across the UK supporting vulnerable people. When the late Captain Tom Moore, a World War II veteran approaching his hundredth birthday, decided to complete one hundred laps of his garden to raise money for NHS Charities Trust, the public donated over £32 million to his cause. The National Emergencies Trust's coronavirus appeal raised close to £100 million.

Entertainers and sportspeople proved to be among the most generous. Grime artist Stormzy pledged £10 million over ten years towards issues affecting Black people, with Children in Need matching this sum. Manchester United and England international footballer Marcus Rashford worked alongside the charity FareShare to raise £20 million for food distributions to vulnerable families. Backed by the public, the then twenty-three-year-old's campaigning twice led the government to change their policies and provide funding for free school meals to low-income families during school holidays.[30] Britain's public had been generous. It felt as if it was fighting back the best way it knew how, not by trying to overthrow but by giving.

But, ultimately, how effective was this way of contributing to change? It was clear that the British government did not want its citizens to imagine a different world or interfere in social policy. It was also clear that they would put party politics and maintenance of power above the well-being of its citizens. Was the social sector, a space that mediates much of our giving, equipped to facilitate the public's challenge to the status quo and lead a 'revolution' of giving? If it were to do so, it would have to reverse a culture that, while well-meaning, had seemingly prioritised financial preservation and growth over people and purpose.

2

My space, my city, my world

> 'Charity and prisons are the two biggest
> signs that our society is failing. A society that
> is functioning wouldn't have charities and
> wouldn't have prisons.'
>
> WHITNEY ILES,
> founder of Project 507, 2020

The two girls were fighting in the dark, narrow hallway of their mum's house when the twelve-year-old grabbed her older sister and put her in a headlock, pulling out the hairband that had been keeping her afro-puff together. The younger sister, Lila,* was wide-eyed and sturdy, with long curly hair. She punched her fourteen-year-old sister, Maddy,† in the face. It wasn't a clean blow. She had not closed her fist quickly or tightly enough before landing a scuffed stroke that would glance off the side of Maddy's forehead.

Maddy, olive-skinned, with sharp features and glazed eyes,

---

* Lila is a pseudonym.
† Maddy is a pseudonym.

was hunched, her grey leggings and baggy red T-shirt loosening. She tried to use her legs to twist her way out of the headlock, left and right, right and left, before the two rotated fully, 360, their backs clattering against the kitchen door. Now Lila's hairband came loose because Maddy was grabbing her hair so viciously it created a grating sound, like a comb scraping through the roots of dreadlocks.

While the fight had been going on, the mother, who was white, with a perpetually worn expression on her face and sagging features, continued cooking. She did not turn around even when she shouted at them to stop fighting, even when she could hear their bodies slamming against stationary objects. I stood, frozen, not knowing whether to intervene or wait for their mother to show some interest. I tentatively tried to break them apart but to no avail. As in most fights, they did not throw many punches. It was a scrappy encounter, full of holding, tugging and wrestling. The victor was unclear; the purpose seemingly lost the more the battle continued. While there were no outward signs of physical damage, the brawl was fierce; they were fierce; you could tell by the piercing sounds, the hair pulls, the banging door, the pace in which they would to and fro.

It was only when the mother turned around and intervened that the two swapped brawling for verbal sparring. Lila, who seemingly got the better of the fight, was upset and emotional, but there were no tears. Amid the commotion, the shouting, the glares, there were smirks as the two sisters appeared to stare through each other. Maddy seemed to be in more control, her voice not so loud or shaken, while looking as though she had just got out of bed with a hangover. It did not appear as if she felt any emotions about what had just occurred. It was almost as if she knew her young sister could not hurt her.

I first visited this London-based family around a month before the fight. I was a project worker for a mentoring scheme supporting 'at risk' teenagers and Maddy had been referred to us for truanting from her school. She had previously run away from home and the school suspected that she was hanging out with older boys, which elicited concerns that she may be sexually active. I visited her home to carry out an initial assessment to see whether we could provide support and if her mother, a single parent, would be happy for us to do so.

The idea would be to find the girl a suitable mentor and involve her in a range of activities that would help her on the right pathway, like regularly attending school, finding a healthy peer group and perhaps repairing fractured relationships within her family. In truth, I spent most of the early months working with her mediating between the school and the mother. The relationship between the two had broken down. The mother had changed her phone number without notifying the school. Her connection with Maddy's father was also strained, which resulted in frequent clashes between mother and child.

Lost in this was the girl herself, who was quiet and timid when we first met. She looked older than her age, rarely made eye contact, and spoke in half-sentences, in a deep, breathy tone. All the men in her life had either left, died or entered correctional facilities. While she was polite enough, it was difficult to know what was going through her mind most of the time as she greeted each discussion with indifference. Underneath her calm was a fiery temper and little self-regulation. When someone annoyed her, commonly her mother, she would lash out before retreating into her shell. Away from home, I would discover that she was far from timid, comfortable roaming around in unfamiliar spaces with restless energy.

While I understood that the mentoring scheme was not a long-term solution to this girl's problems, there did not appear to be a coordinated, systemic approach to supporting her. The authorities made many assumptions about the issues that may have led to her poor behaviour and decision-making. State structures were not in place to support her and help break the cycle of destructive behaviour, nor to help those of us running the scheme to know whether mentoring was a good fit for her or not.

More profound emotional problems required rigorous analysis and a more intensive intervention than we could offer. Given that there was no evidence of abuse within the household, social services did not intervene. But the school knew she was hanging out with older boys, who she appeared to turn to when she ran away from home. It also appeared that the teachers and administrators did not want her to become an exclusion statistic on their record but were not active in reintegrating her back into school.

It felt as if something terrible would have to happen to her before she received the appropriate support. I am not saying that the people involved in the care of this girl were all negligent or destructive. At times, we were all operating in siloed systems that seemed to carve her into an educational risk, a health risk and a homelessness risk, but nobody's responsibility. Just because we were all trying to do good, it did not mean that all of our actions were helpful or effective. While my organisation was well-meaning, taking on this young person was probably the wrong thing to do. However, at the time, we didn't know what else was on offer that could prevent her life from spiralling out of control.

In the months that followed, we failed to match her with an appropriate mentor. She ran away again. I had built enough trust with her that she would accept my calls while away from her home. I liaised between her mother and the missing persons unit during this time, and she eventually returned home. But the reality was that we failed her, and the system failed her.

I do not know what happened to Maddy in the end. I left the organisation through which I was working with her. She was just one of many young people I worked with who appeared to fall through the system's cracks. Like others, she bounced from one agency to another, deviant enough to make her a risk but not risky enough for public services to intervene in a coordinated manner to prevent a potentially more destructive fate. Whitney Iles, founder of Project 507, once told me that our services resemble vulnerable young people's harsh childhood experiences, often defined by abrupt losses, be it their homes, their peers, a parent or a loved one. Similarly, as young people are building a relationship with someone who is there to help them, often, the service runs out of money, the worker is burnt out and leaves or the young person is referred to another provision. I could have picked many more stories of young people I encountered over the years: the uncontrollable pre-teens on khat, the teenager who pulled a machete on my colleague, the self-harmers, the gang members, the young woman who couldn't leave her house, the young boy who couldn't control his sexual urges.

But for some reason, Maddy's story stayed with me. It felt as if those of us being paid to build a relationship with this girl did not understand her needs as much as those older boys. Part of that had been because we were only really engaging with the child's relationship with her mother and sibling and not considering the broader context: her peers, her environment. Part of it was due to the fact we may not have been skilled enough to support her.

As a social sector organisation, we were unsupervised and had heavier caseloads than your average social worker. I say this in hindsight due to much of what I've learned from pioneers like Professor Carlene Firmin and Whitney Iles about the importance of contextual safeguarding and trauma-informed practice, respectively, when working with young people. Funding also restricted us: short-term income, impractical outcomes for the young people we worked with, and lots of paperwork. In essence, we didn't have the time or space to work out what was best for Maddy because targets trumped need, reporting eclipsed appropriate management of young people. We were stuck in a bureaucratic web of ineffective rules, practices and resourcing.

During my time as a youth worker and mentor, there were flashes of what could be. The right for a child or vulnerable adult to have a trusted and long-term relationship with a peer or an adult who is not a relative or a state authority. Someone who cannot take you away, someone who will also provide emotional support, practical tools, information, listen without judgement, advise without demands, bridge without rage.

It is not the solution to young people's problems, but it is a vital role. It is often undervalued, underpaid and unsupervised. It is often the case that the first role to go during funding cuts is this function, which every council or consultant wants to professionalise or redefine. I don't know whether it's the same for NHS workers, care-home staff or teachers, but I defy any youth worker who gave a damn about their job to tell me that they cannot see the faces of practically all of the young people they have worked with over the years.

Had this fourteen-year-old come from a wealthier family, she may have been able to buy her way out of trouble – therapy, boarding school, a move abroad, private care, legal representation, better-resourced support, less reliance on social services. I am not saying that any of this support would necessarily have worked. Still, Maddy's socio-economic status and environment significantly limited her opportunities and severely reduced her life chances.

There was little about her situation – excluded from school, estranged from her mother, hanging out with young people positioned to exploit her, emotional instability, potentially sexually active – where she was the root of the problem. Yet the money and resources did not appear to be directed to her needs.

This is not the story of charity. But, to my earlier point, we were applying a sticking plaster to a far deeper problem. We were a piece of the puzzle that was swiftly elevated to being the complete puzzle. It was my first taste of what was wrong in the social sector. I reported some of these incidences but didn't stay in these roles long enough to learn the outcomes of these complaints.

* * * * *

I witnessed similar patterns to my experiences with Maddy while designing and delivering youth programmes throughout the noughties. The most vital element of each of these programmes tended to be the relationship between me or the youth worker and the young people. But the value of these connections was compromised by the systems that governed the delivery of our work.

In 2004, I worked with Tokunbo Ajasa-Oluwa at Children's Express, where we co-founded a journalism programme called Project Subway. It was a sixteen-week course that worked with young people, using journalism to enhance their employability and personal skills. We hoped that some of the best young people would go on to careers in the media, while others would develop their confidence, writing and social skills enough to find work.

The programme was due to begin several months before Tokunbo and I started, which meant that we were already behind on the targets to accredit 120 young people. For the first few months, we worked outreach four evenings a week, at times doing sessions at two separate youth clubs on a given evening. We worked alternate Saturdays too.

We wrote an accredited programme, supported by Children's Express staff during the daytime, gave presentations to various partners, and managed the extensive bureaucracy that came with managing and delivering a programme behind on its targets. We eventually achieved the target and watched change happen with our young people as the course took them from an introduction to journalism to theory, experiential learning, work placements, and producing a magazine, all while being mentored by the two of us. We also brought young people from different backgrounds and different parts of London together.

While the programme we developed was strong, the element that appeared to be most helpful was the support that came from Tokunbo and me. We were two young Black men, both professional journalists and trained youth workers. We could get interviews with famous people, like dancehall DJ Beenie Man and rapper-singer Est'elle. We also knew how to work effectively with young people referred to us from youth offending teams or pupil referral units.

We achieved our aims even with the funder's potential to withdraw money from the programme due to the fact we were initially behind on targets. Many Project Subway members would become participants of Children's Express and some would move on to careers in the media. We secured follow-on funding to re-run the project and it expanded to the Express's other bureaus. But the new funding terms provided little incentive for growth.

While our students achieved the aims outlined in our funding agreement – certificates, placements, further education – the young people we worked with appeared to be little more than statistics to our grants managers. There was little room to capture the progression of young people who didn't achieve these aims but, in many ways, travelled greater distances than those who accessed further or higher education.

Those who struggled to get out of bed each morning when we first met them attended regularly and started actively and independently pursuing their interests once the course had finished. The young people who couldn't access writing or journalism pathways, generally through lack of money and networks, suddenly had a route to develop their own initiatives. Some participants found new friends from different areas and circles. Due to the way the course was funded – the rigidity of the terms, the lack of capacity to do anything more than grind out outcomes by any means – meant I could not envisage a point where there would be space to improve.

It happened again when I worked at the Stephen Lawrence Charitable Trust (the Trust). When we opened the Stephen Lawrence Centre in 2008, we decided to concentrate our efforts on Stephen's aspirations, not his death. We quickly recognised that our best role was as brokers rather than solely as direct providers of programmes. So, we partnered with close to one hundred institutions, from schools and universities to architecture firms and businesses, to use our name and building to ensure that young people from the inner city would access the best educational activities imaginable.

Stella Dadzie, a co-founder of the Organisation of Women of African and Asian Descent (OWAAD), led our consultation, which informed our services. But we quickly ran into problems. First, there was no value placed on us as brokers; funders were only interested in service delivery with 'at risk' groups. Second, our creative programming was highly aspirational, enabling young people to dare to dream. In my discussions with them, this appeared to be a problem for many funders who tended to favour unenterprising mentoring or CV-writing approaches.

When I started at the Trust, I visited many careers fairs in Lewisham and Greenwich and found them depressing. It seemed that the only pathways available to young people were to university or to enter services like the police or the NHS. Not knocking those routes, but what about careers in the built environment or the arts? The fairs all carried the same format: tables, stands and two-minute sales pitches.

We worked in partnership with Rick Hall of Ignite! and Veda Harrison, who created My Space, My City, My World, which looked at careers fairs from an aspirational perspective. It was a three-day event featuring young creatives and innovators like poet Nick Makoha, designer Catherine Greig and Emily Cummins, who developed the solar-powered fridge.

They helped young people realise that there were pathways to their dreams. It was powerful, inspirational and gave participants a sense that there was more to their spaces, that the city was indeed theirs and that the world, while huge, was accessible. Yet I quickly found myself responding to our funders' confines and less to the needs of those we canvassed – young people, schools, the local community. Ruth Ibegbuna calls this 'dimming your light' to gain funding.

Every few months, grants managers from these funders would visit our projects. I didn't know who these people were, where they'd come from, or what qualified them to inspect our work. I cannot remember coming across any grants manager who had run a project like mine or came from the same background as the young people I worked with. There wasn't a qualification attached to being a grants manager and while I accepted that it was their job to account for their funders' money, it wasn't as if there were standard regulations. Every funder had its own reporting mechanisms, which meant that we had to amend our documents to meet varying requirements. We understood that they had the power to withdraw the funding that paid our wages.

The scenario looked like this. The grants manager contacts us stating that they'd like to visit to see how we're doing. It sounds like a casual visit. A coffee. A catch-up. A conversation. But they arrive with a stack of forms. You offer them tea or coffee. 'How do you take it?' You take them on a tour of the building or the centre. You introduce them to the chief exec, the fundraiser and anyone else who understands the importance of the visit.

As we move through the building or centre, they will see young people diligently at work. Some of it is planned. This is something we've rehearsed. The pupils in these sessions will be the ones we are most familiar with and while they are perhaps a little quieter than usual in this facade, their performance is not an outright lie, more an extension of the truth.

You do this because, despite running sessions outside the school gates, where attendance is voluntary and in young people's spare time, where the primary penalty for bad behaviour is removal from the courses, where young people from different backgrounds and schools are mixing, where the boundaries between educator and pupils are mildly looser, where we have a higher tolerance for pupils from 'troubled' backgrounds and their behaviour than their schools, there was still an expectation from the grants manager for this setting to be as orderly as a school. Inevitably, at some point, they will encounter someone you haven't prepped.

'Hey Dan,' I'd say, 'this is Belinda from the Bam Bam Foundation.'*

'Hi,' says Dan, looking at me as if to say, *And?*

'They fund our summer project,' I continue.

Dan automatically kicks into a charm offensive, telling Belinda how extraordinary the project has been and how it has enhanced his employability prospects, but this wouldn't be the case without their funding.

By this point, Belinda doesn't give a damn. She has forms to fill in. Reports to file. In her world, she probably dreaded the visit too. The difference is, there is little to no accountability related to her role. She could be horrible, condescending and dismissive, and she would remain in post. Her job would not be at stake, unlike mine. All she wants to know is whether we have worked with five hundred kids, how long we had worked with them for, whether they were 'at risk', NEET (Not in Education, Employment or Training), how we had spent the money and if we had the paperwork to verify this.

They appeared faceless, unaware of their power, and lacked empathy for what it took to work with young people productively. The bureaucracy required was too often meaningless and endless. It said nothing about the quality of our service. It was just stats to account for the money the funders had given us with some sense that an actual human being had attended our services.

---

* This is a fictional account, using a fake name and institution. But it constitutes an amalgam of many conversations and situations the author has experienced or observed.

They reduced our young people to eight-page forms. At one point, we were contracted by a funder to work with each young person for a total of six hours each. We didn't feel we could achieve much in such a limited time. So, we created longer and more beneficial programmes for young people, ensuring they received more than six hours. We hustled some short-term pro-bono support to ensure we didn't spend any money inappropriately. For this, we received an unofficial slap on the wrist. I know not of many professions where you are condemned for going the extra mile.

When I interviewed human rights lawyer Harpreet Kaur Paul for this book, I realised I was not alone in my frustrations in running social sector programmes:

> The charities I later became involved in would run small projects that I invested a lot into, and then suddenly the funding would disappear and I would feel a lot of uncertainty about my own job security, whether I was doing the right thing strategically, or whether I was simply looking for scraps of future funding and creating projects that were perceived as more fundable – regardless of whether they sustained the previous work that had been done and enabled it to grow and make the impact that was possible. Directions would quickly change, and the pace of the work – the expectations of what to deliver – the constant aiming for more funding with more outputs and deliverables in a precarious environment, it wasn't good for the work, the charities, or for me.

Despite the evaluations and audits that met our targets, funding always remained precarious. The grant-making world, the bureaucratic layer that sits between institutions distributing wealth to good causes and those receiving it, remained a myth. How do you become a grant-maker? It certainly was not a career I was aware of. What qualifies someone to do this job? Is there a qualification to do it? How are decisions made? What's the criteria for gaining funding? Who are the people behind these funding institutions and who exactly are they giving money to?

Why is there such an imbalance between financial wealth, and those who hold it, and community 'wealth', those who directly serve and understand low-socio-economic communities? Why is it that there are supposedly hundreds of institutions allocating funding, yet it is so hard to find out who they are, what they fund? While I could see that the social sector had limitations, I felt that these projects I had run could grow, be more sustainable, be mainstreamed, replicated, or have a wider impact with the right funding conditions. Maybe, just maybe, we could stay in our jobs a little longer too. But that never appeared to be the case. Funding was always short-term and bureaucratic. I wanted to find what sat behind the myth.

3

Secret service

I entered institutional philanthropy, as a grant-maker, to try to demystify this secret world. I had already designed and delivered programmes at Children's Express and the Stephen Lawrence Charitable Trust, so I had some idea of what a 'good' project or organisation looked like. I knew I would be more empathetic to the needs of applicants and that this would involve creating conditions for them to thrive. This would mean longer-term funding, more realistic targets, paying for staffing costs and building honest relationships with grantees. Problems would not result in a withdrawal of funding but an amendment to the grant agreement. There would be an understanding, on my part, that these charities were often under-resourced and under-staffed but meeting the needs of people who had been failed by far wealthier statutory agencies.

I also recognised the limitations of charities replicating social services, providing direct training, support, mentoring, or development to vulnerable people. But I was also keen to help programmes that were genuinely ambitious for their beneficiaries. At the Stephen Lawrence Charitable Trust, we offered programmes public services couldn't provide. We wanted to break the chain of poor university retention of Black and minority ethnic architecture students. So we tried to address some of the key factors, like poor careers advice, lack of financial support, geographic immobility, lack of parental backing, universities' lack of support and understanding of working-class young people and other factors that limited access to careers in architecture.

I listened to the Trust's bursary students, a brilliant and dynamic set of young people, who offered their time, talent and wisdom to open the doors for future generations of designers. I wanted to set up an architecture scheme encompassing summer courses for young people aged fourteen and above, bespoke support from sixteen to eighteen, mentoring through university with opportunities for bursaries and work placements. The Trust would act as an 'auntie' to young people, helping them navigate their way to becoming architects.

Ultimately, a ten-year programme would influence how marginalised kids entered the architecture profession. If we could change the landscape, literally, of how cities are designed through greater retention of talent entering the trade, we felt we had a good opportunity to influence policy, not just people. I was keen to see how I could direct funding towards projects with deeper ambitions, going beyond changing individuals towards altering practices and policies. I learned a lot from a charity called IntoUniversity, led by Rachel Carr, which provides long-term support to young people from diverse backgrounds through its local learning centres.

I also wanted to know how money flowed in the charitable sector, why success did not lead to more funding, how decisions were made, and why small organisations' innovations and activism rarely trumped large institutions' power and bureaucracy. I wanted to show that I could work in a mainstream organisation as I had previously been typecast as someone who could only work with 'at risk' Black youth. I was also intrigued to discover new projects, campaigning organisations, innovators with bright ideas, people tackling the root causes of issues or those working with multiple partners to change policies and create more equitable services. While delivering courses at the Trust and Children's Express, I didn't have enough time to network to learn more about other charities providing similar or perhaps better work. Rest was a luxury.* Funding agreements rarely allow time for respite. There wasn't time to do lunch when you had teenagers landing on your doorstep because of domestic violence, debt, depression, or not getting their first university choice.

I still knew little about philanthropy and its role in fuelling the social sector. My only experience, as mentioned, had come through my relationships with grant managers. I didn't know what skills were required. Rarely would I see jobs advertised for this profession. And even people I knew

---

* I worked in one organisation where I went to work on a Saturday morning and had to open up the building and play the role of a security guard. There were sessions going on that day as well as a trustees' meeting in the afternoon. Having fulfilled my security-guard duties, I cleaned up, put on my suit and went into the trustees' meeting to present an update about our education programme. Once the trustees left, I went into the office to do some paperwork related to funding and changed again to deliver an afternoon workshop to some prospective mentors. Once the workshop concluded, I cleaned up some of the premises so it would be ready for Monday's activities, then locked up.

who had held grants management posts struggled to describe what they did and why.

I always had the impression that they were perceived as glorified administrators. Bureaucrats, ticking boxes, checking databases, and being thankful for the arrival of the internet as it meant that they wouldn't need to leave their desk, meet with anyone, or work a minute past 5 p.m. I would discover, primarily from the brilliant people I worked with at Esmée Fairbairn, that the role, at its best, was more than that. But rare was the grants manager who enters this profession to work above their pay grade and do anything more than administer grants.

Upon announcing my departure from the Stephen Lawrence Charitable Trust to Esmée Fairbairn Foundation, which specialised in granting in the arts, education, social change and environment, it came as a surprise that a few of my ex-colleagues at the Trust thought I wouldn't last in this world. One senior colleague described me as a 'programmer', meaning someone who creates projects, and therefore funding projects was not my skillset. Another senior colleague flat out told me that I wouldn't last long.

I thought that being a 'programmer' gave me the ideal skills to assess proposals. My most significant battle would be with myself, being more deskbound, dealing with the monotony of repetition, living vicariously through the achievements of the projects I funded and being one step removed from the instant gratification of helping people more directly. But I would also have more power than in any previous role to help projects that were rarely supported and do so in a way that gave them the 'freedom to fail'. I used to say this phrase a lot, but it is not the correct term in retrospect. If good projects had the freedom and space to achieve their ambitions, and navigate the bumps in the road along the way, then the probability of them succeeding would be far greater. But I still did not know enough about the history of philanthropy and its role in British society to fully understand how best to demystify it.

In his book, *Public Good By Private Means: How Philanthropy Shapes Britain*, Rhodri Davies documents the history and influence of philanthropy in Britain. He speaks of the creation of modern philanthropy, shifting from 'religious almsgiving, where the focus was primarily on what it meant for the donor and their immortal soul, towards giving that was focused on addressing the problems of society'.[1] According to Davies, the Poor Laws of 1598 and 1601 placed more emphasis on the role of philanthropy and voluntary action in tackling poverty than in previous times. The Poor Laws were not, however, adequate to address the changes in society. The agricultural and industrial revolutions transformed Great Britain but these were also periods of coerced labour, disease, trauma and poor health from working conditions, and a population increase. While the state had a great deal of responsibility to provide some relief to those in dire need, it wasn't enough. The role of philanthropy increased during the mid-Victorian era when viewed as the ideal way to supplement and even supplant state provision.

In the nineteenth century, the influence of voluntary organisations in conceiving ways to address poverty, identifying unmet needs, campaigning and moulding the state's services grew to a point where the modern charitable sector was established. The wealthy were now donating more to voluntary organisations to tackle Britain's social problems. In turn, voluntary or charitable organisations became core providers of welfare, which would last through to the twentieth century. There was a strong culture of giving during this period. In the 1890s, middle-class people spent more money on charity than on any other thing, bar food.[2] In reality, poverty was too significant a problem for philanthropic and charitable action alone.

A further shift in the relationship between the state and civil society occurred after World War II, following the creation of Britain's welfare state. Philanthropy and voluntary action had been hugely influential in developing the NHS, but it was clear that the government would now be primarily responsible for addressing social problems. By the 1960s, philanthropy and charity redefined their relationship with the government by challenging the state, holding it to account for how it delivered social services.

By the 1980s, challenge had turned to cooperation. Under Thatcher, the Tories started to lessen the role of government in part by co-opting and outsourcing services to charities. These charities got paid and played. They became institutionalised by money (large state contracts and grants), scaled their services, grew financially, gained a seat at the table but danced to the government's tune.

These charities became extensions of the state, their independence compromised. It's a trend that has continued to this day. 'It's become another arm of the state. It feels like the relationship is far too close,' says Yvonne Field, founder of the Ubele Initiative, who I interviewed for this book. 'It seems like you don't have the space to criticise and critique. It feels like the space to criticise and critique is so low in the pecking order of the system that you can't actually really hear that voice of criticism ... I guess what I'm thinking about is the professionalisation of the whole sector, which for me has lost that energy, that push and that possibility for being where you can facilitate social change.'

More than anything, the gap between ordinary citizens protesting and using their voice for change and the mainstream social sector grew to the point that there was a widespread perception that charities served the government more than the public. Moreover, these mainstream charities viewed the delivery of their work through the market-and-growth lens. This isn't to suggest that all large charities and not-for-profits are bad. But it became an industry powered by money and expansion more than by mission.

British philanthropists and the social sector have evolved from being core welfare providers to campaigning against the government to being an extension of the state. They have shifted from serving marginalised people to challenging the government to appeasing the oppressed. Yet, given its mutable history, there is no clear conception of the social sector's role in society today. Much of this is symbolised by the ambiguity over what the sector should be called. As Ruth Ibegbuna, founder of Rekindle, said to me, 'The fact that it doesn't even have a name that people recognise; we're saying civil society, if you took it out of here, people would say, "what's that?" Is it a social sector? Is it philanthropy? What does it even mean?'

4

What do you call it?

Anyone working in philanthropy (i.e., trusts and foundations, public funding, etc.), charities or social enterprises, or campaigning will recognise these as distinct functions: they do not sit comfortably within any singular definition or term. Other than civil society, people often use the term the third sector to indicate, I guess, that beyond the public and private sectors, this is the third one, a bit like a fifth wheel, possibly surplus to requirements. As with civil society, the third sector is a bit of a non-descript term.

Calling it the charitable sector is not entirely accurate either, mainly because charities are only one of many constituted mechanisms used to 'do good'. We have social enterprises less reliant on donations, generating their own money to do good; unregistered groups and cooperatives, among many other not-for-profit structures. This brings us to the phrase not-for-profits or non-profits, which is only partially accurate as a term describing this sector. Many social sector organisations, like social businesses, generate profit and accumulate wealth through 'charitable' means. I have used the term the social sector throughout, which is a little bland but perhaps remains the most easily identifiable way to describe what I'm struggling to explain.

Most people will understand philanthropy to describe monetary giving, particularly by the wealthy, although it does encompass other forms of voluntary action. So, how about calling it the voluntary sector or voluntary action? But, while many people in this field do not do this work for profit or because the state has told them to do it, some are well paid. The social sector features many people who are driven by profit and status more than doing good. Some people will use the clunky acronym VCSE (Voluntary, Community and Social Enterprise), which may be the most encompassing term but not the most charming. Others will refer to it as the NGO (Non-Governmental Organisations) sector, given that these organisations operate independently from the government, although, as I've said, this is not wholly true.

We have a 'sector' (although some people hate calling it a sector) with an identity crisis. Its lack of a recognisable name reflects the confusion related to its purpose. 'Civil society feels like a "gap filler" for where public services are failing and where there is no profit for private companies to swoop in,' says Nikki Clegg, Director of Operations and Grants at Thirty Percy, who I spoke to for this book. 'However, civil society (particularly in terms of people in communities rather than charities) really creates most of the "real world" value that we need. They create the social connections and relationships, they want to look after the environment, they teach next generations and pass on wisdom. People and communities are supporting people to live with happiness, dignity and purpose. It is the hidden economy and the under-valued work that are needed in the world I hope to live in one day.'

Upon entering philanthropy, I started to see more clearly why the social sector elicited such confusion from those who did not work in it. There have been many events and family gatherings where I have told people what I do for a living. Blank responses were typical; praise for doing such worthy work or surprise that I get paid for doing it were also common. Being paid for charitable or 'voluntary' work remains one of the core reasons the public struggles to relate to this world.

There was greater clarity among my family and friends when I worked for the Stephen Lawrence Charitable Trust because it had been such an influential and well-documented campaign, one that touched the hearts of so many people in Britain. But few non-profit activities stimulated such universal affection unless there was some personal or local connection. Unfortunately, it had become an industry, one that helped us in crisis and provided channels for us to give, but that no longer engaged with us and therefore could not authentically speak on our behalf. However, the more I worked in philanthropy, the more I understood why this sector had drifted so far from the public's regard and why, like so many other industries, privilege and not proximity to communities dictated how far you would go in this field.

Fundamentally, the social sector suffers from Band-Aid, also known as the white saviour complex. White, privileged, well-meaning saviours are positioned to use their resources and wealth to help the poor and needy. All very admirable. Extremely generous. Not saying that folks should stop giving because of what I'm about to say. But here are a few reasons why it's problematic. And it is not only a problem faced by people of colour or those in the international aid sector.

There are often community-based organisations and local people who are already working towards alleviating the issues these saviours or mainstream social sector organisations are coming in to relieve. But instead of backing existing efforts, these large entities and privileged people tend to parachute in with their ideas of tackling the problem with little or no consideration of local partners.

The Band-Aid approach tends to feed off people's pain and provides little to no dignity for those facing disadvantage, those being 'saved'. Poverty-pimping. Such efforts can be patronising. 'Poverty porn and the microaggressions sap that imagination about people of colour,' says Bonnie Chiu, director of The Social Investment Consultancy, who I interviewed for this book. Without sufficient consultation or partnerships with local people, the delivery of these projects is often culturally inappropriate, created through a privileged lens with little or no recognition for the needs of those receiving support.

The white saviour complex depends on mainstream social sector organisations instead of building independence for people on the front lines. The problem is, you cannot criticise the saviours for doing what appears to be good because they're doing good, and you'll be accused of being ungrateful. The self-righteousness and a non-self-reflective attitude to doing good leave no room for criticism. How can you improve the way you give? How can you ensure that you're not complicit in reinforcing systems of inequality?

While these efforts are well-meaning, they rarely go to the heart of the issue. Back to my sticking-plaster point, they are essentially buying sticking plasters in bulk to try and stem an impossible stream that also happens to enhance their cash flow. By not tackling the root causes of the problem, these large organisations cannot create a sustainable way of supporting communities facing disadvantages.

The leaders of these large entities will receive their MBEs, OBEs and knighthoods for services to humanity. These accolades position them to move into more powerful roles. Yet often lost are the many people on the ground whose tireless work goes unrecognised despite creating the conditions for the saviours' success. Finally, international social sector organisations (commonly known as international non-governmental organisations or INGOs) have done little to erase the prevailing narrative that the Global South needs saving. The Band-Aid approach dims it, dulls it, saps it, creating a picture of dependency, a world of 'haves' and 'have-nots'. It's a game that wasn't designed for those facing disadvantage to succeed.

5

The way, by charities

I understood that the mainstream social sector mirrored society's inequities. I've already mentioned the lack of diversity, the overemphasis on services over systemic change, and the charity mentality over justice. However, it was not just the composition of the sector's leadership and its approach that was a problem. While I could see these dynamics at play, other issues emerged:

- *Down by law.* Campaign groups and charities often meeting their communities' otherwise unmet needs did not stand much chance of surviving the Coalition and Tory governments' years. The Single Identity Bill in 2008 (under Labour) and Lobbying Act in 2014 reduced the income and restricted the voice and advocacy of many campaign groups, particularly those providing targeted issues and culturally based interventions to their communities. Many of these organisations had to broaden their remit to work with a wider set of constituents or adopt a government-defined community cohesion lens (essentially, assimilation at the expense of your culture) to fit into funding streams, pushing them away from their mission. For many who didn't broaden their work, they often lost income or closed.

- *Stop paying taxes.* The richer you are, the more tax breaks you will receive for your giving. For people earning over £150,000 in England and Wales, 45 per cent of their donations are subsidised by the government through taxpayers' money. Some philanthropists create endowed trusts and foundations or use Donor Advised Funds (DAFs),* among other vehicles, for their giving. There are billions of dollars sitting in DAFs in the United States that are not being distributed to good causes. It is often an off-the-road vehicle waiting for its MOT. Trusts and foundations, as an example, are exempt from paying taxes on the original and investment income.[1] In addition, many philanthropists hold their assets in offshore accounts. The government's tax benefits are there to incentivise giving by the wealthy, but this reduces public spending. Why is this important?

---

* According to the Charities Aid Foundation, 'A donor advised fund or DAF is a wrapper or a vehicle for charitable giving. It is an alternative to someone having their own (or family) standalone charitable foundation. DAFs offer several advantages over charitable foundations, namely cost savings, tax-efficiency, flexibility, and ease of administrative, fiduciary, and reporting requirements. Instead of registering a charitable foundation with the Charity Commission, you can set up a fund with a DAF provider like our CAF Charitable Trust. This gives you everything you get from a standalone foundation but it comes under the provider's umbrella. It takes out a lot of the hassle associated with running your own foundation. This allows you to focus on the meaningful side of giving, from working with the charities and talking to beneficiaries to finding out about the impact that their giving is having.' (https://www.cafonline.org/my-personal-giving/long-term-giving/donor-advised-funds)

- *Undemocratic.* The giving of private philanthropists and the trusts and foundations are undemocratic. The composition of most UK foundations' boards resembles a traditional corporation, as they comprise primarily white men aged over sixty-five.[2] To note, charity-sector governance wasn't much different. There's more diversity on the boards of FTSE-100 organisations than the major charities. Given that a significant amount of private philanthropic money is tied to our taxes (subsidised by us or reduced public spending), who decides where this money goes matters, particularly if they have been elected to senior positions based on their wealth and social status more than their knowledge of social issues. So, how much of this income actually goes to organisations that are challenging such hierarchal models of decision-making in our society?

- *Philanthropy for the elite.* Paul Vallely, the author of *Philanthropy – from Aristotle to Zuckerberg*, discovered that 'in the 10-year period to 2017, more than two-thirds of all millionaire donations – £4.79bn – went to higher education, and half of these went to just two universities: Oxford and Cambridge'. During the same period, British millionaires 'gave £1.04bn to the arts, and just £222m to alleviating poverty'.[3] This is just an example of the substantial amount of private and independent giving goes to institutions that serve a small section of society, such as private schools, universities, large museums and theatres. These are often already wealthy institutions that receive significant income from publicly funded bodies such as the Arts Council and the National Lottery Heritage Fund.

- *Two dead and the other dying.* The late former Manchester United manager Tommy Docherty once declared that an ideal directors' board would comprise three men, of whom two would be dead and the other one dying. Even when you had funding organisations giving money to good and not self-interested causes, the composition of those making decisions remains problematic. Just because you may happen to be successful in business or you've inherited wealth, or you've been in the civil service for seventy-five years, this does not automatically qualify you to know the needs of gang-affected girls or cleaners. I wonder why people without knowledge or experience of their organisations' social missions always had the privilege to decide who received the money. The governance of the social sector remains a club for an elite and privileged few who make decisions on our behalf. There is little interest among this group to rock the boat. It is paternalistic. It is still the case that social sector leadership, narrow as it is, thinks it knows best when it comes to the plight of low socio-economic communities. But then again, the same could be said of most institutions across the globe.

- *Doing good or doing damage?* How can philanthropy from the wealthy be a tool to challenge orthodoxy if it exhibits the same extractive behaviours that govern society? I do not know how many trusts and foundations have direct links to slavery. But I am sure there will be a few. Most have accumulated their wealth through investments that have damaged our environment or abused under-served communities through coercive or exploitative labour. While many trusts and foundations have improved their investment portfolios in recent years, moving away from tobacco and firearms, the vast majority still capitalise from companies that damage our climate and exacerbate racial disparities. Are these funders doing more damage with investments to preserve wealth than doing good with their philanthropic giving? Also worth noting: the top three hundred funders in the UK distribute approximately just 4 per cent of their £67 billion net assets.

- *Dark Money.* More insidious is how philanthropists push their political agendas through their giving. Jane Mayer's book *Dark Money* underlined how American billionaires, such as the Koch brothers and the late Richard Mellon Scaife, had spent millions influencing US politics, pushing their ultra-conservative values. They used their wealth and networks to hire lobbyists and fund academics, think tanks, advocacy and legal groups to shape US voting and thinking. 'They challenged the widely accepted post-World War II consensus that an activist government was a force for public good. Instead they argued for "limited government," drastically lower personal and corporate taxes, minimal social services for the needy, and much less oversight of industry, particularly in the environment arena. They said they were driven by principle, but their positions dovetailed seamlessly with their personal financial interests.'[4]

- *Economic inequality*. During austerity, the mega charities continued to prosper while smaller charities' income decreased. 'In some (many!) ways the VCSE sector has ended up here mirroring the corporate world, we see this in the professionalisation of the sector and organisation cultures,' says Fatima Iftikhar, a founding organiser of the #CharitySoWhite campaign, who I interviewed for this book. 'We see this in the existential question of the purpose of VCSE. Its prioritisation of service provision over advocacy has contributed to the growth of "large" and "super" charities, with grassroots groups disproportionately neglected and losing funding over the last decade of austerity, but even before this.' The Charity Income Spotlight Report in June 2020 found that in 2018–19, 74 per cent of charities had an annual income of £100k or less, but generated just 2.7 per cent of the total annual income. In contrast, 89 organisations (less than 0.1 per cent of charities), each generating over £100 million, generated almost a third of the total annual income.[5]

- *One-size-fits-all*. There are simply not many social sector organisations that take an anti-racist and intersectional approach to distributing their money or delivering their services. These organisations effectively design projects that cannot meet the needs of a broad cross-section of Britain's public. I wonder why so many of these organisations do not see the interconnections between issues. Why does their problem analysis appear confined to single areas, be it health, education or employability? Do they approach their work in this way because it aligns with government policies or funding? This siloed approach, combined with an obsession with clear, hard outcomes, ignores multiple needs, complexity and the deeper, multi-systemic approaches required to tackle embedded social problems. Immy Kaur told me about the government's work on obesity, which seemed to reflect this narrow approach to resourcing complex social issues.

> The Cabinet Office's Obesity Systems Mapwork from ten years ago made me go, 'OK, right, we've got to design differently, we've got to design for multiple benefits. We've got to have narratives that are not zero-sum, that are not binary, and that recognise many truths at once.' It's quite hard to do that work when the money coming down from government even now is not encouraging us to do that. It encourages us to have an answer, to have a shovel ready project, to have a simple solution – a straightforward 'do this one thing and it will be fixed'.

- *B(ureaucracy)-side wins again.* Funders are to blame. Make no mistake. They have loaded the decks against applicants, forcing them to 'achieve' outcomes in unnatural time frames, ignoring complexities, turning real people into products and innovators into bureau-crats. They ask for too much information (which they don't use), they ask for loads of reports (which they rarely read) and they often ask the wrong questions (because they do not have sufficient experience about the issues they are asked to assess). They expect miracles within time frames shorter than an election cycle. 'The sector (in the UK) is misregulated and misgoverned. The amount of time and effort which is wasted on all kinds of tedious administration, from starting up a new charity to making what are usually quite simple funding decisions, is enormously waste-ful,' says Dan Paskins, UK Impact Director at Save the Children UK, who I interviewed for this book. 'There is a focus on short-termism driven by a broken funding system. Grassroots organisations providing a lifeline for their communities have to keep going week by week or month by month. Funders with endowments choose to partially fund organisations and leaders and force them to spend time and effort on approaching many different funders, and only fund for short, time-limited projects. The causes that phi-lanthropy and civil society seek to address are often ones that require efforts over decades, and are rarely ones that can be solved with a one-year or three-year grant which expects '"sustainability" at the end of it.'

- *Gentrification.* Through the 2000s and beyond, busi-ness types and Russell Group graduates displaced grassroots activists, practitioners, and people with lived or proximate experience. I remember when

Connexions emerged in 2000 to professionalise youth work. It was a careers service that aimed to provide information, advice and guidance to thirteen- to nineteen-year-olds. One-to-one contact with young people became more deskbound; it became more transactional and less relational; it became more about serving 'low-hanging fruit' than helping endangered young people. Young people became NEETs, 'hard to reach', 'at risk'. I had already seen a proliferation of suit-and-tie business-sector types infiltrate the social sector. They brought in private-sector terminology and techniques to professionalise the sector. They mirrored in class and colour those regulating, governing and directing the money. Soon after, I started to see more Russell Group graduates being fast-tracked into senior positions. Now, polished middle-class folks constituted the primary pipeline for sector talent. Soon, it became the answer for charities delivering their services. This approach merely coated the fatal cracks in the social sector. These newcomers rarely took an equitable approach to tackling disadvantage; they devalued lived experiences. They focused on individual behavioural change programmes and created frameworks that essentially maintained their stranglehold on and web of power and influence. Their organisations grew. They helped loads of individuals. But systems were rarely challenged as a result.

- *B-Side wins again and again.* Due to the demands on social sector organisations to meet the different needs, priorities, conditions and expectations of multiple funders, many charities found themselves hiring as many bureaucrats as frontline workers to stay operational through the 2010s. The bureaucrats served the funders while the frontline workers helped the service-users. The bureaucrats were often paid more too. Without funding, there would be no services, and money talks. When there were funding cuts, the retention of those who can generate money appeared to become a higher priority. It became more important to serve the needs of funders than constituents.

- *Erasure.* Fundraising success is mainly dependent on your relationships. Large charities have greater visibility through advertising, shops, social media campaigns and celebrity endorsements. It is easy for us to donate to these charities because they have won our trust through their profile, familiarity and age. These social sector organisations also have the resource to hire people whose sole job is meeting with funders and who regularly network. Their job is to find out what the funder is thinking and sell it back to them. They have the resource to stalk grassroots organisations too. They will try to co-opt the grassroots organisation (and call it a partnership) or misappropriate it (without providing due credit or resources to the originator). They will sell their often-diluted version (through their marketing campaigns) of the grassroots organisation's work to you, erasing the idea's originators. Baljeet Sandhu's 2017 report 'The Value of Lived Experience in Social Change' was a game-changer. The report shifted the paradigm, expressing why the social sector needed more people from the communities most impacted by social issues to lead change. Many of the larger charities (often with little or no senior leadership from the communities they were serving) misappropriated Sandhu's work to submit substantial funding bids. Networks and relationships drive funding and smaller organisations have the least access to them.

- *Game of theory.* Imagine declining a proposal from Martin Luther King because he didn't have a theory of change? Sounds ridiculous. But the funding 'industry' is such that validated tools in the 2000s and 2010s became more meaningful than the difference an organisation or individual could make. Yes, tools are essential. But they should be secondary. Meaningful difference is vital. And it is challenging to achieve significant, long-term difference by only filling public service gaps. But this is where the social sector has ended up; reams of money going out to serve public sector gaps, led by slick organisations with great tools but short-term impact. What we should really value is not being measured or assessed.

- *Outsiders.* A Eurocentric frame defines the social sector. Everything from the hierarchal organisational models to the 'accepted' forms of evaluation, from access to positions of power to language, all derive from a Eurocentric lens that fundamentally mar-ginalises communities of colour while creating tools and services that are not fit-for-purpose in a multi-cultural society.

- *Pimping ain't easy, but charities often do it.* Death and deprivation sell. Sounds cruel, but the social sector feeds off the pain of people and communities facing disadvantages. I have covered this earlier in the book, but the public has been fed images of the 'have-nots' to raise money for years, often deleting those with inspirational visions of change. 'We talk about, "this feels bad at the moment, so let's do something small to make us feel less bad." We don't talk about what feeling good would feel like for everyone in the country and I think we need to start naming what good is and now what the new normal is. I hate that phrase. What is good? What is better? What is aspirational? What is inspirational? Why are we just aiming to recreate a normal?' says Ruth Ibegbuna, founder of RECLAIM, The Roots Programme and Rekindle.

- *Charity over justice.* Despite the professionalisation of the social sector, the continued growth of the super-major and major charities and the proliferation of philanthropic foundations, economic and social disparities continue to widen. For all the world changes over the last hundred years, 'the charity mindset' prevails.[6] For philanthropy, as an institution, to exist, there has to be an under-class – the wealthy giving to the poor. Investments, however, are based on the preservation of wealth and the status quo. Surely success would mean that philanthropic organisations invest in a way to work their way out of existence rather than continue to grow? Foundations have longer-term plans on how to maintain their wealth than their grant-giving strategies. As Stephanie

Brobbey, founder of The Good Ancestor Movement, pointed out in an article on Medium, there are more food banks in the UK than branches of McDonald's.[7] While food banks meet an immediate need and are crucial, there is something desperately wrong in a society where charity's growth is based on people's pain. Charity is not a sustainable or ethical approach to alleviating problems in society. Justice is.

- *Too much jargon from too many intermediaries.* The phrases 'holistic', 'systems change', 'co-production', 'theory of change' and 'diversity' are overused, over-theorised and rarely effectively practised. If they were effectively practised, there would be far more social sector organisations challenging the academisation of schools or the ineffectiveness of incarceration as a rehabilitation method. Charities would have been at the forefront of the Stephen Lawrence and Hillsborough campaigns. They would have mobilised the thousands that attended the Black Lives Matter and Extinction Rebellion protests. Instead, round tables trump action. These are facilitated by many intermediaries, organisations that sit between funders and charities and social enterprises. They are brokers, advisors, researchers, etc., tasked with making the sector more effective, efficient and impactful. It's a big industry that continues to grow. These organisations are given endless amounts of money to think, write reports, navel gaze and tell funders and charities what they are doing right or wrong. They are 'extractor fans'. They make friends with and then extract from grassroots organisations, and then sell what they learn back to funders. These intermediaries also tend to create impenetrable language. It is difficult to know how effective they are because it's difficult to understand what the hell they are telling us.

- *20 per cent.* I'll be honest. On most of the portfolios I have managed, I would not consider more than 20 per cent of the grants to be exceptional. Exceptional meaning that they were learning organisations with either substantial evidence or innovators with huge potential; organisations led by or grounded in the voices of those closest to the issue, projects tackling root causes, speaking truth to power, challenging the norm, etc. Not to say the other 80 per cent are bad. Just not exceptional. That special 20 per cent are worth supporting properly. I once pitched for ten-year grants for such charities. Didn't work. I got five-year core-cost grants with 10 per cent unrestricted funds thrown on top for organisations to use as they pleased. This would ease cash flow, support succession planning, rapid response (to emergent social issues), backfill, research and development, experimentation, thinking time, etc. Always the starting point for me. If you have great organisations – the 20 per cent – create favourable conditions, support wholeheartedly, and give them the space to succeed.

- *Collective intelligence.* Research tells us that diversity (demographics, cognitive) leads to a team's rich, deep, dynamic collective intelligence. This leads to improved decision-making, better problem-solving and more innovation. The lack of diversity in the mainstream social sector is shocking. In grant-making, collective intelligence should include lived experience, field/proximate expertise (i.e., practitioners, local awareness, thematic know-how), creatives, technical skills and someone with experience delivering work through an equity lens. They may not agree much. May not be five individual people. But the absence of these people in decision-making severely compromises an organisation's ability to make firm and well-informed judgements on complex proposals.

- *Challenging the glass ceiling.* Probably heard this story before, but worth telling again. In the 1970s, women comprised less than 5 per cent of musicians within the US's top five orchestras. By 1997 this had increased to about 25 per cent. The primary reason was that in the 1980s, these orchestras started using blind auditions (putting a curtain up so judges could not tell the sex of the players).[8] Despite predominantly male judges' insistence to the contrary, the new approach confirmed that bias had heavily influenced their judgements. I have encountered this frequently in the funding world. Bias severely impacts decisions, often without us knowing it. This requires significant cultural change. Unfortunately, too few organisations are willing to go on this uncomfortable ride.

- *Policy-based evidence and data.* At one foundation, I inherited an education funding strand that supported academic research to develop evidence-based practice about learning in the primary and secondary school systems. We found that much of the research, as good as it may have been, had not led to sustained implementation or impact when we reviewed the strand. The academics' ambitions were often different from ours. For them, having their work peer reviewed was a priority. For us, we wanted to see the results of good research practised and implemented in more schools. In addition, it appeared that most universities were poor at dissemination. However, the biggest issue was that most headteachers rarely used robust evidence to influence their decisions. Maybe this was due to lack of time, there being no central place to compare and contrast evidence; perhaps their decisions were more instinctive, nepotistic or cost-effective. Either way, as a result, much of the research we had been funding didn't stand a chance unless it had political weight and will behind it to make it policy. And even then, these decisions, like those of headteachers, were not strictly based on evidence.

By the time the COVID-19 crisis hit, it was clear that the social sector would struggle to meet the needs of the most marginalised groups in our society from a resource and ethical perspective. Bad publicity was the only thing that tended to drive a fundamental shift in the social sector's behaviours and practice. Something drastic needed to change. Was the mainstream social sector, the large institutions, finally willing to sacrifice survival for fundamental change?

Dimming the lights

It is often the case that the social sector dims the light of marginalised communities to get money from the public. This is probably the best way to describe the Band-Aid mentality. It darkens the light of those facing disadvantage as well as those proximate to tackling these social issues. For many people from marginalised communities entering these spaces, these everyday experiences can be damaging. If you're an outsider, your racial background or ability are not things you can switch on and off. You live with it. It may not define you. But often, people will define you by it. And this has an impact on your well-being, work opportunities, and the way people respond to you. I asked a few people from racially minoritised backgrounds what it had been like to work in the social sector.

'I was an award-winning CEO and was asked to give a high-profile keynote speech to an assembled group of philanthropists. I stood at the front, being introduced with warm words when a blonde woman raced in late, took off her coat and hurled it at me to hang up for her as she rushed to her seat. It hadn't crossed her mind that a Black woman could be in that space other than to serve her. I delivered the whole speech deliberately holding her coat and have never forgotten how that felt.'

'I called out a white staff member for making an institutional decision about a race-related issue without consulting any Black or Asian members of staff. When I said this to her, she was offended and defensive. She didn't acknowledge her oversight and the following day suggested that I had a problem and offered to find me a mentor. Within twenty-four hours, she had gone from white supremacy (ignoring Black and Asian folks) to white fragility (being defensive about being called out for ignoring us) to white saviour (trying to help me even though she had the problem).'

'Told by my charity boss that "I should be very careful with any applicant with an African name, as unfortunately there was a lot of fraud within that society." How many levels of wrong in that statement . . . also stupidity, as what is an African society? She was just as bad about Muslims, especially Muslim men and how they dominated women: "Why else would a woman cover herself?"'

'Why are people of colour silenced – unable to be ourselves? Because it makes you [white people] uncomfortable? I see so much trauma in the eyes of my people – working in a system which is designed to oppress them and take away their humanity by denying the reality of our past and present. By ignoring the colonial history of the wealth of our sector, do you think we will forget where we came from and what was done to us? The ghosts of my ancestors walk beside me, waiting to be acknowledged and waiting to see justice. The passion for change courses through our veins and we will not rest until we see it happen – each of us, working with this system, sacrifices a small part of our humanity and a small part of our soul, which deadens in this whitespace. But we keep walking, and we keep provoking and we keep challenging because just like those before us, we take on the burden from our ancestors to dismantle the system which oppresses us.'

'I cannot tell you how many times I have sat waiting on someone to come and get me from reception, even when I'm the only person sitting in the waiting room. My name gets called out and the young white woman [usually] looks through me as if I wasn't there. You see, I couldn't possibly have a German surname.'

'A grants officer once accused a Bengali woman of being "belligerent" for mentioning white privilege in her application. The following week, another colleague described a white male chief exec as a "thought leader" for talking about white privilege.'

'"So, how do we feel about those poor BAME people who depend on us white saviours? So problematic, aren't they? They do nothing to help themselves.

What do YOU think?" Eyes turn, testing, gauging, judging. To speak for a thousand communities. Our complexity simplified to BAME to make it easier for you. You want to speak of systems of mass oppression, histories of subjugation, centuries of blood. But instead, you bite your tongue to subdue the inner voice, to ensure your survival.'

'When you say that something is problematic or racist and white people say they don't see it, and then turn to another white person to confirm this, like we all have equal votes on race.'

'When people finally see your point on race but still dominate the conversation and make you the bad person for not making them see this point in a way that feels kinder. Even though it wasn't what you said or how you said it. In reality it's how their own shame feels, which you can do nothing about.'

'I was employed to be half of a job-share but was paid less than my white counterpart. I was told it was because she had been in the post before me and had more experience. A year later she left the role and I did the job solo for eight months before another white person was hired to be my job-share. That person was paid £10k more than me for the same role. When I asked my white male manager, I was told that she had come from a law firm and was on a higher salary than I was, so they had to match that. There was no suggestion that my salary would be uplifted to match hers and, in this case, we both had the same level of experience.'

'It is shocking to see the manoeuvres some white people make to secure their position as the expert on the Black experience. Black people's ideas are scrutinised and undermined publicly, in secret they are pillaged and presented to the world as if they were their own. I mean . . . this is just the tip of the iceberg!!'

'I was speaking to some white well-to-do graduates who were interested in volunteering at a charity I worked for. The charity worked with young people on the edge of gang involvement. Earlier in the day, they had participated in a workshop facilitated by one of our young people [a young Black male], who was once a service user but had gone on to become a trainer. The well-to-do graduates talked freely. They talked about the workshop. One of them said, "I was so surprised, he's such a big lad, was quite scared at first, but so softly spoken, and funny." It struck me how the Black body elicits fear among white people as an almost natural response and how, in a different context, say, on the high road or in a job interview, this would always be a barrier that this young man would have to overcome before he'd even opened his mouth.'

6

The wrong side of history

'Alternatives that fail to address racism, male dominance, homophobia, class bias and other structures of domination will not, in the final analysis, lead to decarceration and will not advance the goal of abolition.'[1]

ANGELA DAVIS,
American activist, author and scholar, 2003

In the summer of 2020, I received a message from a former colleague, a woman of colour and grant-maker. She said that her 'anger had turned to heartbreak'. She was referring to how her employer, a funder, had been behaving during the COVID-19 outbreak concerning race. I could feel her point.

During the early stages of the lockdown, social sector organisations had to adjust their operations to meet increasing demands, despite facing financial insecurity and reduced ability to serve their users' needs. It was clear that the longer the lockdown continued, the more people would be cut off from vital services, while many of the charities helping those people would potentially face closure. On 20 March 2020,

National Council for Voluntary Organisation's (NCVO) then chief executive Karl Wilding said that voluntary sector organisations would lose £4.3 billion in income over the next twelve weeks.

It wasn't until 8 April that the Chancellor of the Exchequer, Rishi Sunak, unveiled a £750 million financial package for charities. Ten years after then Prime Minister David Cameron launched the 'Big Society' plan focusing on localism, empowering communities, greater support to charities and volunteering, civil society appeared to become an afterthought to the current government. The £750 million pledge fell significantly short of the required £4.3 billion and came some time after the financial bailouts for businesses. While £220 million of the charity stimulus package was ring-fenced for small social sector organisations, we entered a period of the survival of the richest, not survival of the best.

In 2016, Lloyds Bank Foundation reported that since the financial crash in 2008, 'small and medium-sized charities lost a higher proportion of their income than large charities. Income from local and central government fell by up to 44 per cent for small and medium-sized charities.'[2] Over 23,000 charities closed during this period, while government commissioning and contracting models favoured private-sector providers or large charities.[3] The Big Society years had not been about people power, as suggested by David Cameron in 2010, but private-sector power, enabled by the government. During the outbreak, where local support and an understanding of community was critical, the government had turned its back on local communities, true to its performance of the past decade.

This lack of community support was particularly true of the government's response to supporting groups most affected during the initial outbreak, like women at risk of domestic violence or young people facing domestic abuse. This was also the case with many funders. There was little to no talk of targeted funding to reach those most in need. I didn't hear of many trusts and foundations willing to release a higher percentage of the wealth held in their endowments to meet the demand. There was much talk about pooling funds with other funders, protecting their grant-holders, enabling the sector to connect better.

There wasn't much in the way of bold leadership or swift, direct action. Like the government, when independent and high-net-worth funders held a mirror in front of themselves, they did not see the daughter of a Black nurse or the face of a disabled youth worker. If you don't live it, you can leave it. Those who can leave a problem may empathise with the issue, but will they ever have the same level of urgency to try and change it?

The social sector had been warned. For years, many reports urged charities to address the lack of diversity, structural racism and other issues that were disregarding marginalised people. Unfortunately, these reports, the data, and the evidence did not significantly increase funding to specialist groups. In general, there were not many intentional, user-led or strategic responses by large charities to address diversity issues, be it in their approaches, staffing or portfolio, nor many targeted approaches to reach communities furthest away from support. More charities said they valued people's lived experiences; some cleaned up their policies, others confessed that they needed to shift the power, but nothing fundamentally changed. No urgency. No accountability. No long-term vision. No devolvement. No engagement with people on the ground that didn't lead to greater profits for large organisations. There was no change to the toxic dynamic of requiring a white male voice (and, in the social sector, the white female voice) to give the subjects of race, ability, immigration, diversity and inclusion credence.

Through the tireless campaigning of The Ubele Initiative and Charity So White and others through much of 2020, funders and social sector organisations started to take notice. In April 2020, Ubele released the report 'Impact of COVID-19 on the BAME Community and Voluntary Sector'. The report warned that close to nine out of ten BAME-led organisations could close if the COVID-19 crisis continued beyond three months.[4]

Austerity measures had already decimated the BAME voluntary sector. Many of the approximately 10,000 BAME-led charitable groups in the UK had a turnover of less than £10,000. With COVID-19, the majority could be forced to cease operations when their communities needed them most. Ubele's stark 87 per cent prediction became one of the most frequently cited statistics when funders eventually started to think about targeting funding to organisations led by people of colour. An important point raised by the report was that the people of colour leading these charities were also more likely to have lost relatives or friends during the outbreak; they were more likely to be ill, grieving or self-isolating during the lockdown. Their trauma and isolation made it even more challenging for them to support their communities and keep their organisations afloat.

Charity So White launched a paper on 6 April called *Racial Injustice in the COVID-19 Response*. The #CharitySoWhite campaign started in August 2019 when they called out a Citizen's Advice Bureau training document for propagating racist stereotypes.[5] Their paper called for 'civil society and funders to put Black, Asian and Minority Ethnic (BAME) communities at the heart of their response to COVID-19 to address root issues and maximise impact.'[6] Charity So White rightly highlighted that COVID-19 would exacerbate existing disparities across education, health, housing and employment. The paper stressed that BAME groups are over-represented in low-income groups and key worker status while migrants would struggle to have their basic needs met due to having no recourse to public funds.

However, it was only after the death of George Floyd and the subsequent protests that the narrative shifted. The social sector suddenly developed a conscience. It was the first time since the Macpherson Report in 1999 (commissioned after the death of Stephen Lawrence) changed race equality laws that these social sector organisations found themselves under the spotlight if they did not respond to racism. While I'm sure some charities were empathetic, many wanted to mitigate the risk of bad publicity. Unfortunately, the declarations of support for Black Lives Matter did not convert into rapid action.

In July 2020, I spoke at a conference organised by the Association of Charitable Foundations (ACF) – a membership body for UK foundations and grant-making charities. I said that it genuinely felt as if philanthropy had turned its back on Black people. Our pain was high, but our expectations of funders were low, and it shouldn't have been that way. I also said:

'I think the following statements are obvious, but they keep popping into my mind as I think about philanthropy in the UK:

As people of colour, we experience British society entirely differently from how most of the people who govern and run foundations experience life in Britain. They don't understand us or our experience. And this disconnect fundamentally undermines foundations' abilities to distribute funding equitably and competently.

We are still in a situation where Black people generally have to ask white people for money. Trust and honesty will always be problematic because of this dynamic. On the whole, funders' inability to invest boldly has shown that they do not trust us. If they did, there would be more action and less fragility.

Racism only ever springs to light when focused on our pain and never on our abundance or our innovation. CIVIC SQUARE's Immy Kaur and MAIA's Amahra Spence appeared on my Just Cause podcast in 2019. They spoke of ground-breaking work in Black and brown communities and how so few funders understood this. Thus, donors ignore our innovation, or we are subject to different 'rules', a narrower lens, longer processes, little trust, no risk. It shouldn't take George Floyd's murder for there to be an interest in or concern about racism or for there to be an investment in Black or brown-led social change. Over the last three years, we've had numerous reports about structural racism and the lack of diversity in the charitable sector. We have yet to see significant change or investment, barring the work of a few small foundations.

We're living through unprecedented times, which calls for unprecedented responses. Are we sure that funders have started to do anything fundamentally different or radical to respond to this issue adequately?

Future Foundations UK,* Charity So White, Ubele and others have tried various tactics to get the funding sector to move. We've sat in on endless consultations. We've been polite. We've been antagonistic. We've provided practical solutions. We've supplied endless lists. We've provided data. Through it all, we've endured painful conversations and little action. Quite frankly, it has probably been one of the most undignified periods I've suffered in my professional career.

Evidence, data and learning have been ignored, which makes it a fallacy that the funding sector values these things. The lack of urgency is a conscious act. We've gone through Brexit, Grenfell, Windrush, George Floyd, COVID-19 – it has been a relentless onslaught over the last four years, and I'm not even going to go into the historical injustices. It is a conscious act to ignore it, to ignore us. When we look at racial disparities in society, and when race intersects with other issues and other identities, then the

---

* Future Foundations UK is a community of people of colour working in philanthropy in the UK.

It is a supportive network for those working in the UK philanthropic sector to connect, create and lead change within the space. Core to its purpose is ensuring the safety, care, healing and dignity of its community as they move through the sector.

inequalities faced by Black and brown people are frightening. But apparently not scary enough.'

I think back to an incident when I turned down two older white men for funding. One of them responded by saying, 'Do you realise that Black people were happier when they were in subservient positions?' I didn't know who to speak to about this comment within my organisation. I didn't know whether anyone in power would understand. There wasn't a safe space. Every day, people of colour in funding are experiencing racism; seeing actions and inactions that are harming communities of colour.

Structural racism runs through the lifeblood of Britain. Philanthropy is no different. So it requires an entirely different approach if the social sector is to do justice to justice. During my ACF speech, I outlined a few thoughts about how the sector could be more productive in its response. First, I mentioned the need for reconciliation, acknowledging and admitting the systemic failures around funding and structural and historical racism. Second, I spoke of reparations and the need for substantial investment, which is long-term, flexible and varied (not just service delivery, but research, start-ups, infrastructure, capital, tech, etc.) to Black and brown-led organisations. I also mentioned the need for trusts and foundations to divest from companies that exacerbate racial inequalities.

I added:

As a final point, I think back to the civil rights movement. Civil rights theorist Lani Guinier once used the comparison of Black men as 'canaries in the mine'. When bad things happen, they tend to affect Black, brown and indigenous communities first. The civil rights movement didn't just benefit Black people. It benefited everyone. Its success liberated everybody, particularly the marginalised. I, like many others, always say that our liberation and our dignity are tied together. To reinterpret Guinier's words, if Black and brown people are the 'canaries', then we need to heed the canary, 'not focus on simply fixing the canary'. And I don't just mean heeding the canaries in their pain, but to heed the canaries in their abundance.[7]

Philanthropy and the social sector tend to support Black causes through three lenses: our pain, institutionalising us, or elevating charismatic leaders. Pain, because it reinforces the 'haves'-and-'have-nots' Band-Aid nature of philanthropy. Institutionalisation – because the money and funding terms control our activities. And charismatic leaders, a play on the 'Magical Negro' trope, which elevates individuals as almost superhuman and atypical.

Fozia Irfan, then the CEO of Bedfordshire and Luton Community Foundation, wrote a piece for *Alliance Magazine* in June 2020, which would prove prophetic. She said that foundations risked being on the 'wrong side of history' when tackling racial injustice. She added that foundations are 'at a tipping point of becoming part of the problem in perpetuating that inequality' and 'adding to the issues marginalised communities face.'[8]

*

There were some highlights. Resourcing Racial Justice, a fund led by a coalition of activists and artists, including Farzana Khan and Nusrat Faizullah, distributed over £1 million to Black and brown-led charities and movements, as well as individuals. The National Lottery Community Fund launched the Phoenix Fund, a £1.4 million COVID-19 relief programme for charities led by people of colour, pioneered by its then deputy director Shane Ryan, Ubele's Yvonne Field and a coalition of leaders across England, including Naz Zaman (Lancashire BME Network), Joy Warmington (brap), Kamran Rashid (Impact Hub Bradford) and Sado Jirde (Black South West Network), among others. This work led to a £50 million collaboration between the Phoenix Way Partnership and the Community Fund. We also saw the emergence of a plethora of independent Black and brown-led funding entities, including the Baobab Foundation, the Black Funding Network and Common Call Fund led by Do It Now Now's Bayo Adelaja.

The National Trust published its interim report, titled 'Connections Between Colonialism and Properties now in the Care of the National Trust, Including Links with Historic Slavery'. The report shows connections between ninety-three of its eight hundred historic country houses and UK properties to colonialism and slavery.[9] As a result, the Common Sense Group, comprising sixty Tory MPs, wrote to the Charity Commission demanding it reconsiders the National Trust's charitable status.

Barnardo's, the UK's largest children's charity, published a guide for parents on white privilege. The guide outlines how white privilege impacts most of us, recognising the intersection of our collective struggles. It refers to the gender pay gap remaining close to 20 per cent and that 26 per working-age disabled people live in poverty. The guide tions the percentage (35 per cent) of LGBT people who hid or disguise their sexuality at work through fear of discrimination, how Pakistani women are paid less than British women and that 12 per cent of BAME LGBT employees have 'lost a job because of being LGBT when compared to 4 per cent of white LGBT staff'.[10] In response, twelve Tory MPs wrote a letter to the then chief executive of Barnardo's, Javed Khan, expressing their 'concern and disappointment'.

The Charity Commission's chair, Baroness (Tina) Stowell of Beeston, responded to charities like The National Trust with an article in the *Mail on Sunday* (28 November). Widely condemned by charity leaders, Stowell's commentary warned charities to leave party politics and culture wars out of any attempts to improve lives and that they should be careful while implying that these voices are drowning out those who seek charities as an antidote to politics.[11]

Stowell's article did not appear to demonstrate the political impartiality required of the charities that the Commission regulates. Her language was divisive, threatening and out of touch. The regulator had shown itself to be more concerned with preservation than the lived realities of the many people who donate to or benefit from charities. Our struggles, histories, and liberation are bound together as minoritised racial groups, LGBTQ+ communities, disabled people, women, working-class people and British citizens. The Charity Commission, like the government, does not see it this way. Rather than being a force for unity, it is a source of partition, which is, to be fair, true to Britain's history.

financial or reputational interests of als to disrupt the status quo to a point ast – responses to the needs of the mar- iven by those on the margins. During I reflected on the mainstream social vould we say about the social sector's response to Brexit in twenty years' time? With the climate crisis, was it doing enough to challenge structures instead of individual behaviours? Now, with COVID-19, I realised that the mainstream social sector and philanthropy had been tentative, slow, ill-prepared, too fearful of government, and, on the whole, in danger of being bad ancestors. During a time of heightened crisis, these revelations had proven true. It was now a time for radical change or to face a slow pathway to extinction. The choice was theirs.

7

Conclusion

American comedian Chris Rock once described America as 'the uncle who paid your way through college, but who molested you'.[1] Philanthropy as an institution has similar qualities. Philanthropic culture does good, no doubt. But it also breeds an unhealthy culture: one of competition over collaboration, individualism over community or collectivism, preservation over progression, extractivism over regenerative resourcing, charity over justice, and colourblind over anti-racism, white supremacy over intersectionality. It is an extension of capitalist culture.

Philanthropy is an institution that reinforces the status quo instead of disrupting it while patting itself on the back for 'doing good'. It appeases the masses, institutionalises activism, maintains control and rarely challenges the structures responsible for society's problems. Author and activist Arundhati Roy has argued for many years that NGOs* 'defuse

---

* As mentioned, I use the term social sector organisations, but in this context, Roy often uses the term NGO.

political anger and dole out as aid or benevolence what people ought to have by right'.[2] People of colour are presented as 'pathological victims' in need of white saviours, philanthropists and NGOs who act as a buffer between the 'Empire and its subjects', 'de-politicising resistance'.[3]

Whitney Iles spoke of the ethical dilemmas faced by social sector leaders trying to resource social justice work:

> We have a whole charity sector that is a business within itself. If we got rid of charities today, think of how many people will be out of a job. It's the fact that it is a sector. It's the fact that people actively go to school and go to universities and get degrees to go work in the charity sector ... This is business. This isn't charity, this is business ... What's [the] difference between that and capitalism, and putting out a marketing campaign, and getting people to buy your product? It's the same. It's capitalism, just within charity. If I am really against the criminal justice system, how can I take the money from Her Majesty's Prison Service (HMPS) and Ministry of Justice (MOJ) to work in the prison? Am I not just keeping the beast alive? How can I say defund the police? How can I say Black lives matter if I'm then taking funding from the Mayor's Office for Policing And Crime?

Edgar Villanueva, philanthropy executive and author of *Decolonizing Wealth*, believes that philanthropy reinforces colonial divisions. Like the UK, philanthropy in the United States is overwhelmingly white-led. As a result, it strengthens its role as saviours of the 'poor', the 'needy', the 'disadvantaged', and 'at-risk people'.[4] People who know anything about

philanthropy often mention the Scottish-American indus-
trialist Andrew Carnegie, who gave away $350 million. His
most significant philanthropic legacy was expanding public
libraries across the US and, eventually, the globe.

Some may also know of American businessman and oil
magnate John D. Rockefeller. He donated around $550 mil-
lion, including what would eventually be known as Spelman
College (the maiden name of his wife Laura), a historical
Black college for women in Atlanta. From the late nineteenth
century through to the early twentieth century, Carnegie
and Rockefeller became the beacons of philanthropy. They
achieved a great deal of social impact across the globe. Yet,
over a hundred years on, the dynamic of wealthy white philanthropists using wealth derived from extractive means to
do good persists. Giving with one finger and taking with the
other hand.

Villanueva points out that it is still the case that many white
people feel that we (Black, brown and indigenous people)
were better off under white rule. In *Decolonizing Wealth*, he
states that 56 per cent of British people are still proud of the
Empire. The British Prime Minister, Boris Johnson, once said
of Africa, 'The continent may be a blot, but it is not a blot
upon our conscience. The problem is not that we were once
in charge, but that we are not in charge any more.'[5]

Like colonialists intent on building empires that enslaved
and subjugated Black and brown people and maintained white
supremacy, philanthropists and social sector organisations
strive to use their wealth to maintain power, influence and
control of resources and policy by creating dependency on
the services they deliver. They often do so with little to no

accountability, few evidence-driven policies and no meaningful or equitable engagement with those directly impacted by
the social issues they address. Black, brown and indigenous
people and other marginalised communities have little or no
power or say because of the threat of financial withdrawal.
There is a culture of compliance because they are so dependent on white funders or large social sector organisations for
money and resources.

I knew I was complicit. The terrible misery of being a Black
man entering a boardroom comprising the white great and
good, with every type of knowledge imaginable except lived
or proximate expertise of the social issues I was now – as a
grant-maker – proposing for funding, often felt degrading.
These board members, these elected officials, had the power
to decide but not necessarily the knowledge to make the
right decisions. This isn't personal or a judgement of their
skills. But there was often a significant gap between what was
happening in low-income communities and the experience
of the decision-makers. As such, it was unlikely that they
would fund any application truly challenging the status quo.
As Ruth Ibegbuna once said to me, 'The people who believe
the most in social transformation are the very people who
are being asked to turn up with their begging bowls and fill
in boxes.'

In essence, those with the power to make the decisions
do not seem to believe that we need to transform things.
On the whole, they are doing well in life. By sitting on these
boards, they believe they are contributing to a better world.
As Ibegbuna says, they think, 'I'm OK, and I will do my bit

to help these people get better. Not that they should have what I have. Not that their world can ever be like my world. But we can make it less painful for them.'

Grant-making brought on a deep melancholy for me. Always. I knew I was complicit, but I also learned that I could open the doors to more resources for my community. I understood I was in a privileged position, on the inside, capable of influencing in ways that were unimaginable to me. But the day before I'd present an application was the worst feeling because I knew that the conversations between me and the decision-makers were not equal. They had the power to say no, but not necessarily the knowledge to reach such a conclusion. So these interactions became more of a game, one where you aim to create the conditions for potentially transformational work to get funded in spite of, not necessarily because of those who might be making the decisions.

They may have had some respect for my knowledge, but ultimately there was no relationship because they could not connect to the issues I was passionate about supporting. But I played the game. Did the dance because the end game was worth it, right? I'm in a position of privilege, so I have to use it to fund promising projects. Hustle things through. So, I pronounced my T's, cracked a joke or two and fake smiled. I was assertive but non-threatening. I did not interrupt, even if I had been interrupted, and I listened to the reasons for turning down my proposals even if they were wholly unjustifiable.

I watched as they circled on me at times, so I could not win this game. I allowed them to talk to me in ways that I could never have spoken to them. Their privilege, in some cases inherited and unearned, meant that they had power over me. I have no room for mistakes or the perception that I was disrespectful or arrogant because the only people who would lose out are the social sector organisations I advocated for. I couldn't rock the boat too much because I would harm grantees' potential to get paid. I couldn't be too bright because I would embarrass the decision-makers. And all the while I'd watch as, in some cases, their favourite charities flew through with little to no scrutiny. My relationship with those with wealth was never equal in such a scenario, even though I held my own, when required.

In *Decolonizing Wealth*, Villanueva described a person of colour in the role of grants manager as a 'house negro'; a term used to describe a house slave who had closer proximity to power than enslaved people working the fields. The house negro's compliance and unwillingness to stir things up brought privileges and a higher status than their field peers. Villanueva was not far from the truth. Any 'relatively conscious'* person of colour filling a role where they cannot bring their whole self to work will likely have a traumatic experience. This is often the case in philanthropy.

Villanueva argues that wealth can play a significant role in alleviating society's problems but that we need to stop the 'cycles of abuse' while 'healing ourselves from trauma'. According to Villanueva, we need a new paradigm to distribute resources more evenly, one that rejects the colonised elements of our society. The white saviour syndrome, white

---

* 'To be a Negro in this country and to be relatively conscious is to be in a rage almost all the time.' – James Baldwin, *Time* magazine, August 1965.

supremacy and colonial culture, as described by Arundhati Roy and Villanueva, were all too familiar to me while working in philanthropy. I found it most harmful that many people in powerful positions did not self-reflect on these norms. Instead, they actively harmed by failing to change the white saviour dynamics, exacerbating disparities and slowly depreciating the social sector's value as an independent force to challenge the public and private sectors' poor practices.

Through all the changes in British society during the 2010s – from austerity to COVID-19 – philanthropy was, to use a phrase from Rob Reich's book *Just Giving*, at the 'trailing edge, not the cutting edge, of change'.[6] As I re-read the Civil Society Futures 'The Story of Our Times: shifting power, bridging divides, transforming society' report, it occurred that people across England, where the inquiry had been conducted, did not feel that anyone was listening to their concerns. Had the social sector done enough to amplify the public's solutions in a decade of crisis and mass division?

The report urged the social sector to start shifting power, hold itself accountable to the communities it served, deepen its connections to people, and build trust or risk irrelevance. Risk irrelevance. Civil Society Futures stated that 'It (civil society) lacks confidence, skills and credibility and there are far too many examples of charities and institutions being part of the problem.'[7] More than anything, the report had been clear that the government will not fix civil society's problems and that change was in our hands. It was right. And bold with its words.

While social sector leaders publicly endorsed the report,

I suspect many secretly detested it because it did not shift the blame onto the government or the failure of The Big Society. Sector leaders quietly wanted a statement that would urge the government to work more closely with civil society. Instead, after listening to the voices of over 3,000 people consulted for the report, the inquiry responded by demanding that civil society look at itself first. Yet when it did so, it chose to blame others. The mainstream social sector's fear of compromising its relationship and contracts with the government, its fear of regulation and its fear of bad publicity had been a factor in diluting its voice and its ability to serve people's needs. The sector had been complicit in reinforcing divisions and the culture of blame in British society by being so passive.

In *Just Giving*, Reich questioned whether philanthropy should be understood as 'an individual act or a social practice'. As an individual act, philanthropy can be flexible, offer variety and go against the norms. But it can also lack direction. It rarely tackles the root causes of problems. Instead, it is often driven by the personal choices of the elite, who reinforce capitalist culture. Reich argues for a framework of social practice so that these funds address a genuine need. He also argues that philanthropy's role is best suited to foster pluralism and discovery, saying, 'It is an important contribution that individual giving can make to pluralism and the limitation of governmental orthodoxy on associational life and the definition and production of public goods. It is an important contribution that private philanthropic foundations can make in taking an experimentalist long-time-horizon approach to policy innovation that state agencies and marketplace firms are structurally unlikely to undertake.'[8]

When I was young, the police frightened me far more than the kids who'd stare at me as I walked past them on the street. Today, those people in suits, the decision-makers who abuse power without consideration, those who compromise the politics of intersectional justice to retain control and status, gatekeeping on behalf of the elite, frighten me more. What made these people more frightening is that they did not know that their 'isms', ideologies and inertia were doing more harm than good. As a result, they could not move out of the way or challenge their mindsets.

True, it's difficult to change one's beliefs. But when you are in a position of power, in charge of millions designated to doing good, failure to challenge oneself is a failure in your role. I also felt that their refusal to do anything about it came down to a fear that radical change may invalidate much of what they had built during their working lives, therefore compromising the status they had established through their careers. Understandable. Who would want to compromise their position? Or give up their privileges? Perhaps, then, the type of people that should be in charge should be those capable of putting their careers at risk because that's what the best people delivering services in the social sector do regularly.

If you work in the social sector and are unwilling to acknowledge that you might be complicit in reinforcing the status quo, you are a part of the problem. You are a willing participant in oppressing marginalised people. Recognising this made me question why I had entered the sector in the first place. Why I felt so disappointed being a part of it and what I needed to readdress in my understanding of why I was giving. If I knew I had been complicit, was I doing enough with what little power I had? Had I been actively trying to decolonise philanthropy, helping the sector move towards a space where it listened to people, challenged government and rediscovered its imagination? I had to look back at what motivated me to discover where I'd gone wrong and what I needed to do about it.

Part 2

That's why I'm giving

8

Locked, down

I can tell you about the moment. I was around nine years of age, and a white friend and I entered a newsagent on the busy Romford Road. As we left the shop, no doubt opening packets of sweets, two policemen appeared and stopped me. They think I've stolen something. Not my friend. Just me. They tell me so. Accusingly, condescendingly and without a shred of evidence. I was scared. Confused. Not as nervous as I would be had I actually nicked something and my parents had found out, but scared enough. I denied their claims. I cooperated. So, with late afternoon dawning, cars buzzing by, the police frisked me. They searched me for a long time. Couldn't find anything. They did not search my friend. They didn't even talk to my friend. Just me. They let us go. No apology, no admittance that they had made a mistake or were just doing their job, no justification for why they had frisked me, just me, in the first place.

I was lucky. The situation did not escalate. It was daytime, with too many people around, I guess. While racism was an everyday thing for me in my childhood, fortunately only a few incidents involved the police. Baljeet Sandhu, founder of the Centre for Knowledge Equity, once said to me, 'when you've got human beings who've lived something and they don't want that to happen to anyone else, that's when community action happens. It's because either you've lived it or someone you love has lived it. You just don't want anyone else to go through it. So that's how you naturally give back.'

My everyday experiences of racism – with the police, shop-keepers, teachers, prospective employers – shaped my giving. My fortune – stable family background, the realisation that my experiences were neither unique nor as extreme as many others' – also influenced how I'd give. But, while the quest for racial justice always underpinned my work, I realised, during lockdown, that many other factors contributed. Some of it was good, some of it bad.

In the summer of 2020, there I was, a 6ft 2in Black male coiled on a compact grey sofa bed like a mouse in a matchbox. It was 4.30 a.m., and I had been awake all night, thinking about all the negative things I had done in my life. The depressing timeline came in painful waves, like irritable mind syndrome. I remembered the moment I punched a man after he pushed me off a train, the times I'd cheated on partners and another incident when I'd almost run over a disoriented guy who nearly stumbled in front of my car. Each vivid, dis-torted, reinterpreted occurrence made me feel like twisting myself into a ball and disposing my body into the trash.

I tried to cover my thoughts with the duvet. I have been hiding my feelings in this way since I was a child. Back then, it was minor incidents, stealing money from my father's jacket to buy sweets, cheating in an exam, fights at school, pornography. I always found a way to excuse my behaviour under the cover of bed sheets and compare my ills to others I knew were doing far worse. I could be remorseful without challenging my behaviour based on my standing in the league table of poor conduct, which I would conclude was not so bad after all, compared to others. This reaction was no way to learn from my mistakes. I would also try to hide any poor behaviour by doing good deeds, which I'd hope would some- how help me deal with my inadequacies. It didn't work then. It wasn't working now.

Still, I tried. I curled up on the bed, in the loft, away from my two children and partner, covered by an old, thinning, brown-beige duvet – a glorified, all-purpose bed sheet. The bedding is always in the wash because we use it when watch- ing television when it is cold; it is the sheet we used to wrap our kids in when their blankets were not keeping them warm enough. On this night, the duvet had a smell like an old vest because I had slept in the loft for several nights.

I could smell me. Sweat, mainly. This familiarity was not reassuring but reinforcing the state I had been in through much of lockdown, feelings of paranoia, guilt, of being lonely with my thoughts, and my inability or unwillingness to con- front my inadequacies weighing more frequently on my mind. And how trying to make myself a better person through my actions – *trying to be everything to everyone* – exhausted me, haunted me and drained me. I was in a non-resolution and survival cycle, a familiar pattern, all because honesty was more painful and being myself almost unattainable.

With the comparisons to others not working and good

deeds ineffective, I sank under the cover to create fantasies. I would be an outspoken activist, an award-winning writer; I'd sink into the illusory lyrics of my favourite rappers or transport women I'm attracted to on television into my real life. Of course, there would need to be some minor semblance of reality to the fantasy. But now, in lockdown, the fantasies were too far from reality. There had been little to fuel my dreams. My imagination was fatigued. Worse still, underneath it all, I knew I had no right to do anything bad. While I had faced problems with racism and bullying growing up, I had had a good start to life. I came from a good home with unconditional love from my parents and sisters, good food, friendships, and enough popularity to be in the middle of a crowd more than on the margins.

I began to question the line between wicked men's actions and my moral compass and ability to self-regulate. I started to crave being what I once was; I dreamt of the times when I stood for what I believed in without question or compromise. A time when I didn't have to be so damn pragmatic or to play games to progress. How did I become so desensitised yet so sensitive? How did I get to a place of seeking approval from everyone other than myself, finding power only through fantasies to escape the facade, the masquerade I had paraded just to get through the working day?

Minor and major incidents started to roam in my mind. Endless thoughts roved but failed to embed as firmly as the doubts, as every incident I'd like to conceal, those where I feel guilt, from the confrontations with police to moments I've yelled in rage at faulty drivers, surfaced over and over. Then the thoughts of daylight, the dread of the following day, the respite that may come from a new day, seemed far in the distance. I need to change. I need a change. Will disaster have to strike me before I make that transformation? Is it too late? Is it worth it? Who or what will I lose if I attempt to make this shift?

Another wave. This time it was the moment I shouted 'MOVE' to the people standing on the left-hand side of an escalator at King's Cross station. No one moved. I realised that they were static because a blind man and his dog were blocking their path. I read the situation wrong. Didn't see the blind man. Typical, I thought, those white folks are judging me with their disapproving looks. Shame. My actions shamed me.

If only those disapproving of my actions knew me. You would know that I rarely complain. You would know that I always get out of people's way. I always give up my seat. I always let folks get off the train first. I am the first to apologise and often apologise for things I am not responsible for. Feels easier that way. Lessening. That had been my way, the more comfortable way of dealing with everyday racism, with racial profiling, with life.

Every time I'd leave my house, there would always be an incident where my body was being judged, policed: teachers, shopkeepers, neighbours, cabbies, people sitting opposite me on a train. Society had had me under surveillance since birth and it was exhausting. So, I'd apologise. But, sometimes, after being hemmed in daily, you lose it. The constant policing becomes part of who you are, not what you are. But in these moments, in King's Cross, for you, it is your everything, it is what I am, what we are.

*

Racism, destructive relationships, ego; I had no idea of the degree to which this accumulation of my flaws and society's failings had taken their toll on me. I had always found a way to hustle through life, but I couldn't quite grasp how life worked or how the two blended. As a Black child, I was told that I needed to be twice as good as my white counterparts. As a man, acknowledging one's feelings and emotions is perceived as a luxury.

In Britain, you are taught to have a stiff upper lip. In work, validation comes through the number of hours you put in. Value comes from wealth. Our lives speak little to the deflating compromises of attaining and maintaining a lifestyle that adheres to these values. And we miss so many things along the way; the subtle changes in our children's lives, finding substance or meaning in our work and pride in our neighbourhoods. And time, time for ourselves, time to think, time to learn, time to assess, time for quality relationships. You swiftly realise that society defines progress as being about growth, not personal growth, but the accumulation of things that will not work or satisfy you for long. Why fight to get my child into the best schools when those with inherited wealth, built off the backs of my forefathers' labour, can buy their way to the top positions in society?

You can say the same about health, housing and everything we pay taxes for that fundamentally does not lead us to live in an equal society. Instead, it contributes to reinforcing a status quo where depreciation in the name of wealth is a consequence for us and our planet.

I didn't cry or grieve. I didn't make any moves to do anything about it either. I relied instead on hope and the promise that the following day would be better. Having enough con-versations and helping other people to refuel may enable me to absorb other people's realities enough to forget my own. I wanted to confess all, to cleanse myself. But I didn't know whether I needed to reveal all. I also wanted to disappear because I had no possibility of cleansing. I didn't understand what cleansing meant, but I wanted to know whether enlight-enment (for want of a better term) would be something I would ever experience.

Who and what am I at this moment? And why is it that I have nothing to say and that I struggle to be coherent, even in front of those who know me well? I'm alone. A lot. Lonely, which is forcing me to think, confess, to start again. I want everyone to know the truth, my truth, but I cannot face telling it. I want everyone to know because I've reached a point where hope has become anti-climactic. I feel as if I now exist within the black lines of the shapes in my son's textbook.

Everything is plain. Black. White. Not even the lines vary in thickness. Just shapes. Brief instructions. No answers, no colour. Even the angles are difficult to detect. I know they are difficult to detect because I have hit a point where my isolation from my feelings has become so deep that I can no longer see beyond my shortcomings. Not about the picture on the page. It's about how I perceive those pictures. And my perceptions, like my imagination, are dull. All these feelings are pouring out because I had time to fill.

More painful was the lack of belief. Lack of curiosity. Words floated. And the blandness of my mind has become more than a moment, more than a transitory feeling that lies between awakening and being awake. It's now a box set of tasteless feelings where honesty is unbearable and pain a more favourable thing to endure. If these negative feelings were constant, I'd be fine. But they aren't. They mount, and as they intensify, I cannot do the things I need to do to survive the day. Work. Eat. Speak to people. Pay stuff. How I live and how I survive, this too mounts. Details of events become vague, nothing works, nothing looks right, and no amount of comparing my pain to other people's sorrow makes me feel better because everything is so distant. I again realise that my imagination has not been strong enough to turn thoughts into reality. Even leaving my house becomes hard because I think everyone can read my thoughts. The images of my peak life moments – the first person I loved and the moment I first realised this, the initial sight of my first child, soft, smooth, lumpy brownness – all sink into a place where no object has any corners, no room has any colours or shape. I once more only exist in black-and-white figures in the textbook.

There were good moments during the lockdown. My then nine-year-old son going out for morning bike rides alone, something he started doing during the first months when COVID-19 paralysed movement and created space. There were the long evening walks down silent streets. The bench in front of my house, a temporary respite, mainly as no cars were grunting down my road.

The cooking, my daughter's Halloween bake-off, the financial savings from not having to travel, Facetiming my parents, strangers saying hello, not having to go on an overcrowded train to Central London every day. The Verzuz clash between

DJ legends Beenie Man and Bounty Killer in Jamaica temporarily had dancehall music trending again. I loved it when my children were writing short stories. Suddenly, I did not feel so anxious about their futures because I was no longer worrying about what schools they'd have to attend, how to understand secondary school grading systems and other parents talking about how great their children were.

But lockdown was self-exposing. It was the first time in years that my mind had stopped for such a sustained period. My work masked feelings of insecurity, constantly questioning what I'm worth, always seeking validation from those who scrutinised me the most; always wondering whether there will ever be a moment when I could be my authentic self again. Now it was all coming out. I had time to think – too much space to fill, not enough people to see. We missed seasons, and it was scary because time was a privilege I didn't want.

This lockdown experience was part of my story. My struggle. A struggle. Our struggle, once we realised that the coronavirus wasn't another country's problem. Our realities and well-being resembled each other in a way that governments or the media could not mask. Kind acts: how we contributed to society, through volunteering or with money or resource, was all we had at times. Perhaps it was OK to be honest in these moments, to face the music, to realise you're not half of what you wanted to be, not a quarter of what people think you are, because being honest with yourself and staying true to that was the only way to move beyond the pain. In Britain and many wealthy countries not used to such disasters, we were finally more than individuals and part of something bigger. Our contributions to society had started to become a part of our daily lives.

Everyone was dealing with loss, death, absence, fear, ill-health – some more than others. Many of us paused for a similar length of time when someone asked, 'how are you?' because most of us didn't know how we were or how to respond. We didn't know, and it felt OK to admit that. But at this moment, these moments, I couldn't think of a time when feelings of loneliness and uncertainty bonded so many of us. We had been experiencing the worst public health crisis in the UK since World War II. Yet, unlike so many around the globe where such predicaments are more common, we had the choice or more options, to change, reset, dictate what type of life we would like to lead and what our reality should be.

This had been a moment when we needed to call on our communities, friends, families, care workers, youth workers or spirituality. And these relationships were more reliable than the institutions that try to govern and dictate these relationships. It was in our mutual interest to reset. We recognised that while there may have been common emotions and everyday experiences during the lockdown, we were not always equal in our pain; we were not similar in our vulnerability. This was the moment to change. To transform. This was a time to do things differently. I wanted to imagine another world. To do so, I had to shift away from my fantasies. I had to dig deeper into my experiences and go back to what fundamentally inspired me to give.

9

Stand tall

My mum is a warrior. She may be surprised, offended even, that I'd describe her as such. Indeed, friends and family who know her well may also be surprised, given my mum's penchant for raucous laughter, introversion in crowds and expert cooking to ease our souls. But when I think of my earliest memories of resistance, of fighting back, I always think of how fiercely she defended us (me and my two sisters) and Black people generally. Of course, my mum, Elle, wouldn't see this as anything more than her duty as a mother. But she is staunch and uncompromising.

My habit of avoiding conflict stopped me from fully recognising that justice was fundamental to how my mother raised my sisters and me. It was only when my brother-in-law Fedja, around 2018, said that my family's politics derived from my mum that I recognised the origins of my sense of justice and fairness. I also think it is all right to be angry; it is OK to always question – even those whose voices carry more weight than mine because of their professional status. It is OK if I don't always have the words to describe my thoughts. It is, however, vital that people know how I feel. I haven't always lived up to these sentiments. But they exist, always.

I remember my mum and me walking down Ilford High Street in the early eighties. The high road was just a short bus ride away from my house and had not been pedestrianised at this point. There was a vast Sainsbury's at the top end of Ilford with what I thought was the mightiest car park imaginable. It was not far from the Ilford Palais, formerly a cinema that became a concert venue and nightclub. Everyone played there, from rock 'n' roll band Bill Haley and the Comets to the hip-hop group Wu-Tang Clan. When the Wu arrived in Ilford, they did so sans every group member barring the late Ol' Dirty Bastard. That night, he wailed his way through a nonsensical set that, to some, was genius but to me and others, was little more than someone drunk or high fulfilling enough of his contractual obligations to get paid.

Besides the Sainsbury's and Palais, Ilford High Road was so full of shops it was like going to Oxford Street. In some ways, I preferred our trips to the West End. My mother and I would take the 86 or 25 bus from Romford Road in Manor Park and once we arrived, she would leave me in the sports section of Foyles while she completed her shopping. It was cool to do so back then. I wouldn't even notice that she had gone. The only thing that was as thrilling for me as a child was going into a library for the first time, a magnificent and grand red brick Carnegie building situated off Romford Road.

In Ilford, however, there was no such place that my mother could leave me. So, she dragged me around shops like British Home Stores, Harrison Gibson, Boots, Argos, and H Samuel jeweller's. As we drifted towards Cranbrook Road, which took you from Ilford into Gants Hill via Valentines Park, you had Bodgers and C&A, where my mum would always go while pulling me like a wheelie-bag behind her. As we walked back to the bus stop one time with my mum checking the receipts, she realised that she had been short-changed. I don't think it was by much. But it was the principle of the matter. She immediately turned and headed back to the shop to reclaim what was rightfully hers. Her fury had subsided by the time she got into the shop, and she was not loud or rude. But she got her money back while I cowered behind her. While I was growing up, my mother's protestations became a familiar pattern.

I witnessed her objections frequently. She could not stand racist commentary, be it comments about the West Indian cricket team or Black entertainers. She was fiercely defensive of any Black person in the public eye, recognising the injustices they faced. I am sure, given the choice, she would much prefer for me to see fighting on television than racism. I grew up with a pure, unconditional love of Blackness. At times, my mother would be so blinded by this love that she could not be subjective.

But I didn't care. She always carried herself with great pride and treated people fairly and this was perhaps my greatest lesson. While no one is without fault, my mother lived her life how she had expressed and lived her politics. There was not a contradiction, a lie, or a facade. My mother's spirit was vital to me growing up and throughout my adult life, even if I had been timid, quiet, ill-equipped to stand up for myself for many years. *Get up, stand up*, ran through my mother's veins even if, fundamentally, she was shy.

Newham was a difficult place to raise a Black child in the seventies and eighties. Racist attacks, thuggish police, low expectations from teachers, a constant. These incidents often went unreported; the perpetrators were allowed to roam free. When the press speaks of serious youth violence in the twenty-first century, I think back to those chilling days. Acts of violence were a daily occurrence in Newham back then.

There was no moral panic from the media because white people and the state were committing violence against Black people. Those early experiences, combined with my mum's spirit, were the first lessons I had in wanting to give back, even if I didn't know how. My mum created a safe space in our house that incubated us from the terrible acts that were going on outside. And there was always laughter. We were not a family without problems. But there was a joy being around each other, making jokes, watching movies together, from *A Stolen Life* starring Bette Davis to cult-gang-classic *The Warriors*.

Our house was a home for others, and somewhere all my mates could hang out in safety, and food was always a bond. From the curry goat with rice 'n' peas and plantain to the many days when we didn't have much money, my mother would make corned beef or Spam with plain rice or dumplings and fried mackerel taste like gourmet dishes.

In my first conversation with cultural producer Amahra Spence, I remember how she described the wonder she felt as a child watching her grandad make dumplings and the joy of experiencing someone create such splendour with so little. So many of us are inspired to give by our morals, values or personal beliefs. My livity [a Rasta term for one's way of living] was formed by my mother's sense of justice, with food and laughter re-fuelling my will to fight. She didn't worry about what she didn't know but acknowledged how she and others felt. She never sat within her own margins.

Among my favourite memories during lockdown was sitting in my parents' garden on a balmy Sunday evening. The food, the humour, the politics, the safety. That familiarity was like being in harmony with nature, freeing, feeling complete. My father's impeccable cool diminished as he delighted in the West Indian cricket team's victory over England in the first test in July. I watched my mother's mounting annoyance as she recounted John Humphrys's unpalatable utterances during ITV's *Stephen Lawrence: Has Britain Changed* debate. Our faces and, for a moment, our lives loosened as we ate her lasagne with its sweet aftertaste and roast chicken with a hint of paprika.

RUTH IBEGBUNA

Founder of RECLAIM, The Roots Programme and Rekindle

'I've been thinking about why I am the way I am. My dad, Gus, used to have a picture of two white kids on the door of our fridge, a girl and boy. Both grinning for the camera. He was a Bradford social worker and they were from a family he was working with and he felt they'd been let down. He'd fought for them, but the system won and he'd not managed what was in their best interests. My mum and dad endlessly discussed them and even considered trying to adopt them at one point because social services were failing them. Even when he moved on from social work, my dad kept their picture on our fridge. Our small family was all about "how do we make society better for them?" [children like these two kids]. That has always really motivated me. I grew up with social-work magazines around the house and used to be fascinated and horrified by the pages at the back that were full of pictures of smiling children, all adverts, pleading for someone to find them a home and to give them a chance. I think that a lot of work that I do, whether it's been RECLAIM or Rekindle, even now with Roots, it's about, how do we listen harder for all those people who do not have a voice? How do we care about those people whose faces are relegated to the back pages? He [my dad] kept their photos as a reminder that we need to think about children like them whenever we're doing anything of worth in the world because no one did think deeply about them. That always fuelled me and I still think about them and hope their lives were OK.

'My entry point into this has always been about young people. For whatever reason, I feel very comfortable engaging with young people, and I loved teaching. I think some people are born teachers.

Darren [Crosdale, a Rekindle elder and educator] is. I am. Whenever people ask me, what is it that you do? I'd say I'm a teacher even when I was a CEO. To me, being a CEO means little, whereas being a teacher was everything to me, and being a good teacher, and seeing the difference that you could make to a young person whose path is already predetermined as far as they are concerned and as far as other people are concerned. Just putting on different lights for them and showing hidden entry points, exploring possibilities and catching them when the confidence wavers.

'When I look at the state of this country, like a lot of black people, I've genuinely thought about leaving. I've even examined my Nigerian passport and genuinely thought, "Is this really what I want to do with my life? Is the UK battle too tough?"

'I've scaled back my ambitions in many ways. Maybe fifteen years ago, I thought, I want to change this awful world, I want to reshape society, I want to create change and do it now and I can't bear the idea of not working towards that change with every ounce of energy I possess. Even though I might talk that talk now, I'm much clearer about what my role is in that change. My place is to work with a group of young people, but to help them find the strength and confidence to navigate through some of the nonsense and some of the challenges they will face. I want these young people, not born into postcodes that suggest leadership, to understand that you might not be expected to be bold, bright, brilliant and visionary, but you can be all those things – and more.

'To be there alongside them as an elder, challenging and pushing them, and ensuring that they find their way authentically into those spaces, but in numbers because I was always the only one [racially minoritised person] in that boardroom or the only one speaking on that stage. It was damaging to me and I'm pretty strong. I know I'm a strong person. When I look back over my career, I think about all the times I've been terrified, or belittled or just looked over, or vilified, it's too much. It's actually too much, and with hindsight, it's traumatic, so what I am aiming to do now is to work with groups of young people rather than individuals and that's why a new supplementary school is a good thing.

'I think working-class youth, especially working-class Black youth, need each other. They need to have the resources of each other to call on and to be each other's essential support network. That's what I'm working on right now, being less of a voice in the media and being more of a voice in the community, using the networks I have and the money I have access to in order to support those young changemakers, quietly. When you are too loud, too obviously intentional in your work, you draw attention to yourself and your plans and that is often counterproductive. I've learnt to do the work more quietly. Not all publicity is good publicity – especially when disrupting powerful systems and disturbing powerful people.'

10

Public Enemy

I must confess to being a little disappointed in Chuck D. It was 1987, and a school friend was about to purchase tickets for the Def Jam gig at Hammersmith Odeon in November. I was fourteen, but I didn't know where Hammersmith was. And I had never been to a concert. I knew my parents would take some convincing to allow me to go. But when my friend asked whether I wanted a ticket, I said yes even though I hadn't yet worked out the logistics, parental approval, money or transport.

LL Cool J (LL) headlined the tour. He was at the peak of his powers coming off his sophomore album *Bigger and Deffer*. LL had established himself as rap's biggest star, arguably its first sex symbol. His Kangol hat had become an identifiable trademark; he was sharp and quick-witted in interviews and loved to proclaim how bad he was. He bragged, boasted, rapped hard, rapped soft and gave peripheral fans what they desired: a palatable entry point to hardcore rap.

While no one considered him the best rapper at the time, LL's mic flow was a thing of beauty. He could deliver lyrics at pace without blurring his words or mistiming the rhythm.

He would walk out on stage from a massive, mini-house-sized radio cassette recorder and strut up and down the set during his live performances as if he were a king walking to his throne. He would be full of sweat, muscles bulging as he thrusted and continuously licked his lips; a man whose ego was so big, you didn't always know whether he was serious or not.

Supporting LL was Eric B. & Rakim, who had just released their debut album *Paid in Full*. Rakim was a genius, a man who shifted the art of rhyming more than any rapper. As a teenager, I didn't quite understand what he had been doing, why he was so different from his peers. But even to a novice's ear, his rhyming sounded utterly different to everyone else's. I thought it was his deep, laid-back drawl and how it didn't matter how swift the beats were, nothing appeared to alter his poise on the mic. I thought it was how every line he uttered sounded like a hook for a chorus. Perhaps it was because he could rhyme about the most trivial topics and make them sound interesting. It was all these things. But the beauty in his rhyming lay in the techniques he employed, how in-sync these were with accompanying rhythms. There wasn't a wasted or meaningless or old-fashioned line.

Instead, internal rhymes, metaphors, similes, imagery, pauses, changes of pace and tone, elongated words, analogies, multi-syllabic rhyming and alliteration created an immersive experience. These techniques are the norm nowadays. Back then, Rakim set a precedent and upped the game like no rapper before or since. LL was the star, but Rakim was the GOAT (greatest of all time).

The least known of the touring party was Public Enemy (PE). Their first album *Yo! Bum Rush the Show* did not entirely convince me that they were any good. It was a little too industrial, too close to Black punk-funk fusion bands like Bad Brains, the Beatnigs and Fishbone, who I admired but whose messages were too distorted, too abstract and too political for me to grasp back then. It was an inaccurate comparison. Truth being, I didn't have a reference point for Public Enemy. I was listening to a future I couldn't quite grasp. I was listening to political issues that were out of my knowledge zone.

I had to work, read and research to understand what their music was trying to tell me. 'Miuzi Weighs a Ton', oh, the uzi [a gun] is a metaphor for the mind. Later, they would talk about the head of the Nation of Islam, Louis Farrakhan. The movie *Night of the Living Dead* became a PE song 'Night of the Living Baseheads'. *Rebel Without a Cause* became 'Rebel Without a Pause'. I got it, but it took time. The white boys in my school got onto PE before I did.

However, I suspect by the time *It Takes a Nation of Millions to Hold Us Back* dropped in 1988, which was much clearer in its political messaging, those boys were not quite as engaged. PE didn't look like other rap groups either. Chuck, dressed in black, looked like a modern-day Black Panther. The S1Ws (Security of the First World) dressed in army fatigues, the clown prince of rap, Flava Flav, had gold teeth and wore a massive clock around his neck and Professor Griff – part political agitator, part revolutionary – roamed the stage like a military general. Chuck D would later tell *New Music Express* that 'Flavor is what America would like to see in a Black man – sad to say, but true – whereas Griff is very much what America would not like to see.'[1]

Public Enemy's performances blew LL and Rakim off the stage, heralding a much-needed change in rap from self-satisfaction to Black politics. I didn't get to go to the show in the end, despite convincing my parents through careful planning. Unfortunately, my school friend couldn't get me a ticket. A major regret, as it remains one of the great concerts performed in this country. However, my disappointment had little to do with not attending the show. I eventually saw footage from the concert on television.

I was disappointed in Chuck D's attire during one of the shows. He donned a soft/off-white tracksuit top and bottoms that looked like pyjamas. Sounds trivial, I know, but it didn't seem appropriate. It didn't seem militant enough. It mattered because PE had been the closest thing that we Black teenagers had at the time to a movement akin to the Black Panther Party in the sixties or Black Lives Matter now. We were reading the Qur'an or getting copies of the Nation of Islam's *Final Call* at a time when our peers were chatting about *RoboCop*, *Innerspace*, *Predator* and *Colors*.

Not only would PE conquer rap in 1988, but they also seized the imagination of the popular market too. As Chuck D prophesised, rap music became the 'Black CNN'.[2] PE birthed a nation of scholars, activists, and artists. Their song *Fight the Power* became a rallying cry for campaigners across the globe. PE was anti-eighties in every way. In an era of Reaganomics and flaunting of wealth, PE was grassroots, community-oriented and political.

In a period full of excessive hair-lacquer and wet looks, pseudo-glam-rock bands, gold chains, synthetic soul and faceless dance music, PE – often dressed in black – with little flash or flair, attacked each issue, each song like Charles Barkley or Giannis Antetokounmpo on a basketball court. At a time when tinny, synthetic sounds were popular, PE's music raged against mellifluous tones with volts of remorseless and suffocatingly funky beats. And they were cool as hell, a movement you wanted to be a part of. We sat in our classrooms at school being drip-fed Eurocentric knowledge, learning little about real-world issues from Thatcherism to apartheid, while being served like meat through a grinder, our only worth being our end-of-year exam grades. PE made us question everything.

It Takes a Nation used out-takes from the Hammersmith concert, immortalising the Def Jam tour and signifying that the Brits championed rap's greatest band before their American counterparts. The most popular hip-hop band at the time – Run DMC – suddenly seemed dated and before long, every rap artist needed to have some political content to remain relevant. More than anything, as young Black men, we started to understand more about the conditions we found ourselves in and we actively started to seek knowledge beyond our school gates. As a result, PE politicised a whole generation of young people.

In 1999, I interviewed Chuck D for *The Voice* newspaper. I conducted the interview in a car as Chuck was being driven to the Nation of Islam's mosque in Hackney in late summer/ early autumn. PE's legend had already been established, with echoes of Chuck's voice present in Lauryn Hill, who had recently released the classic *Miseducation of Lauryn Hill* a year earlier, and with *It Takes A Nation* firmly regarded as rap's GOAT album. By 1999, rap had become more popular. N.W.A.'s (Niggaz Wit Attitudes) strength of nihilistic street knowledge had enticed record execs to invest in Black culture's negative realism.

It was profitable. Tupac and Biggie became rap's biggest stars in the mid-nineties, warring against each other and dying way too early as a result. By 1999, rap music was in the middle of the 'Bling Bling' era: expensive, ultra-coloured videos and a return to the late-eighties tropes of bragging and gold chains. The only respite came from the likes of Lauryn and OutKast. But Chuck was less concerned about the state of rap and more troubled by the rise of the internet and how important it would be for Black people to control tech before it controls us.

Chuck was adamant that he didn't want technology, like television had done previously, to master our race. He implied that this would be one of the biggest battles in the twenty-first century.

The PE frontman also maintained that London was the capital of hip-hop. He felt that Black people in the UK were best equipped to lead change because of the proximity of second-generation Black people to our Caribbean and African roots. 'In the States, you have a slave mentality that predominates over pretty much everybody. Americanisation is inbred once it gets to Black people – a slave mentality.'³ According to Chuck, the most significant threat would be if we gave in to total assimilation at the expense of our Black British community. Chuck's sentiment has always stayed with me.

*

In music, PE was the most significant political influence in my life. Sport could disarm. It was symbolic of change. But music, like literature, could transform. I found a group that gave me political reference points, a library, some ideas for change and damn fine music at a time when I needed explanations for systemic racism in Newham. They preached self-determination; they preached re-evaluating knowledge production.

I also knew that the state (media, government, police) would try to destroy PE. I knew those white journalists who loved PE initially would not be able to angle their articles well enough from the lived experience of being Black to provide measured responses to PE's development as a band and political force. White fear would creep in. I knew that.

They would not be able to rationalise PE's actions if it went against their politics in the way they could white artists, sportspeople, politicians, kings, queens and scientists, who had perpetrated worse ills in their lives. They would continue to laud the great scientists and philosophers like Linnaeus and Kant for their brilliance without acknowledging the harm they committed against Black people through their work. White journalists would not recognise their privilege and how problematic it was to cover Black artists, sportspeople or politicians.

And they would be quick to deem any Black person who defended people of colour in the public eye as extreme, irrational, a minority view, as if their own often-biased perspective formed some kind of benchmark. This is not to say that everything PE did was correct. They made mistakes, and at times their politics were off the mark. But I just couldn't trust a white journalist to be self-reflective enough about their own predispositions to assess PE fairly. I had already seen how distorted the mainstream press could be when it covered Black people.

One thing the mainstream music industry could not do was replicate PE. *Too Black, Too Strong.* Their music was so uncompromisingly Black, so full of imagination, so rooted in visions of where Black people needed to be and how to get there, fuelled by samples of our ancestral past,* that record execs couldn't manufacture their Elvis version. It was ours. It was unexpected. Nuanced. It wasn't perfect. It was patriarchal. They didn't capture the personal. But PE created a movement and music so strong that only profound social change or a significant shift in the power dynamics between Black and white could date it.

The likelihood of anyone or anything diminishing PE's work is remote. Through their influence, I learned that it was my right to challenge the system; I discovered the importance of self-determination and innovation. PE created images of a world I could believe in. They presented more than a world where Black people were wealthy. They offered a world where Black people had power. It was a frequent lesson on the importance of holding a tangible vision when aiming to uproot the system. Simple and plain.

---

* PE's classic single 'Fight the Power', from Spike Lee's *Do The Right Thing* movie soundtrack, is a veritable history of Black music, featuring twenty-one samples, from James Brown's 'Funky Drummer' and Bob Marley's 'I Shot the Sheriff' to Sly & the Family Stone's 'Sing a Simple Song' and Guy's 'Teddy's Jam'. For more on how 'Fight the Power' was put together, go to https://www. whosampled.com/Public-Enemy/Fight-the-Power/samples/.

MICHELLE DALEY

Director, Alliance For Inclusive Education (Allfie)

'Growing up as a Black disabled girl, I could not avoid racism, ableism, sexism and other forms of intersectional discrimination. I often witnessed the discrimination my parents experienced. The area that I lived in had a bad reputation and it was well known that the National Front operated there. From an early age, I was aware of the poor social conditions of the area. However, I wasn't always able to make sense of my different experiences because there were too many compounding and intersecting injustices and inequalities. I was pretty young when I started to politicise myself; this led me to do deeper thinking and question the huge disparity in how people are treated and valued. It was the moment I said "hold on a minute, there's so much unfairness", which felt particularly relevant to my own schooling experiences: I had been placed in a segregated school, away from the ordinary experiences of life. Being in a segregated setting, you become isolated and are exposed to multiple forms of discrimination including racism and sexism. For instance, pupils' names that were non-English sounding were changed to English names. Additionally, bullying was rife and usually based around pupils' impairments.

'I was sent to a segregated school for disabled children with physical impairments. I was sent to that school for one reason; because of my impairment, and that told me that I was rejected by society, which reinforced other forms of rejections. Being sent to a segregated school had disconnected me from non-disabled children, but also other areas of life. I always hated the fact that I was placed in a segregated school for disabled children and I really believe that my schooling affected me emotionally. I was an angry child and as I grew older it became clear that what was building up inside of me was the fire of hurt.

'I strongly believe that it is important we understand the damage and harm caused because of segregated education, to all of us. We must also understand that segregated education is not only about children and young people who identify as disabled, but also, children and young people labelled with Special Educational Needs. Segregated education plays a huge role in shaping people's behaviour and practices. It's this cruel practice that is used to determine who we consider to be part of mainstream education and also other areas of ordinary life. We also know that segregation reproduces racism, sexism and other forms of discrimination. I felt that segregated education erased my different identities, reducing my existence to my impairment, which was framed negatively. As a disabled child at school there was never a moment I can recall where I felt I was encouraged or supported to be proud about my impairment or my other identities. The focus of my schooling experience was centred on pupils' impairments and medical treatment, which I really hated because the treatment was often painful and horrible. You weren't made to feel of "value". There were never discussions about the contribution that we, as pupils, bring to our communities and we were never asked about our ambitions for the future. I know the reason why we were not asked these questions; because the expectation was that we would attend a day centre. This was where some of the students had attended after they left the school, or other forms of segregated provisions, such as a segregated college. Although I had not visited a day centre at the time, the experiences of that school were enough for me to close the door to any other segregated institution. The idea of attending a day centre scared me because, for me, it would be just another dumping ground where disabled people were placed.

'On leaving school, I was determined that I would not attend segregated college. However, I experienced a number of barriers in finding a local accessible mainstream college. Another big issue with segregated schooling was that it did not offer the same curriculum opportunities as mainstream education and no opportunities were offered to take formal qualifications. This meant that I, and many other young people, left our school with no qualifications, nor a record of achievement. The emotional pain still remains that, as young people, we were not equipped to participate in ordinary life opportunities, like our non-disabled peers. We were only suitable for another form of segregated provision.

'I and many other children who were placed in segregated educational provisions have been (and continue to be) seriously failed by the education system, because of labels as Special Educational Needs, our medical diagnosis and assessments that result in recommendations that are designed to remove certain children and young people from mainstream settings. Additionally, disabled young people are viewed as not being able to meaningfully contribute towards society. We know that people are being hurt and failed by segregated education and we can see how segregated education reproduces other forms of segregated practices. Despite this, there still continues to be investment into creating new segregated educational provisions. We know that disabled children are being shut out of mainstream schools, mainstream school budgets are being cut and there is a further list of barriers.

'This is why the work of Alliance for Inclusive Education (ALLFIE) is important because it is the only disabled people's organisation in England that is committed to campaigning for inclusive education as a human right for all disabled people within mainstream settings. ALLFIE creates opportunities to build capacity about the benefits of inclusive education and lobby for change in national law on inclusive education.

'We need everyone to recognise that segregated education of disabled people must be abolished, because it reinforces other discriminatory practices such as in housing and in employment, which is harming all of us.

'The pain of inequalities and the struggles of injustice are not things you want for others. You can't ignore them or turn your head to them. The combination of my different experiences was the driving factor that got me involved in activism, because I wanted to be part of the resistance to end abuse, violence, bring about change and end the segregation of disabled people in all its forms.'

11

10 per cent

Dr Chilver sat with his back to the classroom door, his head lowered, neither looking at the books laid out in front of him nor acknowledging the rampant fifteen- and sixteen-year-olds entering his classroom. The pupils took their seats and quietened. He had laid the classroom tables out in a boardroom style. The doctor, our English teacher, sat on a table in the middle as if he were one of the pupils; the only thing distinguishing him from us, at first sight, was his clothing, usually a dark, aged blazer. I took my seat beside him, to his right. He looked more like a University of Oxford lecturer than an inner-city schoolteacher. A stereotype, I know, but that's how I felt.

He had a narrow face, a haunted expression with loose cheek skin, and a leaden demeanour, a little like Leonard Nimoy. He rarely moved from his seat. He rarely moved in his chair. Only strips of black hair escaped his greased, side-parted hairstyle, which formed a reluctant fringe and shimmered whenever he spoke. To this day, I couldn't tell you how tall he was. He sat, he taught. A man with the gift of eloquence and a voice so gentle yet mildly shaky that, at times, it could be unnerving. The only time his tone would change would be on the rare occasion when he'd get annoyed. I can't remember what would spark his rage, but his voice would erupt. Hair strands would come loose; his emergent fringe would shake before he'd swiftly return to a calm state.

It was spring 1989, my final year at Langdon Comprehensive in East Ham, Newham, a school whose alumni include rapper Kano and singer Kele Le Roc. Exams loomed and indecision crowded my thoughts. *What now?*

My friends and I all remembered our first day of secondary school and we often reminisced about it and other pivotal experiences in Langdon around this time. Soon it would be over. Five years had disappeared in a whirl of conflicts with teachers, after-school 'rows' (fights), break-dancing, Black versus white football matches with tennis balls, death stars made in CDT (now called design and technology), sponsored walks, pupils ending each sentence with 'man' or 'guy', listening to Janet Jackson's *Control* album or funk-soul band Cameo, white kids disparagingly calling Black kids Ethiopians after seeing famine images on television, Leo Gemelli jumpers, BMX bikes, fights with other secondary schools, chip butties, Panini football stickers, everyone supporting Liverpool Football Club, Farah trousers, 'getting off with' (kissing) girls, leg-warmers, perms, teachers sniggering as they looked at our answers during exams,* the shift from

---

* Sniggering was bad, but the teachers were way more hardcore in Jamaica. My mother told me about one of her teachers, Ms Hunter. During a Bible studies exam, my mother hadn't written much. She couldn't remember what she had revised. Ms Hunter came walking by. On seeing my mother's blank exam sheet, she shouted at her. Ms Hunter's hollering frightened my mother into remembering what she had revised and she passed the exam.

Chaka Khan to Public Enemy, *Spitting Image*, Sergio Tacchini tracksuits, Fila trainers and *Grange Hill*. Now we had to think about our future, and I wasn't sure whether any of us had much of a clue about what we would do next.

As we settled into class, the doctor (of philosophy, I believe) asked each pupil what they would do once they had finished school. He started with the pupil to his left. I would be last. It seemed as if more pupils than I expected knew what they would do once they left school. One student wanted to be a newsreader, and another aspired to be a musician. There were also wannabe accountants and lawyers. As my peers spoke of their ambitions, I felt uneasy. Were they honest about their ambitions? Some started their responses with, 'my parents would like me to ...' Others, I thought, had pipe dreams. In truth, I was resentful. Much as I knew I would like to go into the recording industry or maybe even journalism, I never really thought I could make it. Langdon had done little to instil confidence in me.

Langdon was huge, stately and intimidating. As you entered its gates, a massive clock tower divided the school into two; the right-hand side was the lower end for Year-7s to Year-9s, and the left-hand side was the upper part for Year-10s and 11s. The building was grand, aspirational even, but the grounds around the school were even more exhilarating. There was a ditch, an orchard, and a hilly green field that surrounded the school. We'd sneak out of the school gates during lunch-times to climb trees, build hideouts from the branches, and create miniature fantasylands. The field was even better as the teaching staff could not police this vast land. It had a little creek with a wobbly bridge over it and travellers would often chase us off on their motorbikes. On my first day of school, a third-year (Year-9) pupil with long blond highlighted hair and inflamed eyebrows sat with his back against the clock tower building wall. He had one leg limp, the other raised in an upside-down V, as he stared into space while he played with a penknife. He had Chaka Khan's 'I Feel for You' blasting from his radio cassette recorder (which the white kids in the school called a 'wog box', unchallenged by teachers). I wasn't sure of this pupil's status in the school, but he looked like the lower-school sheriff as he sat there.

It was by no means the roughest school in the borough, but what happened outside of the classroom, in the playground, on the way home and on the sports field, appeared way more potent than what occurred in lessons. The teachers barely monitored pupils outside of lesson times. Beyond the frequent fights and everyday racism, misogyny and homophobia, there was a stabbing, an arson attempt, a sexual assault and boys frequently attacking girls during my time at Langdon.

I was a decent cricketer, which likely incubated me from trouble more than my personality or ability to fight. In my first game for Langdon, I scored forty-five runs not out and found myself in the local newspaper, the *Newham Recorder*. While I would never replicate that form with the bat again, that first game brought me the captaincy of the team, attention from the cool people in school, huge expectations every time I played, offers to play for other clubs and a place on the cover of a pamphlet aimed at attracting local primary school pupils to Langdon.

Playing cricket occupied my time and gave me enough

popularity to avoid fights with other pupils. I had a pass. At one point, I went on strike because of what I believed to be the racism of one of my PE teachers. He stripped me of the captaincy and frequently made offensive remarks to me and other teammates of colour. Inspired by the West Indian cricket team, this was my first display of activism. My teammates also went on strike. I was eventually reinstated as co-captain. By the time I got to the fourth year (Year 10), I was one of the few players who had been a part of the school team since the first year (Year 7). Due to my experience, I ended up training and umpiring matches for incoming first-years, which was my first involvement in youth work or volunteering.

When I spoke to campaigner and educator Yvonne Field for this book, she too was first inspired on her giving journey by experiences in school. While Yvonne was being interviewed for a grammar school at eleven years old, a headteacher asked her mother if she was a British citizen. Her mother replied, 'No, I'm not a British citizen, but I have the right to be here – I came here in the fifties. My daughter has a right to have a place at this school if she's seen to be bright. They say she's bright.'

Five of Yvonne's white peers were given a place at the school, but she was the only one who did not get in. Her parents campaigned against the local authority, appealed and went to the local press while enlisting Black students' support from Goldsmiths University to home-school Yvonne. A race relations council took up the case and helped win their appeal. From that moment, Yvonne realised that you could say no to the system. She went on to excel at her new school and, throughout her life, open doors for other people, particularly the young.

While I was finding my voice outside the classroom, inside of it, I struggled. I had an assortment of charismatic educators with variable teaching skills. My sociology teacher I found to be a bit of an aggressive man, passionate about his subject and inspiring at times but with a short fuse. I had an eccentric history teacher with curly sandy-coloured hair surrounding his bald dome, who sweated profusely and completed each sentence with a wide-eyed psychotic glare. I enjoyed his lessons, which were more like performances. The image of his hands aloft as if conducting an orchestra with sweat dripping from his tanned shirt will never leave me.

I also had an art teacher who looked like a cross between Keith Richards and Donald Sutherland. He grumbled his way through lessons as if he'd had a couple of shots of vodka for breakfast and bathed in clay-coloured paint. My maths teacher spent most of his lessons telling us stories instead of teaching. He would start a class talking about Pythagoras and then end with a war story. The bell would ring. 'Oh, is the lesson over already?' he'd say, shaking his head in disbelief. I had another teacher who appeared more interested in talking about Argentinean tennis star Gabriela Sabatini's beauty than the Kalahari bush desert and a physics teacher who seemingly took fifteen minutes to read the register.

But it was also unusual for a teacher to ask about our ambitions. Only our careers advisor would ask such questions and it was her job. She had to find us work placements, often a crushing experience for pupils with ambition. I was no different. In the fourth year, I told her that I would like to be an Artist and Repertoire (A&R) Man. She stared right through me. I don't believe she knew what an A&R Man was.

When I explained, she only responded with options that were readily available to me. Eventually, I asked if I could do a placement in a record shop (I suggested Music Power, which was situated near the old Sainsbury's car park in Ilford) or perhaps with the local newspaper, the *Newham Recorder*. 'I'll see what I can do,' she said, nodding unconvincingly. When I returned, she told me she had found a placement in MFI, a furniture store in Barking.

For close to two weeks, MFI dulled me to the point of bewilderment. I spent most of my days assembling wardrobes, desks and other household furniture – some for display, but most for staff members to pull apart once we finished. Barely any customers came in. They didn't have anything for us to do. MFI's staff were bored. They entertained themselves by sellotaping twenty pence pieces onto the store's entry stairs to see if any customers would try to pick them up. They'd also announce on the Tannoy, 'does anybody have a book on fly fishing, by J. R. Hartley?' after the famous Yellow Pages advert.

It was finally my turn. 'Derek, what are you going to do once you leave school?' the doctor asked. 'I dunno,' I replied, 'I'll probably go on the dole.' The other pupils did not react. There were no sniggers or whispers, which was strange. While I thought I was somewhat realistic, I was also trying to be a little clever. I thought my comment would elicit a minor laugh.

I lowered my head when the doctor refused to accept my answer. He asked again, visibly annoyed at my flippant response. I hated being in the spotlight. I wish I'd just said anything to pass the baton back to the good doctor; a French teacher, a mechanic, a paediatrician, a bus driver, a Renaissance poet, anything. I guess I was more bothered about how my classmates viewed me than being honest.

With my head still bowed, I told the class that I wanted to be an A&R Man. The doctor did not know what this occupation was or what it entailed. 'It means artist and repertoire,' I mumbled. 'They scout music artists.' No one laughed at me. It felt good, even if I wanted to sink into my trouser pockets and hide with my coppers, loose tissues and door keys.

Many years later, I met an incredible educator named Femi Bola MBE, then the Director of Employability at the University of East London. She ran assessment centres for pupils from the Stephen Lawrence Centre, where I was the Director of Education and Learning between 2006 and 2009. While delivering lectures to teachers, legend has it that Bola would ask them how many formal educators had significantly impacted their lives and careers. Often, these teachers would mention no more than a handful of people. Considering the many educators these professionals would have encountered throughout their lives, such a small percentage of inspiring teachers says a lot about the state of the education system.

There are only three formal teachers I can think of who had a significant impact on me. Dr Chilver, an outrageously witty and cynical English teacher from 'up north' at Barking College called John Toolan, and a passionate Turkish sociologist at Middlesex University named Dr Mehmet Ali Dikerdem. Although it took me many years to realise it, I learned a valuable lesson from these teachers.

They cared and were not afraid to show it. They were impassioned and did not impose limitations on my ability based on their own biases. They took heed of my personality, my character. That said, sadly, this is fewer than 10 per cent of all the formal teachers that I have spent a significant amount of time with during many years of gaining certificates from various educational establishments.

My school experiences also taught me that I might be limited to less than 10 per cent of what I should get from the education system. Wealth and power enable mediocrity to rise to positions that few of us can attain. You can have less ability or drive than me but progress further due to your money and resource. Sounds obvious. But then fairness is not considered among the values Britain generally champions, like the rule of law, tolerance and democracy.

I fell into the trap of believing that working harder, gaining more qualifications, being the best citizen I could be would enable me to achieve some parity (in wealth, not well-being) with those who grew up with more resources than me. I also believed that individual responsibility and decisions alone were the main factors for succeeding or failing in society. At the time, I overlooked how people are situated in life – their environment, access to quality employment, wealth, housing, health, information and education – things that are often beyond our control and usually controlled by the state.

The vast majority of those I went to school with, and I

believe most people in this country, were limited to less than 10 per cent of what they were due. It is never solely an individual's actions that dictate their fate. However, it is often the brilliance of individuals, parents, educators, care workers and youth workers that help us become more than 10 per cent. They need more support and resources though.

Nevertheless, we are all operating within a system of limitations and that – the system – is where the focus of change should be. Increasing the number of good teachers will not increase the 10 per cent if we continue to mistreat them and cannot retain them. While I advocate for working harder and following the law, I understand that these actions alone will not lead to a fairer Britain.

WHITNEY ILES
Founder and CEO, Project 507

'I came into the work because of my trauma, and I'm very aware of that. I'm very aware that my trauma was pimped out by a lot of adults in this sector. It got me caught in this sector. It was not until I was about twenty-six or twenty-seven that I was given the opportunity to start processing my trauma, and why I started this work. I lost someone in a very painful way when I was very very young, and it was that [and] a lot of complex childhood experiences that I didn't know how to heal myself from, so I was helping other people. I was taking all of that pain and I was trying to do something good without pain. And, because of my pain, I was incredibly sensitive to other people's pain. You know, you can look past me, and I'll be like, "Yo, you all right?"

'I came into the sector for all the wrong reasons. I was dragged into this sector more than anything. It was never what I wanted to do. I was very happy doing music. I was a trained sound engineer. I wanted a whole different life for myself. At one point I wanted to be a brain surgeon, a very long time [ago]. I didn't have those opportunities, but I had an opportunity to be a youth worker.

'I've just, I've always wanted to feel OK, and I wanted to feel happy, and it's just been a learning of "what do I need to do for myself to heal myself?" I'm constantly putting myself in that journey and wanting to reflect, and wanting to understand more, to understand why I do the things that I do, why I feel the way that I feel. Needing a lot of stimulation, which is a coping mechanism, needing that intellectual stimulation as a way of not being able to cope with being emotionally overwhelmed, or overwhelmed with other things and just channelling it all.

'So, actually, my trauma has been my biggest blessing and my biggest curse in this life. It's taught me so much more than I think I would have learned if I'd never experienced anything like that, but it's also caught me in a lot of these kinds of bad relationships, in a working sense. It wasn't necessarily that I wanted to help people, it's just I wanted to stop feeling as shit as I did.

'I think that's what a lot of people come into this sector with. We never get given the opportunity to reflect and to understand why we do the work. I remember feeling anxious of what happens if I heal because I have to leave this whole identity of mine behind, and now you know I'm on my healing process and I'm leaving this work behind. I won't be in this work for that much longer.

'I'm setting up [Project] 507 and I want it to be sturdy in any way, shape, or form, but this is not where I'm going to be in ten years or twenty years. I have a whole different kind of want for my life now, and that's OK. It took me a long time to learn [that] this is OK. What I want for other people to know is that it's OK to leave the charity sector. The charity sector is a big plaster for a lot of professionals to give us meaning and purpose in life, stop us from healing from our trauma, and leaving our trauma behind because our trauma becomes such a big part of who we are. We feel like we are no one without it. We don't know who we might be without it.'

12

Rude bwoy

Not quite the same satisfying pleasure one gets from watching a YouTube clip of a bully getting his comeuppance and being knocked out with one punch. You know the narrative: a man picks on someone for a reason never quite established; it could be an earlier incident, they could just be showing off in front of people. Either way, it's a David and Goliath situation. You haven't deliberately searched for the clip. It pops up as you're scouting the net for boxing highlights. But it draws you in, morbid as it feels, and you watch the clip repeatedly.

You wonder how the knocked-out bully felt when he recovered. You wonder whether he knew he was being filmed. You wonder whether he kept up the bravado in the face of the sniggering crowd that witnessed his demise. You wonder how someone so brazen could be so easily defeated. You wonder how people could be so arrogant to think that they can get away with treating another person in that way. You wonder whether he ever bullied anyone again. But then you feel this sorrowful pleasure at watching the bully get what he deserves, and while you don't advocate for violence, there are times when you want to use what little power you have to even the score.

I'm sure a therapist would tell me that revenge is just a momentary fix, that it would not help get to the root of my problems. I'm sure they'd say that I would not be able to move on effectively, that revenge is self-destructive. But like addiction, there's something sweet about revenge. That's how I felt when I used to watch the West Indian cricket team in the eighties. Not in the same ballpark as the YouTube punch but a distant family member. Long term, I'm not sure it resolved any ill feelings I have towards England. But cricket became an outlet for my rage. The memory of the West Indies colonising England in the summer of '84 remains vivid and unquenchable.

The English hated it. Did everything in their powers to destroy it. They couldn't compete with the West Indies even though they had far more resources. So they used other means – the media, narrative, policy changes. They complained about the West Indies' use of bouncers or slow over-rate. They wanted to limit the number of overseas players in the English County Cricket League. They remarked about how Caribbean players were physically stronger, almost non-human. Covert racism. Institutional racism. A way of suppressing Black folks to ensure we never got ideas above our stations again.

I wrote about my love of the West Indian cricket team in my first book, *No Win Race*. About how the English maintained rule over West Indian cricket on and off the field for many years. And how a new generation of West Indian cricketers emerged in the seventies. Most of them were brought up during a time when Caribbean nations were gaining independence from the Empire. Many of these players, displaying excellence and discipline, used cricket to avenge years of oppression brought on by colonisation. The West Indian team was a social movement which partly inspired my mini-activism as a teenager. I found solace in that team. Rarely had I felt comfort growing up in London, a place where I was always under the spotlight, under scrutiny as a Black boy. I was the other. As much as I'd try to blend into society, I did not represent England's conception of Englishness. The first and perhaps last time I felt absolute comfort in myself was when I went on holiday to Jamaica for the first time in August 1991.

For years, my parents referred to Jamaica as 'back home'. When we landed in Montego Bay in '91, it was the first time they had gone back to where they were born in thirty-odd years. Throughout my childhood, I heard stories about this small island with big ambitions. *We likkle but we tallawah.* Yet we never had enough money to go as a family. No sooner had I walked from the plane into the suffocating heat of Mo' Bay than I found out I was as much a stranger in Jamaica as I was in England.

As we moved through the sparse, simple airport, I spotted police officers sitting around a tiny circular table playing dominos. Everything and everyone moved slowly. Despite there being a few passengers, we drifted through customs in a lackadaisical haze. A vast billboard picture of Merlene Ottey, regarded as Jamaica's greatest ever sprinter at the time, greeted us. As we left, we were surrounded by baggage hustlers trying to grab our luggage, who moved quicker than anyone else.

It was hot and I had little time to acclimatise before I heard a few touts skylarking outside the airport shouting at me, 'Hinglish, Hinglish' (as in English). I nodded my head as if they were my long-lost brothers, but they smirked and carried on chatting. It wouldn't be the last time I would hear 'Hinglish', a word that became as piercing as a siren in London first thing in the morning.

Culturally, I could not adjust to Jamaica. *Was it my clothes?* I often wore a Red Stripe-branded vest, knee-length black shorts and my black Patrick Ewing 33 Hi basketball trainers. *My hair?* It was relaxed, shoulder-length, and shaved at the sides. Not my best look but hardly extravagant given the many styles I witnessed on Jamaican men at the time. Maybe it was the way I spoke. For the first few days, I tried my Ja-fakan (fake Jamaican) accent. I soon realised – from the bemused looks of locals – how ridiculous I sounded.

Maybe it had been the intensity of my sweat. While the locals' faces glimmered from the sun, mine looked as if I had a pouring showerhead permanently looming over my cranium. Perhaps it had something to do with how swiftly I walked. Even at eighteen, I walked in a sort of bothered and hustled haste. It was likely that all of these factors contributed to why I was not considered kinfolk to people in Jamaica. I just couldn't fit in as well as I had envisaged.

I tried to emulate what I believed to be a Jamaican way of acting throughout my school years. I thought Jamaicans had an uncompromising attitude, so I 'hissed' my teeth a lot, had a bit of a swagger when I walked (although still much quicker than Jamaicans) and acted carefree. When I was angry, I would launch into a dodgy Jamaican accent to accentuate my point. I didn't act this way because of my father, as I cannot remember him ever hissing his teeth, let alone acting care-free. Laid back, yes, but not carefree. I guess I took my lead from older kids and the media. The way I acted wasn't me. I wasn't a Bandelero, even if I harboured desires to be a rude bwoy. I was doing my best act in Jamaica yet coming across like a reality TV star trying to perform in a Shakespearian production.

In Jamaica, locals treated me like a tourist, which made me feel even worse. While I quickly recovered from knowing I was an outsider, I found no significant connection with people outside of my extended family members in Galina, my parents' hometown. The dusty, gravelly streets were lined with rickety wire fences and woozy wooden houses, which merged with more stable brick structures. There were always people out and about, hungry dogs barking on every corner, cars roaming with little intention of stopping.

Everyone knew each other and had stories to tell. There was a church, a school, a grocery store, a tiny shack of a bar (selling warm Heineken, Red Stripe and Kola Champagne), and little else. Yet there was space. It was open. Freeing. The sky unimpeded. No high-rise buildings were surrounding me, as they did in London. Peace. The big towns, Ocho Rios, Montego Bay and Kingston, with endless streams of market stalls, police with machine guns and men in shades and shorts willing to sell you anything from weed to American dollars, became claustrophobic. I tried to hide my 'Hinglish' traits because I knew I didn't belong.

Still, I had an overwhelming sense of calm visiting Jamaica, which is why the trip was so pivotal in my life. I met my half-brother Donald (on my father's side) for the first time. Locals called him King or Mikey. Softly spoken with a narrow face and a piercing glare, Mikey became our guide. He lived in Galina in a simple wooden and zinc-roofed house. By 1991, Mikey was around thirty-five, and the house remained firm despite the various natural disasters Jamaica had endured over the years.

Mikey had built a local cinema from wood, which consisted of little more than four posts, a cloth covering for a roof and some hand-crafted benches. Using a television and video, Mikey charged locals to watch movies, mainly kung-fu flicks. He also sold household goods to supplement his income. The only safety cushion he had was the money that our father and his mother sent him and a community of relatives and friends in Galina. But there was no welfare state, no benefits, not much in the way of job prospects, just his creative mind to enable him to get by. I'm not romanticising his lifestyle. He lived a hard life. But he was an entrepreneur, self-sufficient, close to the land and someone with great humility, loved by everyone in his community.

Amid all of this, I visited my father's birthplace, now just a balding patch of land. I met relatives I had only heard of in stories. Black folks surrounded me with the sun blaring and reggae music blasting from every corner. I went to Reggae Sunsplash and watched Shabba Ranks and the top dancehall artists of the day. A soundtrack of Pinchers's 'Bandelero' and Papa San's 'Strange' rang in my ears throughout the trip. Jamaica was dangerous too. A *stepping razor*. A driver carrying my whole family fell asleep at the wheel, the car roaming onto a lane of oncoming traffic. We once argued with local passengers on a crammed bus, who defended a driver who had deliberately charged us to go to Ocho Rios but decided to take us elsewhere. The police had to intervene.

Despite the drama, I couldn't have felt more peaceful, more relaxed. It was the first time that I did not question the colour of my skin. I may have been a foreigner, and I eventually accepted that, but I was in a space where I did not have to explain myself or my Blackness. The experience made me feel assured, as if I had a home, if only in a spiritual sense. I carried those feelings back to England. I knew I would never be the same again. But I recognised that true happiness would only come by having those feelings and assurance in my day-to-day life.

Upon returning to England, I felt bold and carried myself as if I knew more about life than my peers. I didn't. And the feeling didn't last long. But it reaffirmed my belief that shared experiences can be more important than a shared birthplace. The power that comes with this identity can be stronger than national identity. I would fully grasp and not fear people's right to find comfort in their own minoritised communities.

It didn't mean I opposed my country of birth. It meant that in a country where I was marginalised, comfort and finding a place of belonging were fundamental to my well-being. This had everything to do with my ease in defining who I was and not becoming the state's idea of what I should be. There would be nothing easy about finding comfort and kinship in England. But I discovered that pursuing a peaceful life solely through assimilation provides a rapid path to submission, complacency and trauma.

BONNIE CHIU
Founder and Trustee, Lensational and Managing Director, The Social Investment Consultancy

'The global elite are so connected and Britain also connected the world through colonialism. I was born and raised in Hong Kong, we are not independent, we got handed back over to China in 1997, but up until I was five years old, we were still part of the colonial empire. But I think that Hong Kong is very interesting because it's a hyper-capitalist society.

'There are very low taxes – you don't pay sales tax. It's just capitalism here but times ten. There are no constraints on profits, it's quite wild in that sense. At the same time, it is still relatively new. It really developed in the last three to four decades, so there are quite a lot of emergent narratives that still haven't been constructed. There's a lot of fluidity because we are in between east and west, and there's a lot of fluidity to construct what those narratives are for people in Hong Kong, at least in the past two decades. But right after, actually the year we were handed back over to China, there was the Asian financial crisis, which was really bad.

'Another thing is, Chinese parents do everything for their children, so my parents wanted to get me into a good school. They moved to this district where there was a higher possibility to get me into a good school, and they bought a flat at the peak of the housing crisis. A few months after the housing market crashed, the flat they bought decreased in value by two-thirds. What that meant was that they took out a mortgage on the house's value that was three times the current value. So at the age of five, I had exposure into a capitalist system.

'I knew the concept of house prices, markets and market dynamics and what that meant to me on a personal level, and the inequalities. It just so happened they needed to buy a flat for their child to have a better education, they didn't do anything wrong, but the markets made them lose their money.

'They eventually recovered, but it was really difficult – my mum had three jobs just to get back on track and pay their mortgage. I use this example because I think that how I grew up meant I learnt about the economic system from a very young age. And also, in school, we were encouraged to explore poverty and inequality, so it was a live discussion and I was grateful that we had an opportunity to explore that in school.

'The other dimension is around storytelling. My English literature (or literature in English) teacher was very inspirational and he forced us to read books by women – an equal number of women writers as male writers. I was in an all-Catholic school, but most people weren't really religious. It was more that they had very strong values about education in school. My teacher in literature said to me one thing that really stuck with me: one day, he asked us, "Why do we always say English literature?"

'But he kept on stressing that it wasn't "English literature", it was "literature in English". We never understood why it was different, but he said that it was really important to make that distinction because English is not the exclusive domain of the English. Because of colonialism, we read a lot of Indian writers and African writers and that was because they had as much stake and ownership over the language as the English.

'That was interesting and I had never thought about it before. My education really helped me interrogate the assumptions we find ourselves in the world. I feel very sad right now because I know that this is not the education that my cousins (who are now fourteen) will have in Hong Kong because of the repression that is going on. It does help me reflect on my friends here in the UK and I think I've probably learnt a much more reflective view of the world and of history than my friends here in the UK.'

13

Fanon

I had to read Frantz Fanon's *Black Skin, White Masks* (first published in 1952) three times before I understood its content. Even so, I am not sure that I ever fully grasped the meaning behind everything the Algerian-French psychiatrist, thinker and writer had been trying to say. Yet, except for James Baldwin's *The Fire Next Time* and John Edgar Wideman's *Fatheralong*, I don't think I have read a truer text about race and racism.

Fanon was born in Martinique in 1925. He completed his most famous work, *The Wretched of the Earth*, shortly before his death from leukaemia in 1961. Today, decolonisation movements across the globe reference Fanon's work, recognising how we need to undo colonialism, racism and white supremacy embedded within the structures, language and institutions that govern us. Militaristic means often enforce this ideology. Colonists used violence to wrestle the land and the livelihoods from Black and brown people across the globe. For Fanon, an armed revolution would be vital in liberating the colonised from a life of being 'othered' and perpetually oppressed. Not all decolonisation movements advocate for violence as a means of change, however. Fanon's philosophies also drove the thinking behind some of the most influential anti-racist leaders and movements since his death, from Malcolm X and Stokely Carmichael (Kwame Ture) to the Black Panthers.

I knew little about Fanon's impact when I first read *Black Skin, White Masks* in the early nineties. But for me, nothing before or perhaps since has captured with such clarity the social and psychological condition of growing up as a Black male in a western European country. Fanon conveyed how one of the most significant battles I'd face would be establishing my own identity in the face of the one moulded by white people's stereotypes. Submitting to such stereotypes meant that I would always seek validation from white people while never being entirely comfortable in my skin. I was inescapably the 'other'. Even if I conformed, thereby attaining some level of acceptance for my achievements, a mistake would swiftly result in me being othered again.

But how do I negotiate white lies? If I gave myself a score out of ten based on my performance over the years, I'd likely give myself a six. The results have been patchy, even though I have continued to revisit *Black Skin* to gauge how I'm progressing. To gain a sense of identity, I knew that I needed to know my history. Yet much of Black history had been erased, distorted and re-written.

I didn't think I could go back to a country in Africa, yet the consequences of full integration in Britain appeared to be a price I was not willing to pay. Fanon described it as 'not yet white, no longer fully black'. The conflict between Blackness and Britishness was arguably the most significant battle I faced growing up. The former is not fully defined but based on culture, shared experiences and, often, a sense of belonging. The latter was imposed, based on history and pseudo-scientific racism, portraying me as less-than-human.

As we grow up as Black men, we see that some stereotypes can be advantageous – primarily those related to our physical prowess. We enslave ourselves by reinforcing such stereotypes in our actions, be it a quest for careers in sport over academia, promiscuity, or using our physical strength and power to gain some sort of parity. I saw these dynamics play out with my peers and constantly battled to ensure that I didn't fall into such stereotypes. Too often, I did.

I was preoccupied with my ego, a neurosis that seeks power to make up for feelings of inferiority that I had to confront continuously. Whiteness is the default and my inability to fit into these norms rendered me 'abnormal' in society. I continually tried to attain status, wealth and well-being in a system built to suppress my potential to achieve this. I learned that there is a real and everlasting neurosis that comes with racism and that white people who have little sense of this, who do not have their bodies targeted, who do not understand Black history, cannot provide solutions to this problem.

I learned that our institutions are little more than 'Europe's colonial offices', reinforcing the white power structure. We have an education system that supports the Empire State of Mind and such racialised hierarchies. Capitalism is the son of colonialism. It will bleed Black communities of their resources, never seeking to collaborate but always to own. I would later recognise these behaviours in the charity sector.

*

In reading Fanon, I understood that the teachings from *Black Skin* had been fundamental to my approach to giving. It's political. Cannot separate the two. I also understood that part of white people's fear of us sits with the possibility that we might do to them what they had done to us. In *Black Skin, White Masks*, Fanon quotes Martinican poet and politician Aimé Césaire, who once spoke of how the only baptism a good slave could remember was the day the blood flowed as he slayed his master.

For many years, in moments of anger or frustration, I held the view that violence was a necessary retort to a hostile state structure. It's not a belief I own now, as I hope there is a better way of gaining justice in society. *Black Skin, White Masks* is one of the greatest books I've ever read; its politics were central to formulating my views. But as I grew older, I also realised that I had had a privileged enough upbringing to seek a different kind of baptism.

LILY LEWIS

Founder and CEO, The Pocressi Initiative

'I have been part of a twelve-step programme since I was in my late teens, and being of service to others and having this type of honest human connection is very important to me. There's a saying, "You can only keep what you have by giving it away." I really believe that. Within twelve-step meetings, there often isn't a class divide, which provided me with my first opportunity to listen to experiences and realities that differed from my own in a very real way.

'If it wasn't for the support that my privilege enabled me to have, I know I probably wouldn't be alive and well. And that's just not fair. Why should winning the genetic lottery enable me to have quality mental health care and the luxury of time to heal? I will never be able to express the amount of admiration and respect I have for those who manage to thrive despite experiencing oppression.

'These things, along with the privilege of space and time within my own psychotherapy, have allowed me to see my social responsibility and work through uncomfortable feelings in relation to my class and wealth. I have witnessed many people who inherit wealth or power to feel a lot of shame. Often, ultra-high-net-wealth families are highly dysfunctional but are able to hide it well. There can be a lot of pressure, addiction (including workaholism, power or drugs) and emptiness. Everyone is disconnected.

'Young people in this position can often go into three categories.
1) They pretend it isn't there and act "normal". Living middle-class lives, not telling their friends or partners about the extensive wealth they have.

2) Separate themselves from it, i.e., go work for a bank and build their own material success to prove [an] identity separate from their family. They hide their connection with their family's money/business/power to the outside world.

3) Indulge in the wealth and power to the extreme i.e., drive fast cars, living out the "rich kid" life.

'These are all forms of denial, to an extent. Connecting with the social responsibility and the potential of what it could mean to be an ultra-high-net-wealth individual can be incredibly overwhelming. Often, these families will never even talk about money, to begin with. It is a secret elephant in the room. Most people inheriting these things can often get stuck in unconscious money shame and can struggle to have direction or a sense of purpose.

'It is only when we can honestly examine our relationship and identity in relation to these issues that we are able to break the pattern of accumulating wealth and start to redistribute it in a way that doesn't repeat the patterns of white supremacy.'

14

Black press owes me money

On a sunny weekday afternoon, my friend Errol and I strolled up to Portobello Road upon hearing that the Electric Cinema would be reopening as Britain's first Black-owned cinema. An Edwardian-era building constructed in 1910, it became one of the UK's most famous independent cinemas. I had never heard of it before learning about its revival. It was 1993 and Portobello had not yet become as trendy and exclusive a neighbourhood as it would after the 1999 movie *Notting Hill*.

This part of west London was all about the Carnival for me. Every year, Ladbroke Grove, Westbourne Park, Notting Hill, Kensington, Harrow Road, et al. provided an unflinching celebration of the UK's Caribbean presence and culture. It was also a site of resistance, as the Notting Hill Carnival had proven resilient to the authorities' many attempts to shut it down. For a few hours, we didn't have to compromise; we didn't need to fit in, to code-switch, to contend with the stares, lack of promotions and constant restraint required to get through the day. For a few hours, we felt at ease and a part of an event that became the most joyful and enduring Black political act in Britain.

Builders were still refurbishing the cinema when we arrived, so it was a dusty shell. But we met two of the owners and asked for work; they asked if we had any experience and told us when to start. So in the autumn, we picked up our tangy green work jumpers and became the Electric's first employees, alongside a previously employed projectionist. They launched the cinema with *Passion Fish* starring Alfre Woodard. In my final year at university, I primarily worked weekend shifts, often arriving Saturday afternoon for matinees and working through late-night showings.

The cinema did not last long under part-Black ownership. It had financial problems right from the start; it suffered from shoddy programming and lacked a clear identity, never quite balancing Black audiences with the emergent trendy Notting Hill crowd. But it had its moments. I met Angela Davis – one of the most significant Black American political figures of the last sixty years – when she delivered a speech at the cinema. There were some great movie nights too, from *What's Love Got to Do with It* to Spike Lee's beautifully shot *Crooklyn*, with a brooding lead track by a temporarily assembled supergroup called Crooklyn Dodgers, comprising rappers Buckshot (from the group Black Moon), Special Ed and Masta Ace.

Being at the Electric would prove to be a blessing for my career. I had wanted to go into film but wasn't connected enough in that world to find work upon graduating. It was through a colleague at the Electric that I eventually found film-extra work. Another co-worker connected me to the journalism and PR agency Power Moves. Inspired by Dean Ricketts's Watch-Men Agency, Power Moves was founded by specialist hip-hop writers Justin Onyeka, Lee Pinkerton and Paul 'Rapscallion' Ryan. They edited the music pages of the Black broadsheet the *Weekly Journal*. So, I gave them a call offering my services. Pinkerton answered:

'What do you write about?'

'Hip-hop,' I said.

'Everyone's hip-hop writer, we have hip-hop writers coming to us every day. We don't need hip-hop writers.'

'I can write about other genres too.'

'You'll have to. The industry is overrun with hip-hop writers. Right now, we only have an opening for a reggae writer.'

'I can write about reggae,' I said.

'OK, tomorrow when Justin gets in, have a word.'

I called back and had a brief chat with the softly spoken Onyeka. He told me to write a two-hundred-word review for the following week. 'What of?' I said. 'Anything current,' he replied. I didn't know what was current. I liked reggae, well, dancehall, and had spent the early nineties going to the all-dayers (all-day outdoor concerts) featuring the best Black artists from the UK, Jamaica and the United States. As much as I listened to entertainers such as Buju Banton, Mad Cobra and Terror Fabulous, I was still more of a hip-hop head and didn't know enough about contemporary reggae to provide an informed review on the genre.

After speaking to Onyeka, I ran out to buy the *Reggae Guide* book and then went to Daddy Kool Records in Soho to flick through the latest pre's (pre-release, seven-inch records). As I flicked through endless records, I had no idea what was current and what wasn't. At the time, the volume of records coming out of Jamaica was overwhelming. I called Dennis Rootical, a friend and bass player for dub band Iration Steppers, who told me about his friend Dub Judah.

After buying the reggae book, I didn't have much money left. So I made a deal. I agreed to write Dub Judah's press release and biography for his new LP in exchange for an exclusive copy of his latest album. I figured that if I reviewed a record not yet released, it would appear as if I had connections in the reggae world.

I faxed the piece to Onyeka and he liked it. Power Moves took me on as their reggae specialist. They sent me my first assignment within a week – a review of Bounty Killer's *Down in the Ghetto* – and the piece launched my journalism career. Later, I called the *Caribbean Times* and proposed a weekly basketball column called 'Slam Session', which they accepted.

Within months, records and free tickets to basketball matches flooded through my door. I didn't earn much money. Magazines either took me on without pay or never paid me. I contributed to about ten publications in my first two years of writing but netted around £60. But I didn't care. I was building my portfolio and earning some money at the cinema. Within seven years of the *Down in the Ghetto* review, I had expanded my freelance work to include journalism work-shops, PR and some radio and television work.

Through much of my twenties, freelancing gave me some freedom; my fate was in my own hands. The strength of my portfolio, my willingness to take on assignments at short notice and my ability to meet tight deadlines gave me a good reputation. That's how I liked it. Yet obstacles remained in finding work through more formal routes after graduating and leaving the Electric.

From 1994 to 2002, I continued looking for stable work to support my writing when my freelancing dipped. I struggled to secure a job through official channels. Freelance or part-time employment came through cold-calling or my networks. My degree and ample work experience (I had become a duty manager at the Electric) counted for nothing at job interviews.

In 1996, Onyeka recruited me to *New Nation*, a Black newspaper to rival *The Voice*, and he remained a willing advisor. Rapscallion recommended me to Jet Star Records and I worked as a press officer promoting the best reggae music of the mid-nineties. I ended up doing some PR for legendary south-east London sound-system Saxon Studio after interviewing the founders, Musclehead and Dennis Rowe, for the *Weekly Journal*.

From 1998 to 2001, I worked as the Music Editor of *The Voice* after a recommendation from Pinkerton, then the Arts Editor. While working at *The Voice*, I tried to follow Power Moves's lead by mentoring young people on work placements and responding to students who wanted to shadow me to gain journalism experience. I tried to open doors with what little power I had.

I started conducting journalism workshops at HMP Wormwood Scrubs through another journalist at *The Voice*, Paul Macey. This eventually led me to run after-school sessions and workshops in youth clubs voluntarily. This led to a meeting with Angela Herbert-Richards, who was working in the education department at Scrubs. Herbert-Richards provided me with more freelance work through her Inside-Out Consultancy and much of my grounding in youth and community work. I eventually qualified as a youth worker, which led to a full-time career in the social sector.

It was not until I was twenty-nine that I received a permanent job offer through a formal interview, eight years after graduating. Even then, the person who hired me was a person of colour. My first position where a white employer hired me was with Children's Express in 2003, at thirty. I was lucky as I had helpful mentors at crucial times who opened doors for me when the more formal ones were closed.

Years later, I met cultural producer Sade Banks. Sade was excluded from two secondary schools and homeless by the age of fourteen. Despite a complex background and not having a degree, she progressed to leading positions in the theatre industry. However, the higher she went, the fewer people she saw who looked like her or had similar experiences. Banks had infiltrated an exclusive club where not many people of colour or from working-class backgrounds were in positions of power.

In 2017, she created the charity Sour Lemons, through which she pioneered a leadership programme to nurture diverse talent while tackling the structural barriers to inclusion in the arts. She wanted young people with a similar background to her own to have access to opportunities and networks.

One of the reasons Banks succeeded was because she had mentors at critical stages of her development. She developed a programme that met the individual needs of working-class young people pursuing careers in the arts. Critically, in finding placements for young people in major arts institutions, she worked with her 'Lemons' (Banks's term for her leaders) to tackle the structural issues within their host organisations. Banks is an excellent example of using her lived experience to address the individual and institutional barriers to inclusion to create long-term change.

My experiences taught me many lessons. First, lack of access to opportunities in employment is real for people of colour, working-class folks and most marginalised communities. Self-determination is necessary for minoritised people. If you can't get a fair deal from the institutions tasked with serving your needs, you must create your own. A vibrant social sector is reliant on organisations like Power Moves and Sour Lemons.

Second, Britain, like most of the world, operates on networks. It's all about who you know. I was fortunate in that I met people with access. I was also lucky because countless Black businesses in the nineties enabled me to get a foot on the ladder. It's challenging to know what path I would have taken without them. Third, much of this history – your Power Moves, your Electric Cinemas – has been and continues to be erased.

I remember going to the Electric Cinema in 2005 to watch the film *Capote*. The cinema was under new management and featured luxury reclining seats and a licensed bar. Before the movie started, there was a short feature on the history of the Electric Cinema. This did not mention that Electric had once been the UK's first Black-owned cinema.

It may not have been a glorious or extended part of its history, but it should have been significant enough to gain a mention. I think back to the untold stories. I think about the importance of preserving these narratives, contextualising their relevance to today, learning lessons from them, and how important it is to keep telling these stories. For many people, particularly those in power, self-determination means segregation. But, in most cases, self-determination promotes pride, independence, representation, possibilities and hope. And for many people, myself included, these pathways enabled me to mobilise in my career to prevent myself, like these stories, from being erased.

One of the key roles of the social sector should be to promote self-determination within less fortunate, continually disadvantaged communities. For the social sector to reinforce fears perpetuated by the government and the media around self-determination is to compromise its independence, effectiveness, and ability to represent marginalised voices.

AMAHRA SPENCE

Co-Founder and Creative Director, MAIA and Founder, YARD Arthouse

'There's a couple of things. The first thing that I remember happening was when I was ten; I was voted class valedictorian for the first-ever leavers' fair at my primary school. I didn't know that my classmates trusted me enough or valued my words, so right then, I knew my words held power – there's a strength in the things I have to say. In my leaver's speech, I was speaking about collectivism, and that's what my classmates valued and that's why they voted me as class valedictorian, so I always had that in the back of my mind. That was one of my earliest and proudest moments.

'I was a bit of a naughty fifteen-year-old. I was on the wrong path, I was doing some dodgy things, I was in some dangerous spaces, I was a failing student academically and when I got to Year 11, my English teacher and my maths teacher worked their arses off with me to study. They saw potential in me that deep down I knew was there and they stood with me. I felt like they held me through a moment.

'My GCSE grades are fundamentally the proudest thing I've ever done, not necessarily because of the grades but because I had people with me who believed in me, who held me through it, and we did the damn thing – that is my proudest moment. From that moment on, I've always known whatever you put your mind to, you will work it out with other people.

'My English teacher taught me at that moment what it is to truly show up in service of others. An act that went beyond job titles and pay, that could never adequately reflect what he was instilling in us – confidence, self-determination, agency, worth. I don't know if he realised that consciously. But it felt like witnessing somebody embodying both their hope and their purpose. We were a bunch of kids the rest of the staff had written off, perhaps mirroring how we felt in a society that at best didn't recognise us, at worst didn't care for us. He studied with us, taught us and pushed us well outside of what was expected of him by his own superiors. But also, he created safety within an institution and context that did not feel safe for Black teenagers from endz. By doing so, he challenged the belief we had internalised, that we as Black girls from inner-city Birmingham weren't able to strive for the very best, and that the idea of "very best" is to be self-determined. Essentially, he was tending to the basic conditions so that transformative things could be possible. There is something that feels intentionally care-led about somebody who walks with you through that, and it was the most affirming experience. I think this is what I've been carrying with me ever since. This is what it is to show up to the movement, to be so deeply rooted in your purpose, it is regenerative by design.'

15

The half that is never told

Not Bob Marley's fault. Can't blame him. Can't blame a once-in-a-generation artist. A man who turned sceptics into believers, turned a marginal sound into a popular one, temporarily turned war into peace. He had dreadlocks and praised Haile Selassie. Was odd to folks originally. He turned odd into the norm, odd into cool, odd into a voice for disaffected people around the globe. Wore tight denim shirts and jeans better than anyone, too. He was big. Too big for a genre he used as a platform for protest. Too big for the country from which the music had been born; too big for the artists that would follow him.

Sizzla Kalonji didn't stand a chance really. He's the good, the bad and the ugly of contemporary Jamaican music. A haunting presence, like hollow voices in a housing estate stairwell in the middle of the night, audacious and unpredictable like Ray Leonard's bolo punch against Hagler, the sinister theatre of Walken in *Things to Do in Denver When You're Dead*.

Few people outside of hardcore Reggae fans know much

about Sizzla. A quick scan of the net reveals little about the man. There are few decent articles to be found. You will not see him on the pop charts or on the front page of the iTunes store. No surprise then that the Grammys, the most significant awards in the music industry, continually ignores him. Like most mainstream media, the Grammys acknowledge only three things about *post-Bob Marley-death* Reggae:

- Relatives or former band members of Marley or artists from his era, the seventies. Let's call it 'Nostalgic Mind Enslavement (NME)'.
- Cheeky island idlers or the type of stereotypical studs women holidaying in the Caribbean want to have a fling with. Call it 'A Taste of Paradise'.
- The gay-bashing, nihilistic, misogynist. I will refer to this one as 'Yardie', a term that seems to encompass everything bad about Jamaica.

Some of the story, not all.

A member of the Bobo Ashanti branch of Rastafari, Sizzla's fame rose as dancehall was dying. Dancehall was a gardenia that grew from the garrisons. Times were tough in Jamaica in the seventies and eighties when dancehall became king. Syrupy sounds wouldn't wash. But, by the early nineties, the world got to hear it. Liked it. Well, they liked the taste-of-paradise bit. Not so much the ghetto culture from which it grew.

While the mainstream media were Reggae bashing, roots had re-emerged in the dancehalls, led by the evocative vocals of Garnett Silk in 1992. Buju Banton and Capleton converted to Rastafarianism and created the blueprint for the Roots and Dancehall (R&D) sound, which combined the sweet-sounding militancy of seventies roots with dancehall's inventive but uncompromising ethos. Sing-jaying (singing mixed with deejaying, the Jamaican term for emceeing/rapping) also came back to the fore. Reggae entered another golden period. R&D, by the mid-nineties, was the perfect blend of old and new. *Brown Sugar*, D'Angelo; *Paid in Full*, Rakim. No one did it better than Sizzla.

In 1997, Sizzla released two classic albums in as many months, *Black Woman & Child* and *Praise Ye Jah*, featuring radical but lucid criticisms of western society over shimmering slices of traditional, digital and soulful roots rhythms. At the time, Sizzla was a part of record producer Philip 'Fatis' Burrell's Xterminator label collective, which included roots reggae singer Luciano. These albums and subsequent releases put a mirror right in front of my face. Questioned. When did you start questioning rappers and stop scrutinising those who write their cheques? When did you start thinking that questioning was enough and that acting was for others? Do you exploit Blackness to satisfy your ruthless passions for women? How can I feel so angry watching Leticia getting f**ked by Hank while being turned on watching Halle sleep with Billy Bob? When did you start being more concerned about what you might lose materially than what you might gain spiritually? Are you searching for yourself through the eyes of your oppressors?

It made me uncomfortable. Embarrassed. Slowly, his

music eased me into a place where I started listening again, questioning again, learning again. Took me back to a time when I was least conservative in my thinking.* Liberating. Restrictive.

Sounding like a fan, right? Journalism rule number 4080, don't become a fan.

It wasn't just me though. I worked as a citizenship teacher in prison for a time and listened to my students tell me how much they needed Sizzla's music for relief. Freedom, they said. I worked in a youth club in west London too. The club was nicknamed 'Little Vietnam' by locals. I watched rude bwoys take a pause from profanity-riddled-Grime to listen to tender Sizzla's love songs like *Just One of Those Days (Dry Cry)*. Relief.

Unlike Buju and Capleton, Sizzla had not used 'slack' lyrics to gain notoriety. His choruses sounded more like new wave than dancehall. Like Coltrane, Sizzla's music nibbled its way to your soul at times when you least expected it. Made politics cool too. His messages were not concealed beneath sacred chants and facial hair. Made Biblical references and street language a natural blend. Took sing-jaying to its apex. His lyrics were unrelentingly curious, intuitive, noble, assured. Rage at its most eloquent. *Black Woman & Child* should have been

---

* Adapted from a quote from Mao Tse Tung, Chairman of the Community Party of China (1943–1976), 'The young people are the most active and vital force in society. They are the most eager to learn and the least conservative in their thinking.' Introductory note to 'A Youth Shock Brigade of the No. 9 Agricultural Producers' Co-operative in Hsinping Township, Chungshan County' (1955), *The Socialist Upsurge in China's Countryside*, Chinese ed., Vol. III.

a *Catch-a-Fire* moment, a Usain-Bolt-in-Beijing moment. Didn't happen.

Suddenly, Sizzla changed. Not quite a Chappelle-disappearing-act-move, but similar. He allegedly refused to sign to a major label and for many years snubbed interview requests. When on the verge of chart success, he turned down the opportunity to record a video for *Rain Showers*. It had been Sizzla's most commercial release, a track that saw him freestyling over a rapid but tender hip-hop rhythm. Could have been a breakthrough hit, a track that opened the door to his more credible work. Didn't happen.

Sizzla went on to study architecture and build a commune called Judgement Yard, which has been embroiled in conflict with locals for years. His politics became erratic, more hatred, less love. Sizzla's sing-jaying became shakier, too, with unhinged, angry roars offset by quirky, toneless Curtis Mayfield wails. Some good, some bad.

Sizzla would later be banned across Europe and in Canada for homophobic lyrics, perform at Robert Mugabe's eighty-sixth birthday celebration (a man he refused to condemn or condone) and almost die after being hit by a bus while riding his motorcycle.

No one knows what changed. Did he peak too swiftly, power and ego clouding his beliefs? Perhaps it was the pressure to conform to the needs of dancehall's hardcore audience, which thirsts for 'bad man' lyrics. Maybe he was influenced by Capleton's adoption of a near-maniacal, punk-like flow in the late nineties. Or it may have been Luciano's departure from Burrell's Xterminator Records that caused the transformation. Luciano apparently cited ideological differences with Sizzla as his reason for leaving. 'A conflict of interest,' Luciano told *Vibe* magazine at the time, as he objected to Sizzla's increasingly antagonistic lyrics. Perhaps it's difficult to put a lid on genius, as I believe English writer Geoff Dyer once said of D. H. Lawrence.

Amid the controversy and views I could not defend or condone, there were moments of brilliance. While displaying Fela/Tupac-like energy for creating music (releasing more than eighty albums, including close to forty original studio sets since 1995), Sizzla has experimented more than any Jamaican artist. Used everything from Afrobeats, gothic rock and jazz, to drum and bass, funk and Lionel Richie soul. He inhabited every genre he employed. His 2002 release *Da Real Thing* may be the greatest R&D album of all time,* while 2005's *Soul Deep* was a better vocal performance away from being a classic too. He also found time to cover Dylan's *Subterranean Homesick Blues*, set up an agro-business and recording studio in Zimbabwe and establish the Sizzla Youth Foundation. Could have, should have walked away with half a dozen Grammys.

More than anything, Sizzla's switch told us that he was not going to be what we wanted him to be. For many, he was initially the braver part of us, the articulator of our frustrations, a fantasy in which we could rebel without

---

* A shortlist of R&D's greatest albums also includes Sizzla's *Black Woman & Child* and *Praise Ye Jah*, Buju Banton's *'Til Shiloh*, Damian Marley's *Welcome to Jamrock*, Capleton's *More Fire*, Tony Rebel's *If Jah* and Anthony B's *So Many Things*. All these albums, with the exception of *Welcome to Jamrock*, were released during R&D's golden period between 1995 and 2000.

sacrifice. Gave us a taste and then told us to make the change ourselves. Listening is not enough and dependency is a bigger sin.

Raised another question: do you stop following someone who has given you so much because you no longer believe in or have lost faith in their politics? If you accept unconditionally, what does this say about you? If you neglect, what does that say?

While Sizzla's politics made it easy for the mainstream media to marginalise him, he remains true to his Jamaican audience. His music is rooted in, representative of and perhaps trapped by his community, a gift and a curse. Sizzla fans, those who followed him from the beginning, have forgiven his post-'99 actions. Later fans would often say, *well, Bob wouldn't have done or said that.* A shame.

Like Marley, however, Sizzla is fighting history, or those who write history. He is attempting to make the seemingly insurmountable achievable. Perhaps to the wider world, Sizzla's music comes from a different spiritual place than Marley's. I disagree. Neither is easily boxed. Both artists have proven that reggae is transformational. Sizzla is perhaps less willing to pander to the mainstream media than Marley was. He is less focused on his global responsibility than Marley was. However, the main difference between the two may be that Marley was too big for the media to believe that Jamaica had actually produced a more gifted artist.[1]

MARAI LARASI

Black, African-Caribbean-British Feminist and Former Executive Director, Imkaan

'There've been major transformation moments in my life that I have been conscious of. One was when I first read Angela Davis's *Women, Race & Class*. I was in my late teens and raised in Jamaica. I cut my teeth on a certain type of socialist politics that was very much linked to the Cuban revolution and the way Angela Davis wrote spoke to me in terms of that anti-capitalist politic.

'Then when I encountered Stuart Hall and I encountered his work around hybridity, he helped me gain a sense of belonging in terms of Caribbean identity and the way that that's racialised. What it means to have white ancestors alongside Black ancestors and what it means that my white ancestors would have owned my Black ancestors. His work helped to give me a specific kind of grounding that also helped me to hold a lot of gratitude for the Jamaican country upbringing where you couldn't be eating while somebody else was not able to eat.

'My mom was a nurse ... a midwife. She trained here and had gone back home to Jamaica. It was hard work. There was an expectation that because she was doing that, and she had a certain kind of job outside the home that she needed to employ people. She needed to employ people to grow stuff and care for the land, but she couldn't do that with snobbery. If someone "called out" in the middle of the night after she'd just pulled a long shift, she still had to go to deliver a different baby round the corner at three o'clock in the morning. So I learned "community" in that space.

'Then, through my work at Imkaan, I also had huge opportunities to connect and spend time in different places. So, I spent time in Aotearoa (New Zealand), where I was working with Samoan sisters doing work around ending violence against women and girls, work with Maori sisters, really hearing the synergies in terms of that type of indigenous praxis around the community.

'And I read, I'm a nerd. So, I am always synergising and integrating experiential knowledge with our intellectual and sometimes academic knowledge. I'm always pulling that in and looking at how I practise in my life, how I practise in my family, how I work with the older people in my life, how I work with the young people in my life, how we make social justice meaningful.

'If I don't believe in crime and punishment, if I'm a prison abolitionist, what does it mean for how I deal with the young people in my life when they've harmed? What do I do with my own experiences of harm? I map it on my own body, that's what I'd say. It's really inscribed in my psyche because I think, to me, that's the plantation legacy. There's something around carrying the pain in our bodies all the time and resisting: the Haitian Revolution techniques involved slow poisoning, burning things down, and trickery. We were raised on Anansi stories. There's something about all of it.

'And spirit. For me, I really carry my ancestors with me. For me, I'm learning; I am also synchronising and integrating ancestral wisdom and knowledge all the time.'

16

Ella Baker

I discovered Ella Baker late in my life. In many ways, it was too late, because I would have likely directed my work in the social sector differently had I known about her much earlier. While growing up, the model of leadership was Malcolm X. In many ways, Malcolm was the model of Black masculinity – a former street hustler who spent time in jail, then discovered Elijah Muhammad's teachings and converted to the Nation of Islam.

On release, he swiftly rose through the Nation of Islam's ranks and increased their membership with exceptional leadership, organising and oratory skills. Malcolm's influence saw the Nation of Islam go from a marginal group to a national powerhouse in America. They also became the biggest threat to American national security. His presence and Black nationalist militancy contributed to opening the doors to the more moderate reforms demanded by the civil rights movement. He would later break away from the Nation of Islam and renounce the teachings of Elijah Muhammad and in 1964 he converted to Sunni Islam. Malcolm X influenced the Black Panther movement too.

For years, in my mind, I considered myself an uncompromising Black man, someone who would not turn away from danger or confrontation, someone who would succeed 'by any means necessary', someone who would not compromise in the face of whiteness and Malcolm was my model. Civil rights leader Martin Luther King was church. Malcolm was street. Martin spoke about peace. Malcolm talked about revolution. The differences between the two and their politics were never as blunt as I've just described. But that's how I viewed them as a teenager. Those were the headlines.

In truth, Malcolm was a projection of what I wanted him to be because I was so insecure with my masculinity. I was never stereotypically the most masculine of boys. I am not stereotypically the manliest of men. Not interested in cars, I cannot do DIY, I have no desire to take charge of the barbecue. I can hold a conversation about football, but I'm less interested in scores or games and more interested in the personalities. While I had my share of fights as a youth, any act of violence or conflict makes me retreat. For many years, I tried to lessen my height so as not to be a threat to society.

I also had some typically male traits. I was driven by ego and a desire to be recognised for my work in the social sector. It may not have been evident in my behaviours, but it was present in my feelings. I'd feel like a fraud whenever I'd meet a man who wasn't driven by ego, although I did not meet many of them. I found competition and recognition were never far from the DNA of most of the men I worked with. They craved attention; they craved being a hero; the dependency others had on them was emotional fuel. Envy would leak before praise. I realised that manhood in Britain does not present the ideal attributes required to lead change.

I cultivated an ability to talk well and to deliver good speeches and timely interventions in meetings. I was assertive even when I didn't feel in control and I could make people believe what I was saying was correct by the way I said it. The Malcolm in me. The little bit of Malcolm I could be. A good talker, a motivational speaker who can switch from calm to emotional on a dime. But it is all a facade.

For over five decades, Ella Baker was an activist and organiser, a prominent figure in the civil rights movement. She worked with everyone from W. E. B. Du Bois to Martin Luther King, inspiring generations of Black leaders. Apparently, Baker once disclosed that if she was ever going to write a memoir, she would call it *Making a Life, Not Making a Living*,[1] which is how she viewed activism: as a part of life, not something to monetise, not a career. Baker was the antithesis of the institutionalised social sector.

Through Barbara Ransby's *Ella Baker & the Black Freedom Movement*, I learned about Baker's life and leadership, how she recognised the power of language and wanted to make sure she didn't isolate communities with her words. She was a practitioner at heart, ensuring that her actions had a practical outcome. Baker mentored and guided many leaders, helping them to 'see their own ideas' instead of imposing her views.

She advocated for democratic practice and horizontal operational structures and supported a class and gender analysis of racism. Baker also opened the space for women in the civil rights movement while challenging masculinity in grassroots organising. She embraced the values of collectivism over the colonial mindset. Yet, she did not seek recognition, status or fame but rather lived an activist life with her deeds, actions and ethics in sync with her politics. As much as anything, she was a facilitator and a vessel for others to succeed, which enabled her to grow the movement far more effectively than taking the helm herself. And Baker did so without a speck of the credit received by her male counterparts.

I have yet to see many men display the qualities of Baker. I wanted to be Malcolm; I still love Malcolm. His willingness to challenge his beliefs showed immeasurable bravery. But I realised that I would have been better in my work had I known more about Ella. Would I have had more conviction in my beliefs, been less protective of what I had, less frightened of what people might say and more compassionate? Probably. Would I have been less egotistical, been more gendered in my approach, less concerned with what I thought I knew and keener to learn more about what I don't know? Definitely.

I would not have questioned myself, my actions, my mistakes or my failure to live my values had it not been for the knowledge I gained working with incredible 'leaders'.* Many displayed the qualities exemplified by Ella Baker. This includes Dr Carlene Firmin, pioneer of contextual safeguarding, who, when I met her at Victoria Station, described what needed to change in child protection policy in this country before running off to celebrate her mum's birthday.

Baljeet Sandhu, pioneer of knowledge equity, who, by way

---

* I have used apostrophes here to denote that many of the people listed would not necessarily classify themselves as leaders in the traditional sense of the term.

of introduction, sent me an unimaginably lengthy LinkedIn message but, more than anything, looked beyond my chaotic mind and life and into the contents of my heart. Shane Ryan, whom I met when he became the CEO of Working With Men (now called Future Men), is a model of authenticity and truth. Tara Flood, the former CEO of Alliance for Inclusive Education (ALLFIE), seamlessly blending action and activism.

Whitney Iles, candid and humorous, who in one second could explain the systemic failures of England's criminal justice system and in another could tell me how to track down a cheating partner. I still remember the two of us chatting non-stop while walking from Bond Street to Trafalgar Square in torrential rain. I also think back to meeting Ruth Ibegbuna and the young people from RECLAIM after the London Riots in 2011, and how vulnerable they felt about how the youth were being portrayed in the media.

Writer and cultural studies pioneer Stuart Hall once said that 'feminism taught me the difference between a conviction in the head and a change in the way you live.'[2] My understanding of Ella Baker's approach to social change and my proximity to Ruth Ibegbuna, Baljeet Sandhu, Professor Carlene Firmin and others taught me a similar lesson to Hall's. I cannot separate my beliefs from my actions. I also realised that a man in a suit would not spearhead the level of transformational change required to alleviate poverty and save our planet. I have, quite simply, encountered way more women who live the values prevalent in their work. And that, to me, seems to be the primary attribute of anyone seeking to change society for the better.

YOU

This story may sound familiar. Perhaps not. I asked a friend, one who doesn't work in the social sector, about her giving. I don't know how reflective this may be of your experience. But you may find yourself within some of these answers. I have anonymised this interview.

Do you volunteer or donate money? If so, why?
I don't volunteer, but I would like to and will. But I give money to various places because I feel like I should 'cos I care about things and if I have the spare money to contribute something to help alleviate the issues and sufferings I care about, then I think it's my duty to offer it.

What do you tend to donate to?
I donate to Shelter, a homeless charity. I contribute to NSPCC – abuse of children really upsets me. I also used to work at a young abusers' project (NSPCC) for people who abuse because they have been abused. So I have a personal connection. I also contribute to food banks because people are hungry in this country, which is ridiculous and infuriating.

We all have to try and help if we're in a position not on the end of the suffering, or else it's like we're heartless. In being aware of other people's suffering, there's a natural obligation to help. If you don't feel that obligation, there's something wrong with you. I volunteered after the Grenfell disaster and I encourage my children to give money, which they do. I always feel that it's not impactful enough and you don't know whether [the money is] going to get to people. There's an element of distrust. I'm not sure where [the money is] going. [This is] more the disaster relief, the international work. I'm more trusting [of how charities use money]; even though it may not go to grassroots work, it will support the organisation in some way to keep it going.

How do you tend to give?
Donating money, but I do want to do more and volunteer. I think I'd like to work with older people or kids affected by gangs and knife crime. The young and the very old speak to me as people that I want to help. Helping them deal with this world, strengthening them and helping them keep a hold of who they are and fully manifest who they are in the cruelty of this world because that's all we have to survive this world. And to try to keep these souls good, not corrupted and lost and traumatised.

If you had a chance to donate to a charity tackling the root cause of hunger and not food banks, would you do so?

Yes, I would because it's more useful because the food banks are just a plaster.

Would you know how to donate to a charity that does this type of work?
No, I wouldn't. [Hunger is] something we see happening around us, and the immediacy around [food banks] is persuasive and emotive because you can see it happening and you can see the suffering.

How does it make you feel when you give?
It makes me feel sad 'cos it makes you aware of traumas existing around you and a bit helpless because you're helping, but you don't feel like you're doing enough. The problem is so big you can't [really help] – [you have a] desire for the problem to go away and not exist. There's an element of denial in help. A wish, by performing this act of giving, you can make it less real, which of course is not true. That's where the sadness, no matter what you do, won't go away because it's created by things that are so much bigger than you. But it [giving] makes me feel like I'm a good citizen, makes me feel human, makes me aware of my humanity.

How do you find out where to donate?
Usually via emails, like newsletters I'm subscribed to and TV adverts. Shelter, I just looked it up.

Is this easy?

It's easy to find. It's normally a response to things happening around us. I tend to pick the ones that look the most reliable and legitimate – a trusted name like Shelter and NSPCC. Really established names I'd rather give to. The smaller ones are like an independent shop, fighting for support. When I donate to these, it's normally because a friend of mine has told me about them. Word of mouth is important for trust and some evidence of their work, effectiveness and a sense of longevity, a long-established commitment to their cause.

What do you think about charities?

They're essential. Important. Steeped in altruism. They're the social force that connects us to our humanity. They are an ever-endangered social force that connects us to our humanity and their vulnerability next to the forces of government and the economy makes them all the more valuable.

What purpose do you think charities serve?

They serve the purpose of helping people who have drawn the short straw in our social system. [They're there] to help people in need. They also facilitate impulsion to help, they form a framework and they're reciprocal, they help us help. Really important.

Do you see charities as having a role in challenging injustice, for example, challenging the government or the police?

Yes, of course, they have a role. Every social problem is the result of injustice. Poverty, which is unjust in the fifth richest country in the world and our [Britain's] whole history of domination, it is ludicrous that we are in this position; a country without a conscience on the face of it.

Economically, we don't care; we don't have a conscience, and discrimination, [be it] racial, religious, sexual, gender, which is also exacerbated by an unjust system and reinforced continually. Mental health charities are really crucial, like Mind and Cruse – bereavement counselling. [These issues] are largely the responsibility of government, [it's] their obligation to make [society] fair, to make it healthy and well. They're meant to attend to our well-being, but you feel like your government is so lacking in these obligations that the role of charities is paramount.

If you could donate more, what would enable you to do so?

If I had more money, I would give more and more time. I think I can make the time. There are people that I have huge admiration for who are way more courageous than me. They volunteer. I feel like I should step up more. If I can't give more money I should volunteer. I feel most alive because you're connecting to another human being and you feel like it has some meaning. It's a realisation that it helps them in that moment and your life is worth something in the larger scheme of things.

17

Conclusion

'Proximity has taught me some basic and humbling truths, including this vital lesson: Each of us is more than the worst thing we've ever done. My work with the poor and the incarcerated has persuaded me that the opposite of poverty is not wealth; the opposite of poverty is justice. Finally, I've come to believe that the true measure of our commitment to justice, the character of our society, our commitment to the rule of law, fairness, and equality cannot be measured by how we treat the rich, the powerful, the privileged, and the respected among us. The true measure of our character is how we treat the poor, the disfavored, the accused, the incarcerated, and the condemned.'[1]

—BRYAN STEVENSON, *Just Mercy: A Story of Justice and Redemption*

I got so much wrong. When I think back to what inspired my giving, I realise that I have made many mistakes. I looked at the world through a narrow lens, a patriarchal lens. While working full-time in the social sector, I failed to explore power dynamics fully, and I didn't do enough to understand how my female colleagues and peers were differently situated. I didn't recognise the gendered dynamics fully in the workplace; for example, how it affected the ability of colleagues to perform or how they were treated differently by their peers.

I recognised that my politics were rooted in the eighties, political Blackness that, by 2021, was dated, and needed to be redefined and revised. While my peers viewed Blackness as something that bonded Black and Asians in tackling racism in British society, this was not how younger generations viewed this relationship. Even if I gave space to those with alternative conceptions of racial dynamics in the twenty-first century, in reality, I continued to hold firm to my outlook as a frame for my work. Political Blackness remains a core part of my identity and perhaps always will, but I should have allowed space to critique the term and what it meant. I was defensive to any challenge. I was guilty of what I accused many leaders of doing, putting ideology before other people's experiences.

I understood that I was not the 'leader' I thought I was and didn't live the values I espoused. Often, I'd offset my poor life decisions with good deeds. However, I was still driven, in part, by ego and a competitive spirit. I was also, despite being outspoken, still in deference to white power. I was afraid that I would sink back to where I was in the nineties: unemployed, unemployable. My actions, too often, related to my fear of being disempowered again. Through this proximity to communities and innovators and by observing radical social sector work in different countries, I started questioning my lens and working towards aligning my values, my life and my work. But I'm still a work in progress.

Proximity is everything. And the Charity Commission is out of touch. For a regulatory body to deny or diminish my experiences by trying to divorce acts of giving from my truths, our truths, so often impacted by politicians' behaviours and policies, is a most blatant abuse of power. I had entered the social sector naively because I thought it would be a space where I could effect social change, not recognising that I embodied justice through my actions, regardless of where I worked. By de-politicising me, the social sector separated me from my livity. The most helpful element of being in, volunteering in, working in philanthropy, and the social sector was proximity, which enabled me to start challenging myself, my politics and actions.

Giving is often political, an intentional act towards social justice. It is influenced by our experiences and our feelings, of course, and our biases, ideologies and opinions. Nevertheless, entities like the Charity Commission try to maintain giving in a traditional sense, strictly related to donating time or money, solely an act of compassion. Giving makes us feel good. It's good for our well-being. But it can also help us question ourselves and unlock those positive values within us, which are often buried in the stresses of modern living.

When I interviewed Nikki Clegg, Director of Operations and Grants at Thirty Percy Foundation, she told me about Shalom H. Schwartz's theory of Basic Human Values:

'The premise behind this model is based on quite a lot of research that demonstrates that every one of us holds the same set of values within us and that these different types of values can be enhanced or reduced by the social norms, environments, conversations and situations we find ourselves in.

If we are surrounded by people who talk about making the world a better place, equality and justice, then we find that our "greater than self" values (that are present in everyone) are activated and nourished. However, the majority of people are not in this privileged position all the time and so other values that are more inward-looking and "selfish" are often nurtured and encouraged. Current social norms and conventions are geared towards these extrinsic "self-enhancement" values, such as encouraging continuous consumption and materialism as a way of "empowering" people ('vote with your wallets') or feeling a sense of 'status'.

If we are ever going to be successful in bringing about a just and sustainable world, we must reduce the promotion of these types of values and enhance people's intrinsic "self-transcendence" values (or "greater than self" values). Every advert on TV or discussion with friends will promote certain forms of these values that we all hold within. This always re-affirms to me how impactful the build-up of all the little actions can be and how important it is to keep true to living these values where we can; otherwise, the enormity of the changes required can make you feel quite helpless; as one person.

The enormity of the world's problems can make us feel helpless. As a result, we can withdraw into ourselves and resort to serving only those who look like ourselves. But we are interdependent. And it is often the experiences of those on the margins, even if they represent a small percentage of your local community, that tell us what lies in our future. A failure to recognise these voices is not only remiss, but also contributes to neglecting one's own destiny.

Indeed, the social sector should serve as a tool to help people discover their 'greater than self' values. Suppose the proximity between our 'greater than self' values and livity decreases and the proximity between our livelihoods and understanding of the communities most impacted by social policies shrinks? Wouldn't we have a fundamentally different society?

There are many reasons why we give. It is often deeply personal and connected to our hearts and feelings. Some people respond to emotive narratives, for example, images of starvation and suffering. Television appeals feed off tales of pain, anguish and deprivation. These images suggest that you may have little in life, but others are less fortunate. The tradition of giving is based on the binary concept of the 'haves' and the 'have-nots', an over-simplified mindset that separates us (the givers) from them (the receivers).

For others, religion plays a massive role in their giving. Some are attracted by charismatic or heroic individuals whose courage symbolises the plight of the marginalised. Examples of people who catalysed change across the globe with their bravery and activism include Malala Yousafzai, who was shot in the face in Pakistan for exercising her right to go to school, and Greta Thunberg, who refused to go to school in protest against political leaders' failure to tackle climate change.

Our peers and networks also influence how and to whom we give. We also donate due to personal experiences; for example, we may have survived domestic violence, worked in the NHS, or experienced transphobia. Our pain and sense of injustice from these experiences often compels us to want to support these causes. Most of these motivations are linked to people holding 'doing good' as core to their values and beliefs and their desire to be selfless. Of course, on the negative side, giving can be as much about self-interest as anything else. It may be motivated by tax breaks, reinforcing capitalistic, extractive or even violent political ideologies, having your name on a building, looking good to friends, moving into new markets or gaining honours.

How we donate and what we view as worthy is one part of the picture. But we also have a right to question where the £10 billion+ per year we donate goes and how charities and public funding bodies effectively address society's economic disparities or contribute sufficiently to our well-being. To what degree is our giving a temporary fix, a quick but non-sustainable way of doing good?

What if we donated money, resources, ideas or time differently? What if the smaller charities, the equivalent of independent bookshops, had enough financial support to advertise and gain greater awareness and trust from the public? What if we spent at least one hour a week learning about the many social sector organisations I refer to in this book?

A weekly meditation into hope. What if giving became part

of our day-to-day lives, as it did for many people during the lockdowns? What if giving became more of a cultural or social practice, encouraged through education or employment? What if we heard more stories of local community heroism in the press and less scare-mongering? What if siloed approaches to delivering services were not the norm? What if our services genuinely explored how people's multiple issues intersect and how a more holistic, person-centred way of addressing their problems was a more appropriate response? What if the way we governed the country was different?

Our values, trust and our experiences are so important in influencing how we give. But the norms in our society also contribute to shaping how we donate and to whom. This makes it challenging to give differently or address some of the questions I've raised. For example, we understand, expect and have come to trust hierarchical structures. Most institutions have governors, trustees and shareholders who oversee the headteacher, the chief executive and the director. In turn, these leaders manage a senior management team responsible for running departments and managing the operations and admin. Our minds have been trained to view this as the norm. The way that every business, service, or charity should operate. We are more likely to trust this organisational struc-ture than a horizontal setup, a flat structure, with devolved power and minimal hierarchy. Those people working against these norms will likely struggle to elicit trust from the public, yet their approaches may be better for you and me.

Whether conscious or unconscious, this extends to who we trust in positions of authority. In their book *Messenger: 8 Ways to Get Heard*, Stephen Martin and Joseph Marks speak of how 'the perceived difference in status can be sufficient to drown out what is in fact a poor judgement call'.[2] We tend to trust the white middle-class man in a suit who speaks good English or the scientist in a lab coat. But who we trust and how competent they are, are two completely different things. In a fair and just society, in an equal race, many of the people who run our institutions would probably not be in power.

Following the lead from one's peers is fair and safe if you have a diverse network and bonafide friendships with people from different classes, ethnic backgrounds or parts of the country. What if your giving is solely influenced by those who think just like you, look like you, share the same interests as you, come from the same social class and ethnic background as you? How can you have a broad conception of contributing to society through your giving if your networks remain narrow?

It is better for us to give than to hoard. But the very same culture that influences how we donate and mediates our giving can also reinforce the disparities in society. What if we focused less on individual failure and more on transforming our systems? What if we thought less about the charismatic leader or those who look the part and more about investing in those most impacted by the issues we are passionate about? What if self-determination or self-sufficiency was more attractive than starvation and suffering? What if we scrutinised the politics of giving and how this relates to our core, 'greater than self' values?

'I think us as a society, we don't like to self-reflect,' says Whitney Iles, who I interviewed for this book. 'We don't like to look at ourselves. We like to box ourselves. We like to fragment ourselves. We like to be good people, and we like to help people that are lesser than ourselves or in lesser conditions because of the dopamine, because it makes us feel good. I think we need to learn how to question ourselves a lot more on why we make the choices that we make.'

The reality was, there were some limitations in my approach to giving. The only way for me to improve was to acknowledge my inadequacies, unlearn so much of what I thought was the truth and radically listen (without judgement) to the outsiders within. Elle. Ella.

If we want to contribute to a fair and just society that prioritises the most vulnerable, it is unlikely that a large, formal institution will lead to that change. Instead, it will be our actions, our behaviours, the movements, cooperatives, collectives, many of whom are often excluded from receiving money from funding institutions, that will transform our society.

'I believe if citizens could act and make decisions in their everyday lives that were aligned with the long-term changes they want to see in society, we would achieve great change (and fast),' says Clegg. It is often the case that we learn through repetition, practice and guidance; what we absorb and when, through listening and our interests, is crucial. If we are to unlearn and retrain ourselves, and if transformative change lies in our hands, what characteristics will we need to make equity, justice and joy a reality?

Part 3

Stand for something

18

Reparatory justice

Adopt a reparative and regenerative frame,
shifting from a lens of giving to one of giving back

'This is really the most extraordinary historical
moment I've experienced, and of course
I've experienced many in my relatively long
lifetime. I think that finally there is a popular
awareness of the need to acknowledge our
historical situatedness. For such a long time
there has been a reluctance to engage with
issues that were first opposed at the end of
the civil war and was the abolition of slavery.
And, of course, issues that emerged out of the
whole period of colonisation and the assault
on indigenous people, we have lived with these
realities without really understanding the
extent to which our present is shaped by the
failure to address these questions in the past.'[1]

ANGELA DAVIS, 2020

October 2014, in Manhattan, and I couldn't sleep for three
nights. Even after that, my sleep was disturbed; the faintest

noises sounded like banging. Tried writing about it. I consulted my notes, then threw them away. I couldn't quite describe the two-and-a-half days I had spent taking part in the Undoing Racism workshop. Tried talking about it and explaining it. Fruitless. I just wanted everyone to be there, friends, family, work colleagues, anyone who knows me, knew me, wants to know the real me; to be there, a place where anyone Black, white, Latino, queer, young, old, male, female confronted their feelings and fears about racism.

No hiding place, just a circle of strangers. Our closest ally, us, irrespective of politics. Confronting it together. Time to say what you got to say, the pain, the ignorance, the hate, nobody will scorn, point the finger, get personal. Say it so you can confront it, so that you can do something about it; two-and-a-half days talking about an addiction, a mental illness called racism, a condition that exists in the collective unconscious of the world[2] – no time for whispering.

People's Institute for Survival and Beyond (PISAB), founded by Ron Chisom and the late Dr Jim Dunn, has been delivering the Undoing Racism workshop since 1980. Chisom learned much of what he knew about community organising from the doyen of community organising, Saul Alinsky. But Chisom saw a gap. He felt that organisers had been learning about political analysis, approaches to and techniques in organising. But they were not being taught about racism, its history, the practices and the structures that reinforce it. While organisers were developing more skills, the absence of any analysis of racism was enabling participants to become more skilled racists.[3]

Alongside Dunn, Chisom created the Undoing Racism workshop. The workshop, grounded in the experiences of

Black people in the US, trains people to undo racism from within themselves and in their institutions. It's not your typical HR approach to tackling discrimination; it's not diversity and inclusion or unconscious bias training, a bit of paperwork, a few units, a tick box for your equal opportunities policy. No. The workshop helps participants confront their assumptions and biases and prevents them from reinforcing racist attitudes in their practices.

PISAB teaches participants to think structurally, not individually, to think about their institutions as a starting point for exploration and see where these inequalities are reinforced. Regular follow-up support meetings help participants continue their learning, provide a safe space, and ensure that they do not slip into old unconscious racist behaviour patterns.

During the workshop, PISAB described racism in the following way: 'Race prejudice + Power = Racism'. Race is a social construct. Not real. Doesn't exist. Fake. Race by PISAB's definition is 'a specious classification of humans being created at a time of colonization [sic] by Europeans and European Americans, later known as white, placing themselves as the model of humanity and the height of human achievement for the purpose of establishing and maintaining social status, privilege and power'.[4]

It was a system created by white people for white people at a time when racism was legal. Prejudice is prejudging, having an idea before you have the experience; power is legitimate (legal) access to and collective control of systems sanctioned by the state. An 'ism' is an ideology, a belief system.

*

PISAB's workshops cover the legacy of racism and how this plays out in today's society. These sessions also tackle, among other things:

- The history of individual, institutional and cultural racism, how race science and the law justified and validated racial hierarchy and slavery.
- The practice of gatekeeping – how those with power stop others from attaining power using colourblind approaches or diverting conversations away from race. The workshop addresses our role as gatekeepers, ensuring that we are aware of our accountability to the people we are servicing, not just our bosses.
- Internalised racial superiority – denial of or being defensive about racism, distancing from racist individuals, treating it as ahistorical, acting in entitled and paternalistic ways, shaming each other, exhibiting fragility, misappropriation of Black culture and appropriated oppression (white victimhood).
- Internalised racial oppression – feelings of inferiority, denial of racism, code-switching or acting typically white, competition with fellow Black people, colourism (preferential treatment of lighter-skinned Black people), self-doubt, exaggerated visibility (outlandish behaviour, rage).

Gatekeeping, internalised racial superiority and internalised racial oppression are behaviours present in the social sector. PISAB has trained almost one million people, from social workers to educators, from health practitioners to community organisers. Its work has spawned numerous movements across the United States, including the Anti-Racist Alliance (ARA) based in New York, founded by Sandra Bernabei, a Liberation Psychotherapist and President of the National Association of Social Workers, NYC Chapter.

I attended a workshop in 2014 led by the ARA, which had – to that point – worked with over 8,000 social workers and other professionals and had been organising over twenty engagements a month for practitioners intent on undoing racism within their institutions.

PISAB's focus on unconscious racism was pioneering. It highlighted the impact of unconscious bias many years before the term started trending. PISAB also addresses how racism contaminates every institution. For example, in education, this manifests through a narrow curriculum that silences Black people's history through an absence of anti-racist teacher-training or the high numbers of Black pupils unfairly excluded. In the media, we see it through negative images of Black people on television, demonising people from low-income backgrounds, particularly people of colour, and a lack of diversity in positions of influence. PISAB's work clearly articulates how historical racial injustice infects our structures, systems and institutions, and disadvantages people of colour.

Funny, isn't it. Funny how most social sector activities target 'fixing the poor'. Yet the people who decide who receives the money, often white, male and privileged, come from similar backgrounds to those with political and economic power. What would happen if the sector featured more organisations tackling power and privilege? Or root causes?

We can talk about poverty, work on helping the needy get employment, get training. But you cannot alleviate poverty until you address racism, power and privilege.

This is PISAB's starting point. It's not about the baby; it's about the people who throw the babies in the river: the advantaged, the over-served, the high income, the elite. PISAB also targets us. Yeah, you and me. It's about our power too. We all play a role in reinforcing the status quo.

'This country [America] values individualism, they speak of the individualism of it, so "catch the racist, catch the Ku Klux Klan" [and] what that does is keep us crazy,' says Bernabei, who I interviewed as part of my Churchill Fellowship in 2014. 'So [we're] always looking for the racist but we're not doing the work of institutional equity. You could take every racist you know, put them in a rocket ship, ship them out and the system will remain the same. That's why you have President Obama and it just doesn't matter, every constituency behaves the same way. Racism was invented in the fabric of our nation and we're having a hell of a time getting it out.'

So why do we still ignore structural, systemic and institutional racism? Why are people so afraid to rock the boat? Fear of disruption, fear of dismantling? Is it because of denial by our governments and the media? Is it about the intolerance of others' views? Pain? Avoiding conflict? *Who am I to disrupt?* Is the problem too big? We can't force everyone to change, can we? *Can we?*

The underlying themes of PISAB's workshops are a love for humanity and the fact that racism hurts and controls Black people, advantages white people (opportunities, resources), and, ultimately, damages everyone. Eventually, there will be no winners, even those who currently profit from Black pain. The destruction of us will at some point lead to the ruin of you.

'This is undoing racism 101,' says Bernabei. The workshop prompts thoughts on race and racism and how to become an actor, irrespective of perspective. What part do you play? Are you an extra reinforcing the system or an actor trying to change the system? Are you doing more harm than good? Can you honestly say that your decision-making is in no way stained or uncontaminated? Is hitting your KPIs [key performance indicators] more important than challenging your assumptions and tackling your biases?

The regular meetings after PISAB's workshops are essential in helping reinforce the values of the training. The workshops are the start of the journey. It empowers people; it unties disempowerment. The workshops help participants get an intrinsic sense of their power, enabling them to effect change constructively. Another message was evident through the training.

Black people in America may have race prejudice, but often, they do not have the financial, political or institutional power to enforce and reinforce it out systematically. Nothing will change unless white people are an integral part of the journey because they have the power to do something about it. PISAB is not advocating for white people to lead that change. But they need to be a part of it. If white people do nothing, nothing will change. A sorrowful message indeed, but perhaps a unifying one.

* * * * *

The legacy of slavery and colonisation, the guilt, ignorance, and denial run deep in the British psyche. I call it the Empire State of Mind, a form of white and national supremacy that considers the British superior to all. The UK played a significant role, alongside other European nations, in displacing over 12 million Africans over four hundred years, with between two and five million captives, perhaps more, dying.

After abolishing slavery in 1833, the British government paid enslavers £20 million, the equivalent of £2.4 billion today.[5] It was the British treasury's biggest pay-out in history until 2008, when it bailed out the banks after the financial crisis. And crucially, we (as taxpayers) didn't pay off our debt to enslavers until 2015.

The roots of the highly racialised economic and social disparities are historic. In 2020, the writer Kimberly Jones compared the link between slavery and the present day to the board game Monopoly: 'For 400 rounds of Monopoly you don't get to play at all. Not only do you not get to play, you have to play on behalf of the person that you're playing against. You have to play and make money and earn wealth for them and then you have to turn it over to them.'[6] Jones's use of Monopoly to illustrate her point was poignant in more ways than one, given that the original conception of the game was invented by left-wing feminist Lizzie Magie in 1903 to provide a practical demonstration of how awful capitalism and land grabbing were.[7]

It was true. When we finally had an opportunity to play (through 'freedom'), our opponent (white folks) got all the money; they owned the banks and all the properties, they also got to set the rules. They had the power to create a narrative that questioned our ability to win. They didn't explain the history behind the game nor compensate for the trauma faced by Black communities.

'Colonisation did a number on us,' says Marai Larasi, former executive director of Imkaan. 'It had us think that Black men run faster. It has us invest in narratives about us that focus on whether we've got more rhythm or not. It renders us magical or beast, or magical beast. It has us doubt our capacities to lead our countries, to lead our organisations. We have to deal with that for ourselves and with each other. For me, that comes in the same with the self-emancipatory work.'

On 22–23 November 2019, I attended the Interdependence Festival* at Toynbee Hall, curated by Healing Justice London co-founder Farzana Khan, writer and community organiser Lena Mohamed and Thirty Percy Foundation. Colombian activist Sebastian Ordoñez Muñoz examined the origins of the climate crisis and how colonialism's son, capitalism, is a threat to humanity:

'It's rooted in European colonialism and a simple way to try and unpack the complexity and the depth of colonialism is

---

* Interdependence Festival was a two-day festival hosted by the Thirty Percy Foundation in 2019 that focused on listening, learning, visioning and actioning 'Climate Just' futures. The festival centred the solutions and strategies of Black, brown and lived-experience leaders, thinkers, innovators, activists and artists working on climate justice from a systemic and frontline positioning. Through a decolonial climate framing, it explored interconnecting issues including the Hostile Environment, youth violence, energy democracy, housing, artwashing and land reparations. It is often the case that major companies will sponsor cultural institutions or exhibitions to artwash any extractive or negative practices related to their business.

if it's understood as a triple violence. It's cultural violence through negation, political violence through repression and economical violence through exploitation. I just want to highlight two points that are related to this. On the one hand, that colonialism is still going on today in many places materially, physically, discursively and mentally. But also, that part of the justification for colonialism was this notion of the advancement of conquering land in order to tame nature and in order to humanise savages, essentially'.[8]

At the same festival, lawyer Harpreet Kaur Paul told the story of the plight of Native Americans:

'If you take the story back to 1492, what you see is ships arriving in the Americas and people, indigenous peoples going from estimated numbers of 50 to 100 million to 3.5 million. Why did that happen? Silver is a part of that story. Gold is a part of that story. What we see is environments being ruined to make way for quarries and plantations and we see that story told again through the African continent and Asia as well. When we say countries that are not responsible for climate change are disproportionately feeling the impacts, what we are saying is countries that were experiencing ethnocide and ecocide to pay for an industrial revolution that caused our current crisis, are the same countries that bear the greatest impacts of climate change today'.[9]

Few of the major western efforts to tackle the climate crisis, for example, acknowledge the impact of slavery and colonialism and where accountability lies. Slavery and colonialism disenfranchised and displaced Black, brown and indigenous people and planted the seeds of a global crisis that affects everybody.

For Britain to contribute to a fair and just society, a reparatory justice frame must underpin our donations, actions, activism and how the social sector functions. We need to move beyond giving towards giving back. We need to start by ethically resourcing and repairing the harm inflicted on the most acutely marginalised groups, the historically disenfranchised and those most impacted by the continued extractive practices of major international corporations. But what does reparatory justice look like for us in practice?

* * * * *

Truth and reconciliation. In 2020, Chris Grant, then a Sport England trustee, advocated for a truth and reconciliation-style commission to address the structural disparities prominent in UK sport. Grant's proposition derived from South Africa's Truth and Reconciliation Commission, which emerged after the end of apartheid. The Commission took a restorative justice approach, enabling victims and perpetrators to share their experiences of the offence.

Together, they came up with a solution for how the culprit can repair the damage they caused. While the impact of South Africa's Truth and Reconciliation Commission, now called the Institute for Justice and Reconciliation, has been variable, the principles of restorative justice offer significant learning. It has proven particularly effective in the criminal justice and education systems.

'There has to be a reconciliation of multiple histories,' says

Amahra Spence, co-founder of MAIA and founder of YARD, who I interviewed for this book. 'That's as much about people as it is about place and environment. At the centre of that has to be those who are most approximate to those challenges, those who are most approximate to injustice, they have to be the ones who determine how that conversation goes.'

The International Center for Transitional Justice (ICTJ), based in New York, is an organisation that supports the transition process in places where major human rights violations have taken place. ICTJ aims to restore trust in institutions complicit in such atrocities by establishing accountability to the most harmed. It centres women and marginalised groups in re-establishing a just society or community. It cultivates a peace and reconciliation process where the solutions are sustainable and fair, which is not always the case in existing judicial systems. While this can result in criminal prosecutions, the transition may also mean legal reform or reparations. ICTJ attempts to bring survivors and perpetrators or people in power together to create meaningful solutions.

ICTJ has worked worldwide, operating in extreme circumstances, from Israel and the Occupied Palestinian Territories to Sierra Leone. The operational principles provide a model of how collaboration, deep listening and reconciliation lead to long-term policy change. Acknowledgement of atrocities by those responsible for such reprehensible deeds is an integral part of the process. It indicates the seriousness of the violations to the victims and survivors.

Those in power legitimately invest in righting their wrongs. There have been reparations programmes in Chile and Argentina.[10] Policies to repair past transgressions have been implemented. There has also been a concerted effort to ensure that there's no erasure of victims' narratives. It isn't just about paying victims and survivors; reparations also support people's futures through improved health care, university scholarships and pension plans.

Cultural studies pioneer Stuart Hall famously said:

> People like me who came to England in the 1950s have been there for centuries; symbolically, we have been there for centuries. I was coming home. I am the sugar at the bottom of the English cup of tea. I am the sweet tooth, the sugar plantations that rotted generations of English children's teeth. There are thousands of others beside me that are, you know, the cup of tea itself.
>
> Because they don't grow it in Lancashire, you know. Not a single tea plantation exists within the United Kingdom. This is the symbolisation of English identity – I mean, what does anybody in the world know about an English person except that they can't get through the day without a cup of tea? Where does it come from? Ceylon – Sri Lanka, India. That is the outside history that is inside the history of the English. There is no English history without that other history.[11]

Ruth Ibegbuna believes, in general, that there needs to be a national conversation exploring English values:

> For me, what I would love to see happen is for us to have a really deep reimaging about what our values are and what we want them to be and to have that national conversation,

not led by government. That has got to be kind of grass-roots to find out what kind of country are we, what kind of country do we want to be, what kind of values do we hold and do we cherish. Who are we? I think until we have the honest conversation about who we are and who we want to be, and what kind of society we're building for our children, all children, I just think we get stuck in this.

As a nation, we're just not honest about what kind of people we are and what kind of society we're building, so we just push ourselves further and further to the right without ever stopping ourselves and thinking, "What's happened to us, why has it happened, and who do we want to be going forward. Is this who we want to be?"

Imagine if the truth and reconciliation process laid the foundation of a national conversation about English and British values? What if the major institutions started their journeys toward change by exploring how they'd accumulated wealth? What if they placed power for this process in the hands of those most impacted by their exploitation?

Reparations. We cannot wait for our institutions to find enlightenment before changes occur. The climate crisis is often framed as a lifestyle or scientific issue in Britain, not a life or death problem. While small acts of giving and lifestyle change are imperative towards building a more climate-just future, we cannot ignore that people are dying now, across the globe, because of capitalism. While Britain should go through a truth and reconciliation and decolonisation over time, it must also act with urgency now.

It must work with the communities most affected by extractive private enterprise to put actions to repair the damage. The case for reparations grew stronger in 2020 and 2021. For example, multiple cities in North Carolina approved reparations and race equity policies, acknowledging their roles in slavery, Jim Crow laws and sustained systemic racism. These reparations (well, more like reparative initiatives) primarily address the failure to compensate Black people after the abolition of slavery. The descendants of slaves will benefit from investment in Black-owned farms and businesses.[12]

The case for developing 'baby bonds' programmes to reduce economic disparities resulting from historical racist government policies also gathered momentum in 2020. Professor Darrick Hamilton of The New School has been developing a policy that would create a trust fund for babies born to low-income families.[13] As Hamilton once said, 'In a capitalist system, if you lack capital, it just locks in inequality.'[14] With 'baby bonds' all babies would be entitled to these funds, but the poorest would receive more considerable sums. As with the UK's Child Trust Fund,* young people would access these funds on becoming adults. The difference is, parents would not have to pay into it, and it would be means-tested; those with less would receive more.

Baby bonds are not the elixir for repairing atrocities of

---

* The Child Trust Fund is a tax-free savings account for children launched by the Labour government in 2005. Babies born between 2002 and 2011 were eligible for £250 (in some cases up to £500), which parents could 'top-up' each year until their child was 18. The Fund was meant to incentivise saving, as a high-interest, tax-free account.

the past by any means. While it may reduce the wealth gap in the long run, I am not sure how it supports the health and well-being of parents from low socio-economic backgrounds while they are raising their children. If tasked to the government to drive as a policy, race or intersectionality wouldn't inform it, therefore invalidating it as a fair programme.

But I mention it as one of many models worthy of exploration if converting the concept of reconciliation to policy. When City University of New York's Naomi Zewde ran a hypothetical baby bond programme, she found that it could profoundly reduce the wealth gap. Annie Lowrey's article in *The Atlantic* (29 June 2020) suggested that it would cost around $80 billion a year in the United States.[15] The annual cost of Social Security in the United States in 2019 was approximately $1.059 trillion, so the baby bond would consume less than 10 per cent.

The CARICOM Reparations Commission (CRC), created by Caribbean heads of government in 2013, has put together a ten-point reparations plan. The CRC is calling for a formal apology from the European governments. It also demands help with the healing process, debt cancellation for Caribbean governments who inherited the ruins of the Empire, funding towards illiteracy and health problems stemming from slavery, and programmes to even the technological and scientific knowledge and resource gap, among other measures. The plans suggested by the CRC offer a firm foundation for a reparations process grounded in the experiences and needs of Caribbean people.

*

Decolonisation. The collective Voices that Shake!, which supports young people to challenge social, racial and climate injustice, describes its decolonial practice as such: 'We challenge the pervasive, hierarchical and historical dualisms that take white, male, straight, able-bodied experiences and perspectives to be more valid than the experiences of womxn,* of Black and brown people, and of queer and disabled people.'[16]

Decoloniality rejects the enduring presence of coloniality in our society – from wealth generation through extraction and exploitation of land, labour, education and science through a Eurocentric lens to the preservation of white supremacy and racial hierarchies. Decolonisation situates and centres knowledge, history and production through those on the frontline of intersectional oppression and seeks to 'undo colonial mechanisms of power, economics, language, culture, and thinking that shapes contemporary life: interrogating the provenance and legitimacy of dominant forms of knowledge, values, norms and assumptions.'[17]

Decolonisation will lead to a shift in power and resources, and our society's functions, away from individual gain towards a vision of collective growth. But to do so, Britain has to start by reconciling with its past. It has to start by dismantling the

---

* 'While there are valid reasons to reject the term, for many, it is an important way to signal inclusion and to acknowledge differences between different groups of women. Dr. Danai Mupotsa, senior lecturer in African literature at the University of the Witwatersrand, uses "womxn" to signal inclusion of cisgender and transgender women. "Womxn" also has significance within Black feminism, says Dr. Mupotsa. "The term came into very popular use in the last few years in Black public feminisms, to think and practice in ways where difference becomes a productive site of struggle."' Karpinski, Monica (19 August 2020). 'What You Need To Know About The Intersectional Term Womxn'. Source: Daye, https://yourdaye.com/vitals/cultural-musings/what-is-the-meaning-of-womxn/.

Empire State of Mind. It has to formally apologise and set about a course of reparations for the enduring damage of slavery and colonisation.

Sounds big. Unobtainable. Unimaginable. Perhaps. And it is unlikely that any British government would willingly shift towards something that does not protect its assets and ideologies. But the protection of government interests and ideologies has caused more harm during the COVID-19 outbreak than a response that prioritised the most susceptible people.

There was a noticeable difference in then Prime Minister Jacinda Ardern's management of the pandemic than Boris Johnson's. Of course, New Zealand is different from Great Britain. There's no straight parallel. However, according to the Australian think tank Lowy Institute, New Zealand had the best response to the coronavirus of any country. Ardern acted swiftly by closing the country's borders, implementing early lockdown plans and providing the public with clear actions.[18]

Underpinning this, however, was, it appeared, a great deal of trust in Ardern's leadership, perhaps born from her putting people before business. To be clear, Ardern's approach was not decolonisation in practice. More an illustration of someone with immense power deprioritising money. In Britain, during the COVID-19 outbreak, we saw the same patterns we observe when we look at the roots of the climate crisis. We saw the most vivid illustration of what capitalism seeks to do, prioritising money over humanity. Decolonisation practice, at its best, prioritises humanity over money, reducing, therefore, harm to people and the planet. Everyone benefits in the long run.

*

Healing. Reparatory justice is not merely about acknowledgement, payback, accountability and a move towards shifting
the power base. Recovery is essential within communities of
colour and other marginalised groups who've suffered the
most historically.

It goes deeper than evidencing the scale of generational
trauma accumulated through decades of discrimination in
housing, health, education and every other institution we
contribute taxes to maintaining. As people of colour, we
have been interfered with by Britain, in ways often too brutal
to confront. It is an insult of the most seismic proportions
when politicians or those in power deny complicity, therefore
rejecting our lived experiences. It hurts so bad.

When I interviewed Marai Larasi, former executive director of Imkaan, for this book, she told me something that I
haven't been able to shake. She said:

'I have good people in my life, really good people. I've
got a couple of really close friends who are like sisters,
colleagues, warriors. I have children now who are like
warriors. Literally, they are there. They are adult children
who were like, 'we are a community. We hold each other.'

I come from where the dirt is red, so there is also something for me about not trying to oversimplify this hybridity.
My dad's dad was white, and my understanding is that he
was a deeply unpleasant man who had acted as an overseer
of a plantation in Trelawny [in Jamaica]. I met him when
I was little. He was 102. When I encountered the painful
truth about how that white bloodline had interacted with
my black bloodline, I had to deal with what the hybridity

means, and it's [a] fact that it is complicated. Something is
freeing by doing it.'

The work of organisations like Healing Justice London
(HJL) feels like an important part of this process as we
move through healing, reparatory and restorative justice
processes. It provides healing and a safe space for racially
minoritised and marginalised people. HJL offers culturally
sensitive workshops focused on reproductive health, training
for those enduring racialised and lived-experience trauma,
research on loss and grief, and men's healing circles, among
other things.

HJL's work is holistic and informed by a disability-justice
framework; it adheres to a trauma-informed and somatic
approach, draws on the arts, and centres on people of colour
and lived experience. The work recognises historical, colonial
and intersectional issues and uses body-oriented practices.
This is very much a different approach to England's public
health systems, but one that offers a more culturally appropriate and person-centred slant to well-being. An essential
ingredient too, to protecting those changemakers who are on
the front lines.

'Nothing outside of you can really give your life meaning or
determine your worthiness,' says Farzana Khan, co-founder
of Healing Justice London.

'It means that you are ready, and I hope curious about
what the potential of that is. This is why trauma work is
so important. If you come from a traumatised community
or those that experience oppression-based chronic trauma,

change from any precarity, even internally, is destabilising/ feels risky. Even being able to visualise yourself long-term or in the future is hard. We often find that same thing with people wanting to hold on to power in our communities because they find it difficult to embrace change.

'There's a survival response attached to that, created as a result of our contexts. So, with this as a coping mechanism, what do we do to create safety or resourcing within oneself to be able embrace or move towards change? When we do trauma work, we support facilitating access to safety in one's own body, trust in one's own body, trust in one's own emotions, trust in one's own experience, so when you are experiencing different types of change or transformation, you can participate in it and still feel your agency in it. From here we are more able [to] surface and enact new choices or responses with less overwhelm, shutting down and without only having to default to what already is. I think that work around trauma specifically, and I've seen people engage in that deeper internal work; including myself, we are practising how can we safely support or build towards our presence or integrating more of our bodies/selves without absolving the structural changes that also need to happen for real safety. Since we can't fully, justly or equitably participate, if we are not able to be present (or even be present with as much of ourselves is safely available to us in that moment).'

Without healing from trauma, those moving into power may be in danger of replicating the behaviours of our oppressors.

*

Regenerative justice. It will also be important in the process of shifting power towards the historically disenfranchised, that the rightful beneficiaries do not replicate the deeds of current power holders. Adopting a reparative frame to giving must lead to a regenerative system, one where wealth is distributed evenly, one that solidifies a new paradigm of giving back.

While the details fail me, I remember hearing about a school in East Africa based on a farm. The school combined typical desk-based work with experiential and project-based learning. The pupils would learn to farm, but they also created a business to sell local produce to consumers (through markets) and shops. Profits from the industry went back to the school to pay the teachers' wages. In return, this incentivised the teachers to do a good job, in part because their livelihoods depended on it.

In this school system, everyone is reliant on each other. While I am sure there may be issues around perverse incentives, the idea of a more circular education system, where the system is accountable to pupils, parents, and educators, not a government-controlled regulatory body, strikes me as a healthier platform.

Cooperation Jackson is a worker-owned cooperative based in Jackson, Mississippi, that operates a series of ecologically friendly businesses. Their ventures include an organic vegetarian farm, a community centre, and a community land trust,* which it will use to construct houses. It creates community wealth and work distributed among its members,

---

* A community land trust enables ordinary citizens to hold land and to develop and manage affordable homes for their local communities.

prioritising the most economically marginalised, which in this case is Black and Latino communities.

Founder Kali Akuno wants to create an alternative economy from these worker-owned enterprises, all of which have been funded by donations. Mondragon, which started in the Basque region of Spain in 1956, inspired Cooperation Jackson's approach. The Mondragon model now comprises ninety-six cooperatives with 81,000 members employed in over 250 companies.

Akuno aims to expand by developing restaurants, banks and housing, but not at the expense of people or the planet. This alternative model shifts away from reproducing capitalism's harms, one that leaves too many of us behind. Cooperatives like Cooperation Jackson work towards an equitable vision, a fairer system, and a reparatory approach, where wealth works for those most in need. A healthier system for all.

This level of change takes time. It takes deep work. You're talking about a significant mindset shift. But all over the globe, there are many more examples of people and projects, movements and collectives delivering circular models, providing examples of what healthier communities could look like. While we are working towards a better future, a reparatory and regenerative future, we can now contribute in more practical ways. Individuals and foundations can give back by supporting or finding out more about initiatives benefitting the most marginalised operating a regenerative model, such as those described above. You should also invest time, money, and ideas in the space and scaffolding required to enable communities to imagine and manifest these models.

Reparatory justice, for me, underpins the following inter-connecting principles: truth and reconciliation, reparations, decolonisation, healing and regenerative justice. For trusts and foundations and business, this means exploring the DNA of how you accumulated wealth, moving away from grant-making and philanthropy as an antidote for the rich and an institutional practice, working towards reversing systems of extraction and exploitation and donors and foundations absorbing risk on behalf of, and finding ways of investing directly in, communities most impacted by the harms of your wealth. A reparatory frame is a start to giving back. Reparations is giving everything back.

For individuals, it is about exploring colonialism, empire and slavery, understanding who has been harmed the most by excessive wealth accumulation and shifting our minds from giving to giving back. Read the works of Sir Hilary Beckles and Walter Rodney. Learn more about the Grenadian Revolution in 1979. We may not see a change in our times. But anything we can do in our lives and roles that does not contribute to our current systems of extraction will be one of the most powerful ways for us to give.

19

Knowledge equity

Value the wisdom and expertise of those with lived experiences of unfair and inequitable systems

All he wanted was a bike. His mum sensed that the promise of a bicycle would help him deal with the wrenching pain of separation. She said it would be waiting for him when he arrived in England. He didn't know where he was going. She didn't know whether he'd ever get there. But she was sure that her nine-year-old son had a better chance of surviving a perilous journey across continents than staying at home.

He didn't arrive. He didn't find himself cycling, a cool breeze tickling his coarsened skin. Instead, he found himself crouched in mud, his body crawling with bugs in a make-shift 'jungle' border between French and English-speaking worlds. He was trapped in a vicious system at the mercy of adult strangers, moving his young body between the jungle, at times leaving him swaying in cold boxes or stuck in detention cells that were sucking the warmth of his mother's words from his soul.

Three years later, he still hadn't arrived. Now twelve, he

found himself detained in a cell in Dover, Kent. It had been four days since he had any food, frightened by the unknown items on the plastic plates forced in front of him. There must have been times when he thought he was expiring within these four walls, his quest for a bike a fate worse than what seemed inevitable in his Afghan village. He had escaped from the Taliban and the murders that befell his father and brother; he had fled violence and war, crossed several territories and seas. And now he was facing hunger, isolation and hostility in a place that should have safeguarded him.

The adults in suits and uniforms didn't believe him. He missed his mother. He only shared what she'd said about the bike when he heard a familiar voice speaking his mother tongue, once he was finally taken out of his cell. This voice boomed through a box and speaker in the middle of a table in an interview room. He found warmth, a contrast to the humans in uniforms sitting across the table, interrogating his story, scrutinising details of his journey and purpose of arrival, shuffling papers, dissecting his contact with enforcement officials in France and the UK.

The suits asked why he had left. He spoke of the bike. They inquired as to why he wasn't telling the truth about his prior port arrivals to the UK; he was confused. He didn't know. He wasn't sure quite where he was, given he'd been carted in the equivalent of refrigerated boxes, back and forth across the English Channel. His young mind unaware that the swaying lorries he'd been forced into over months were bouncing him between French and UK ports.

They didn't think his story was plausible or worthy of a refugee-protection assessment. A bike? *The liar.* They wanted to send him back. Back to Calais, back to Afghanistan, back to anywhere that's not here. Those were the rules. *We are only doing our jobs*, they probably said. Their entry records told their story, not the boy's truths. The records that refused his claim for refugee protection would later be judged as illegal.

His story was not unique. Thousands of children, thousands of truths had fallen foul of this broken and vicious system for years.

The child may not have been able to speak French or English; he may have been hungry and traumatised. He had fallen victim to a system and process that failed to acknowledge his truths, wisdom, young mind, emotions or language. But he understood the 1951 Refugee Convention – legislation aimed at protecting refugees' rights – better than most. He could tell you what was wrong with the system controlling his body while denying his right to be heard. He could have told you how to improve it because he was experiencing it. So, he did.

When approached by a legal team aiming to represent other young people who had fallen victim to this flawed system, one that should have been there to protect and give sanctuary, he shared his experiences. He wanted to help those young people who were now in a position he had once occupied. He believed them. Eventually, some of these young people would get an opportunity to tell their stories. By the time their case – exploring this unjust system – went to court, the boy was in his late teens. It was a case that would recognise the role of children's social services in supporting a child in need of state protection – a shift from a system of suits and uniforms to care providers, from the transactional to the relational.

He agreed to have his experiences and case filed in this

collective effort, even though he had already secured refugee status by the time it reached the higher courts. When asked why he did it and didn't cut his ties, he uttered a local Afghan saying, 'we are mice fighting the lion'.

* * * * *

She was an explosion of empathy and energy, a proud Nottingham native with an unyielding belief in young people facing disadvantage as fierce as the bright red lipstick she'd often sport. She believed him. The former youth worker and children's rights lawyer had experienced enough unjust systems, personally and professionally, to know that what he was telling her was true.

She unpacked the complexity of the Afghan boy's experiences and emotions and investigated the actors and players in suits. The evidence mounted. She built a case and unveiled the harmful practices and systemic failures. But she wanted to do more; she needed to do more. As gratifying as seeking justice for this child and many others had been, as many laws and policies as she'd challenged and changed as a lawyer, there was a deeper, underlying problem she needed to address.

Baljeet Sandhu describes herself as a recovering human rights lawyer. A former youth worker, her social justice career has spanned nearly two decades, where she has progressed the development of children's rights law, policy and practice in England, winning several awards. Sandhu is the Migrant & Refugee Children's Legal Unit (MiCLU) founder and founding partner of Kids in Need of Defense UK (KIND).

She has served as a Special Adviser to the Children's

Commissioner for England, UN agencies and national and international governing bodies (going onto develop the UK's first national children's rights programme in the migrant and refugee advice sector). She was also an Expert Advisor to the Strategic Legal Fund for Vulnerable Young Migrants, helping shape an innovative funding programme for strategic litigation and policy work in the UK. In recognition of her achievements, she was honoured with the 2017 DVF International Award during the Women in the World Conference at the United Nations. Through all of her life experiences and achievements, Sandhu recognised a key thing:

'The heartbeat for justice is human kindness. It's what ignites and sustains community action. Meeting a poor man on the street who would buy me cup of tea when I was cold. Kindness. Debbie, white working-class Debbie, who let me sleep on her sofa when I was a homeless young person. Kindness. Jabai, a Rasta who was educating me on our indigenous, ancestral civilisations, powers and innovations through Afrocentric education as a sixteen-year-old – to tell me my life, body and mind mattered. Centred in love of our collective humanity and history. You could be white, Black, purple, blue, rich, poor. Kindness drives equity. A white disabled woman understanding her privilege to speak out against disparities faced by disabled Black people. Women's rights and LGBTQ activists organising to support one another against tyranny. That for me was the true moment. I knew that it's that human connection that matters.'

In 2014, while still an active lawyer, Sandhu – dismayed by the inability of national and international charities and agencies to mobilise and respond effectively to the growing refugee crisis and inspired by the work of disability and civil rights leaders from the 1960s – started to shift away from the bounds of human rights law. She wanted to address one question. Why did well-meaning professionals and technical experts find it impossible to understand and work alongside change-makers on the hard edges of unjust systems in an equitable and meaningful manner?

In her ground-breaking report 'The Value of Lived Experience in Social Change'.[2] she argues for a fundamental shift in attitude towards people with lived experiences, how a new form of leadership is required to tackle major social issues, and how transformative change has historically been powered by those at the forefront of the social problems they tackled. She told me:

> 'First of all, the natural thing to do is give back, when you think about giving. 'I don't want what happened to me to happen to anyone else'. The civil rights movement wasn't going to be started by white people. As much as they love us when they joined us. It would only be started by people of colour. The disability rights movement was only going to be started by people with disabilities. The women's rights movement was only going to be started by women. You can have allies, but change only gets started by the people it impacts. We then connect to move forward, but you ultimately begin something because it affected our lives and we care about it. That is just how it is. Most exact change and progress in the the world is created or crafted by people

experiencing personal struggle – going back to the invention of the wheel – to people that are suffering or have a need to fight for change. They'll either invent something or create something new. That is just how humanity works, and yet for some reason we've forgotten that.'

This is particularly true of the social sector, which, to its detriment, operates on a model where wealth and power know what's best for communities facing disadvantage. The sector does not cultivate the insights and knowledge of experts by experience and tends to treat those most impacted by social harms as little more than service users, not changemakers.[1]

'Right now, we are stifling human ingenuity,' Sandhu says.

'What we have instead are processes, systems, parties, charities, civil society organisations, hell-bent on understanding distant problems when actually, there're people who are living those problems who need and want to be the inventors of the wheel. And this isn't just about whether we're Black or brown or poor or rich. We're talking about people with disabilities who have innovation ideas for a more inclusive world. Survivors of domestic violence or addiction with visions of inclusive policy design. We're talking about people who understand their lives and lived realities ... But we are stifling the potential of humanity to tackle societal problems until we recognise one fundamental thing, that humans will always create. People with direct first-hand experience of a problem understand a problem because they lived it, they will have knowledge, insight and wisdom that someone cannot read from a book or report. The best innovations in the world have happened where people have had agency to action human ingenuity. That for me is where real social transformation happens. And that's all about allowing human wisdom to flourish and that then requires us to question access and agency to create and innovate. Who do we consider as knowledge producers? What knowledge is acknowledged, valued or platformed? Then we go back to structural inequities entrenched in the current systems that silence, suppress or oppress different forms of knowledge. Our history tells us that research, operating models and those frameworks, those carrying out 'future thinking', are being constructed through white, patriarchal, ableist knowledge frames. So, it is no surprise that this privileged knowledge will always get money and resource to drive forward its ideas.'

Sandhu, a Clore Social Fellow, Greenberg Yale World Fellow and a Visiting Fellow at the Skoll Centre for Social Entrepreneurship, Saïd Business School, University of Oxford, coined the term 'knowledge equity' during one of her lectures in 2017. She centred the knowledge and human wisdom of people with lived experiences as the catalyst for transformative social change. During her time as a Yale World Fellow, Sandhu worked across academic disciplines exploring and developing the concept of lived experience, moving it away from traditional research practices towards a concept rooted in social innovation, systems change and social entrepreneurship.

Inspired by her work, she was invited to return to Yale as an inaugural global innovator-in-residence to support the development of the new Tsai Centre for Innovative Thinking at Yale (CITY), where she supported the centre's design. She also launched the Knowledge Equity Initiative (KEI) at Yale, a year-long research, education and practice hub and a pre-cursor to the creation of the Centre for Knowledge Equity. As part of this work, Sandhu carried out further research with social leaders with lived experience. In 2019 she authored the report *Lived Experience Leadership: Rebooting the DNA of Leadership*,[3] developing and codifying the Lived Experience Leadership framework for social, economic and environmental impact work.

In 2019, with a coalition of senior and experienced leaders in the UK, Sandhu co-founded the Lived Experience (LEx) Leaders Movement (also known as LEx Movement), a UK-wide collective impact network connecting, supporting and strengthening the capacity of LEx Leaders to create systems-level change.

With over 1,000 LEx leaders, LEx-led organisations, coalitions and networks as part of its membership, the collective has fast become a vibrant movement working across sectors, industries and social justice issue areas. The LEx Movement now also has sister movements emerging around the world.

Sandhu also launched the Centre for Knowledge Equity, which stimulates change through pioneering collaborations with LEx leaders, funders, academic institutions, social purpose organisations and activist movements that equitably and meaningfully unite lived, learned and practised expertise.

Its catalytic innovations include a partnership with the Skoll Centre for Social Entrepreneurship, including the launch of the Knowledge Equity Fellowship and a new global Knowledge Equity Initiative. CFKE also launched its Imagination Observatory, a collaborative space to bring together systems actors and LEx thought leaders to reimagine systems and visions for the future.

Sandhu says:

'Ultimately when I think about knowledge, it's not just about lived experience. I moved to crafting the concept of knowledge equity later, because first we needed all changemakers to understand the notion of lived experience. As people who have direct personal experience of injustice, we walk through those lives gathering insight and knowledge. So, I wanted to shift the paradigm from people seeing us as external vulnerable identities to understand that we are holders and producers of knowledge that you have long needed. Ultimately, to put a stick in the ground and say it is knowledge. We need lived expertise firmly on the knowledge table. The second step was, now let's talk about knowledge equity – how do we equitably and meaningfully integrate lived, learned and practice expertise in impact? That's why I coined the term. Right now, all forms of human wisdom matter, to this planet, world and our future. But what human wisdom do we value and how do we value it? Do we even acknowledge it? That's the first step. Most of the [social] sector does not even know that it is knowledge, stuck in circles of storytelling and giving voice. Second, if you do start understanding lived expertise as knowledge, then start giving it equitable agency. And if it's about giving it agency, it is then about understanding that the luxury of innovation – designing, failing and testing is not the white male social entrepreneurs' luxury. Many of whom are funded to test out their ideas on our communities, yet communities who have a deep entrenched understanding of root causes and problems, have little or no space or resource to think of solutions.'

Since the launch of her reports and the Centre, Sandhu has supported, designed or pioneered many programmes in the funding world seeking to centre the power of LEx leadership. This includes: the Leaders with Lived Experience Fund at the National Lottery Community Fund; the 2027 Programme – bringing more working-class people with lived experiences into decision-making roles in UK philanthropy; the Challenge and Change Fund – a fund designed by and for young activists; the National Survivor User Network (NSUN) COVID-19 Fund for Black lived-experience leaders supporting communities facing mental distress, trauma or loss; Resourcing Racial Justice and Phoenix Fund – designed by Black and Asian racial justice leaders to resource the work of Black and Asian-led organisations responding to the COVID-19 outbreak.

The Centre has also launched numerous National Leadership Programmes to support and elevate the work of LEx leaders, including work with Clore Social Leadership and other mainstream providers in the fields of criminal justice and migrant and refugee rights and anti-poverty work.'

There are many unbelievable but often underappreciated leaders across the globe, whose work and solutions are informed by their knowledge gained from first-hand experiences of social ills. For example, when I spoke to Rachel Muthoga early in 2021, she told me about her work as a trustee of the Wangu Kanja Foundation in Kenya, which supports survivors of sexual violence. Muthoga is a former human rights lawyer and founder and CEO of On Point Policy Advisers. We first met in 2015 in Kilifi, Kenya, when she was CEO of Moving the Goalposts (MTG), which uses football to unlock the potential of girls and young women.

At the time, the charity worked with over 5,000 girls, supporting their economic independence and creating educational opportunities while developing their leadership skills and safeguarding their physical and sexual health. MTG also challenged men's attitudes in the community, particularly the elders, who would often confine girls to rearing the family from a young age at the expense of their education.

Wangu Kanja is a survivor. In 2002, aged eighteen, she was raped and did not receive the services that survivors of sexual violence are meant to secure, including an effective investigation of her case or professional psychosocial support. But she was inspired to help other girls and women in her predicament and started the foundation in 2005. Kanja has since been an authentic voice for survivors by applying her lived experience and expertise.

According to the 'Violence Against Children' report in 2010, one in three girls experiences sexual violence before the age of eighteen in Kenya.[4] As in so many countries, reporting incidences of sexual assault, violence or abuse rarely results in prosecution. For many women, silence is preferable to the emotional and potentially physical and sexual violence they'd face if they reported the incident.

Kanja's foundation represents the voices and experiences of the most marginalised women, balancing provision with policy. Its survivor-facing work informs its push for policy reform. As Muthoga told me, success does not stem from grants but the foundation's proximity to and experiential understanding of the issues it addresses. The foundation recognises the needs of women seeking state services, the founder's credibility is crucial, and it is willing to speak women's truths to power.

Through comprehensive care, including medical, healing, psychological and legal support, restorative justice, financial aid and dance therapy, the foundation has supported over 20,000 girls and women over the last sixteen years. Its systems advocacy work aims to hold the state authorities accountable, change policy, develop prevention strategies and cultivate more coordinated approaches to supporting survivors. Kanja had to fight to be recognised. But she is an example of a solution that emerged 'from the ground'. Imagine if more funding went to, as Sandhu would term it, LEx leaders to test their ideas, methods, and innovations?

The funding world has changed a lot since I first entered it in 2009. More talk about systems change. More talk of user voice. More talk of collaborations. More jargon. All apparently to make the social sector more effective. Fundamentally though, little has changed. The same people sit around the table, setting the agenda and deciding how and where money flows. No matter how well-meaning, the social sector is still a product of a profoundly unequal society that provides opportunities for few, a society that continually moves the goalposts enough to keep the marginalised from the centre.

The lived expertise* of those closest to the social issues

---

* Lived expertise was a term coined by Sandhu at the time she launched her 2017 report with open access to all at https://thelivedexperience.org/. As she explains, every human has lived, and every human has experiences – but lived expertise is when someone activates their lived experience to move it away from story of self and activates the knowledge, insights and wisdom it provides into their change-making toolbox.

we aim to address should be *the* most vital component in everything we do to transform our society for good, yet it remains on the periphery. Sandhu has provided the most compelling case for shifting power towards people with lived experience. She is creating safe pathways for lived expertise to lead in the social sector's design, delivery and decision-making.

'Right now, there is a whole lot of gatekeeping going on in the middle, largely the mainstream charity sector, that is trying to own and drive the field of lived experience leadership from their service-user lens. This is not only creating a new form of modern-day erasure and co-option of a field created by and being evolved by LEx communities, but it is also not allowing good humans from across sectors and industries to come together with communities to equitably design the futures we all wish to see,' Sandhu says. 'The beauty, I believe, in is the connection between people who care, who have so much different skills and expertise to bring, but have authentic, true, connected spaces to exchange knowledge and build connections in ways we've not seen before. That will only be rooted in values and principles of respect, dignity and mutuality. The one simple thing we can do, is to start to celebrate and credit people knowledge producers from different realms, elevate them, acknowledge their presence.

'Love matters. Kindness matters. Care matters. What you love is what will drive the future.'

20

Collective care

*Support collectives that build the well-being, power
and economic strength of marginalised communities*

Over thirty years ago, Dudley Street in Roxbury, Boston,
was desolate and poverty-stricken. America's garbage can.
Literally. It had become an illegal dumping ground for con-
tractors and people outside the community; the smell was
so bad, kids would throw up on their way to school. Adults
would hold their breath as they drove through the neighbourhood. Businesses and services started 'red-lining' Dudley
Street. They stopped investing, stopped hiring locals, charged
more for their services. They disowned it, abused it.

Residents wanted out too. Homeowners with houses that
had little or no value started burning them down for the
insurance. A fire a week. Virgin arsonists. Heat and sirens
would regularly wake locals. It would frighten them, disturb
them. They couldn't draw their curtains or close their windows to the wrath of burning houses in their neighbourhood.

Many started to look for somewhere else to live. But

equally, many residents wanted to stay or had no option but to stay. Some of those tenants formed the Dudley Street Neighborhood Initiative (DSNI) in 1984. DSNI fought for the neighbourhood's rights, protested against those dumping waste, cleaned up the trash. And when the authorities finally decided to redevelop and regenerate but ignored the community while making these plans, DSNI protested.

They organised themselves, hired planners, built partnerships and created a resident-led vision of what Dudley Street could be. DSNI formed a community land trust. The City adopted their plans. DSNI transformed a wasteland into a desirable location, gained ownership of its neighbourhood and gained political power.

They transformed a once undesirable neighbourhood into an altogether community-owned area. DSNI's work centres on housing, workforce development and youth leadership. It prepares young people to be organisers and planners for the local neighbourhood. In 2014, I met then executive director of the Boston Promise Initiative, Sheena Collier, and Joceline Fidalgo, an example of youth leadership in action.

Joceline grew up in Dudley Street and joined the staff in a fundraising capacity. As a youngster, she started the Dudley Youth Council with her peers to empower youth and drive positive change in their neighbourhood. Collectively, they built leadership within the community. The community is the leader, not an individual.

DSNI's governing board comprised thirty-four people (elected every two years), including four people of Cape Verde heritage, four Latino, four white, four African

American, four youth and members from local businesses and religious and housing institutions. Fully reflective of its demographic. These residents had the power to dictate what happens in their neighbourhood.

DSNI primarily serves the Dudley Triangle (in 2014 it owned 225 homes) and a surrounding area called the Dudley Village Campus. In total, it served almost 25,000 residents, including close to 7,000 children and young people. Under its leadership, the community has kept homeownership affordable, fought off gentrification, and enabled residents to play an integral part in local development without being forced out. DSNI's slogan was 'development without displacement'.

Back in 2014, education in the area remained a problem. Almost 75 per cent of children and young people were still 'bussed' to schools outside Dudley Street. After much illegal resistance, Boston City finally decided to integrate its schools in 1974. Unfortunately, they did this by 'bussing' Black students from Roxbury out to predominantly white schools, causing rage among white parents.

The Soiling of Old Glory, the Pulitzer Prize-winning photograph by Stanley Forman, captures the racial tensions of the time and white residents' resistance to integration. Forman's picture shows a white student, Joseph Rakes, swinging a flagpole with an American flag at Black lawyer and civil rights activist Ted Landsmark. Aside from the resistance from white parents, 'bussing' also entirely failed to improve schools locally, a legacy present in Roxbury into the 2010s.

*

DSNI decided to apply for a Promise Neighbourhood grant to develop a coordinated and community-integrated approach to raising its local schools' attainment. It was awarded a five-year $6 million grant in 2012 to deliver a tailored educational support package like the Harlem Children's Zone, which I speak about later in the book. It supported schools and the local community to develop a culturally responsive educational offer that considers the community's needs.

True to its approach, DSNI consulted the community heavily and asked schools how they could help them perform better. DSNI valued the lived expertise of its residents. 'The end users of the system are the ones you should be empowering to make the changes,' said Collier, for my 'They Just Don't Know' Churchill Fellowship report. She is now the founder and CEO of Boston While Black and The Collier Connection.

DSNI has improved parental engagement, school readiness, reading proficiency, community voice, youth leadership, community service and access to healthy foods, and twenty-first century technology programmes. Its culturally responsive education focused on:

- Taking teachers on tours of the neighbourhood, so they understand where their pupils are coming from, helping them grasp and respect the history of Roxbury.
- Translation services.
- Running a campaign called Caring Adults, where each pupil has a mentor they can identify with (from the same cultural background).

- Supporting schools with teacher recruitment to help diversify their workforce.

DSNI has been successful at giving residents power, giving them a stake in housing and workforce development. It has started to support children through to adulthood under the slogan 'Children born to learn, neighborhoods built to care'. DSNI's local community will propelled the initiative. It has for many years been the glue between the local neighbourhoods' services. Being 'the glue' was fundamental to Boston Promise Initiative's approach to educational reform too.

'The bringing together of people across nonprofits and different sectors? I think that is powerful,' says Collier. 'When people across sectors are invested in something and really understand? The bringing together of partners is an art.'

* * * * *

In 2020, a young trainee architect asked me to name my favourite place in Britain. Rarely has such a simple question left me speechless. First, of course, I assessed where I grew up and where I live now. Then I thought about the many places I had visited, either on holiday or for work. But I couldn't settle on an answer.

Instead, I thought about the areas where I felt most at ease, where I had a sense of belonging. Places where there was a healthy unravelling of my character, an unconditional openness to difference. Areas where I didn't need to become a shadow to fit in or worry about the police harassing my kids. I had had fleeting moments of belonging, in St. Mary, Jamaica, in New Orleans, but never in Britain.

My adult life followed a similar pattern to my parents. They bought their first house in a working-class neighbourhood of Manor Park. Then, as the crime rate rose, they moved to a middle-class area in Essex. Similarly, I bought a house in Lower Sydenham, then moved to the suburbs (Beckenham). Sydenham, like Manor Park, felt more like a community.

The children played out in the street a lot, and the parents looked out for each other's kids. A trampoline was vital. The gardens on my street were small, maybe five by four metres. But one household's garden had a trampoline, which consumed it like a basketball in a shoebox. But it was a magnet for all the kids on the street.

The children interacted with each other, which led to the parents talking to each other and saying hello. There were cultural differences, no doubt. That didn't change. But I knew that when my kids played out on the street, they were safe under the other parents' guardianship. When Sydenham became a hot spot for knife crime, I started to recognise that the parents' values on my street were not as far from my ideals as I once thought. The trampoline broke down many barriers.

I have never spent a significant period of my life in a safe neighbourhood that also felt like a close-knit community. My community is my family and my friends. It has never been a place, which is sad. The closest I came to belonging was living on the fifth floor of a one-bedroom flat in Ladbroke Grove. I lived there from the age of twenty-five until I was thirty-three. When I first moved to the area, I was a freelance journalist. By the time I departed, I was working in the social sector. I had a child, and by the time I left, I had escaped financial precarity.

While my financial situation changed during this period, the social conditions within the flats didn't. When I entered the flats' lifts, I had to scan the floor because it was often covered in piss (sometimes in s**t, buried under cardboard). It was not unusual for phlegm to be dripping from the ceiling. In addition, the building's pipes enabled me to hear everything going on in the flats above and below mine.

Beneath, I could hear a man – it would appear – frequently beating up his spouse. Above, I listened to a man apparently abusing his dog. I believe that a sex worker for a brief time lived next door. There were always men lined up outside of my flat. There were also frequent threats from tenants, a postman who'd dump letters outside the lifts and teenagers smoking weed on the stairwell. It wasn't pleasant.

Yet we knew the neighbours on our floor. Said hello. I asked them if they were all right. I was only ten minutes away from four of my best friends. I worked in a local youth centre – Avenues Youth Project – and for various housing associations in the area.

There was a lovely park just behind the flats, a local West Indian takeaway (Yum Yums), countless North African and Mediterranean cafes and a nightclub called Subterania, where The Fugees and The Roots put on legendary shows, as well as frequent transportation to central London. I would later work for Kensington & Chelsea and Westminster volunteer centres and HMP Wormwood Scrubs, which increased my sense of community and gave me some sense of belonging. But ultimately, we couldn't afford to stay in west London.

What made Ladbroke Grove feel like a community was the opportunities to contribute to the neighbourhood. My flats' problems often appeared too big to tackle, the only option to call the police – there was no middle ground. But finding ways to give back, however small, helped.

It would have helped more if I knew what I was contributing to; how it may have been feeding into longer-term change. That's what was missing for me in Grove. Charities like Paddington Development Trust were trying to piece the various services together, providing a bridge between the public and social sectors, resurrecting the local economy, cultivating community voice and fighting for the rights of locals. They seemed to be more functional versions of the local government but with not nearly the same level of resource (i.e., ownership of housing stock or buildings) to escape income dependency from the state or independent funding.

It wasn't until 2011, when I visited the 2Up 2Down project in Liverpool, that I started to fully grasp what community leadership and ownership could look like and how it didn't need to follow the same top-down, hierarchical government structures. In 2010, Liverpool Biennial, a contemporary arts festival, commissioned Dutch artist Jeanne van Heeswijk to work with community members in Anfield and Breckfield to reimagine their neighbourhoods.

These areas were once part of the Housing Market Renewal Pathfinders regeneration plan. The Pathfinders programme was launched in 2002 under New Labour and aimed to renew failing housing markets across England, but the scheme had its funding cut in 2011 under the Coalition government. As a result, occupants of 1,800 properties had to leave. The scheme had always been controversial, with accusations of community cleansing and gentrification.[1]

When I visited, the Biennial organisers took me to where van Heeswijk would work, near Liverpool's Anfield football stadium. Anfield and Breckfield were broken neighbour-hoods. Rows upon rows of empty houses, windows and front doors boarded up with silver screens with notices stuck on them, vacant streets during a time when kids would be coming home from school; no cars parked or passing through, no colour, no life. These were people's homes, their lives. Nearby, all I could see for the remaining residents were book-ies, pubs and chip shops.

In 2010 van Heeswijk worked with twenty young people and designers to regenerate and refurbish two houses and a local bakery called Mitchell's. Mitchell's had served Liverpool football fans for years. But it had recently closed. When I visited the bakery, I saw health notices and equipment that looked like it was from the 1950s.

At the same time, local people started a community land trust, a cooperative that would enable the community to own the housing and the bakery. The intention was to create a community-led vision of what Anfield and Breckfield could look like if regenerated. The bakery would generate income primarily from Liverpool home matches and train local people in catering. The twenty young people working with van Heeswijk would also go to a local college to gain voca-tional qualifications.

The project became the Homebaked Bakery Co-operative in 2012. Today, the local community runs it. The bakery is now a café, open six days a week, and catering service, employing local people. Homebaked has plans to refurbish more houses and create more businesses and affordable properties for local people. The bakery was the trampoline for its neighbourhood, a central place for community members to gather, connect and create a bigger vision.

There is something magical about place; a sense of alignment, priorities and community and people developing relationships that enable them to see past prejudice. For this book, I interviewed Maria Adebowale-Schwarte, founding director of Living Space and chief executive officer of Foundation for Future London. Adebowale-Schwarte's work ensures that local communities lie at the heart of community development plans. She believes in the importance of place and how local connections between people open 'doors to create social justice and equity'.

But community ownership of the vision and their ability to commission, direct and bring in technical expertise is vital. 'Communities and civil society are not just at the table but are making the decisions and are provided [with] the resources that they need ... ensuring that they can create the places they want to live in ... places that have good local community, good schools and good homes.'

But Adebowale-Schwarte is also quick to point out that the most marginalised need to be prioritised and central to community development:

I think it is about community interest, but that's what you have to lead on – that it's for the community. I think there are certain individuals or groups in society that need to be put forward first: the ones struggling, refugees, asylum seekers, the working class struggling for jobs, struggling for housing, struggling to pay bills.

So I think there's something about putting a certain group of needs forward first. My expectation wouldn't be for a young mum or dad to look after their kids and to survive as an individual, and to put the same amount of time into this neighbourhood approach to someone who actually has their own trust fund. If you want people to really be part of decision making, you have to think about how can they do this without being worried about their very basic needs, about rooms, overheads, food, education for their children. You have to meet that.

Too often, power lies in the hands of those who are furthest away from the community. Adebowale-Schwarte told me about Black feminist poet and essayist June Jordan's interest in architecture and place and her collaboration with architect R. Buckminster Fuller, called 'Skyrise for Harlem'. Jordan was filled with hatred[2] after the Harlem and Bedford-Stuyvesant uprising in 1964 sparked by a white police officer fatally shooting the Black teenager, James Powell.

Jordan's and Fuller's vision was an example of development without displacement. Together, they envisioned a Harlem where conical towers, light-filled apartments and balconies housed residents. 'Every room would have a view.' Fuelled by local people's imaginations, there would be theatres, concert halls, fields for sport, more green space, and communal spaces where Black people would participate 'in the birth of their own reality'. When Jordan wrote an essay for *Esquire* in 1965, she titled it 'Skyrise for Harlem'. The editors retitled her piece 'Instant Slum Clearance'.[3]

Jordan's vision for Harlem was one that the editors of

Esquire could not grasp. But that is often true of those developing policies for urban renewal, be it Boston, Liverpool or Harlem. They just don't understand. 'We can't start from a place of reform and then try and retrofit a big vision. I think we have to start with utopia, with what's the biggest thing, what's the dreamiest thing, what's the closest thing to utopia that we can create?' says cultural producer and co-founder of MAIA and YARD, Amahra Spence.

* * * * *

Immy Kaur's work appears to be a product of dreams, ancestry and tradition. She operates with the belief 'in the infinite capacity of all people' and centring the joy, the tools and experiences that historically disadvantaged people have used to thrive.

In 2012, she co-founded Birmingham Impact Hub, underpinned by the idea of a twenty-first century town hall, a space defined by those who occupied it. The Hub did not start from a rigid definition; it wasn't a community centre, it wasn't a social enterprise, it was a blank canvas inviting people to create. Instead, the space's occupants defined its use, morphing ideas into solutions for local people that could potentially change systems.

One such project was called Radical Childcare. One of Impact Hub's freelancers, Amy Martin, flagged the childcare problems she had been facing. Her issues included the large deposits required, inflexibility and expense. These barriers to inclusion were also real for other potential users of the Hub. So, they set out to see what citizen-led solutions to childcare could be and how this could transform the way we raise children.

They worked with parents and children across all demographics and systems scientists to design a series of interdependent, citizen-led initiatives that they would incrementally implement. This wasn't the sort of piecemeal consultation you get from local government, schools or developers; one where you feel like your participation will not result in change. One where you think the decision has already been made.

The Hub created the conditions to provide a safe space for people to participate on their terms. Everyone locally had a view of the system and understood the challenges. The process enabled the Hub team to address some of the critical issues facing parents around time, money, and the guilt of not spending enough time with their children.

In total, they created ten interdependent investment areas that they felt could transform outcomes for children and their families. Some of the ideas were new, some already evidence-based; others were smaller interventions. Notably, Martin emphasised that investment in all ten areas could lead to social transformation, not in one or two. They used scientist and systems analyst Donella Meadows's Twelve Leverage Points* to

---

* Meadows's places to intervene in a system, in increasing order of effectiveness, are: 12. Constants, parameters, numbers (such as subsidies, taxes, standards). 11. The sizes of buffers and other stabilizing stocks, relative to their flows. 10. The structure of material stocks and flows (such as transport networks, population age structures). 9. The lengths of delays, relative to the rate of system change. 8. The strength of negative feedback loops, relative to the impacts they are trying to correct against. 7. The gain around driving positive feedback loops. 6. The structure of information flows (who does and does not have access to information). 5. The rules of the system (such as incentives, punishments, constraints). 4. The power to add, change, evolve, or self-organize system structure. 3. The goals of the system. 2. The mindset or paradigm out of which the system – its goals, structure, rules, delays, parameters – arises. 1. The power to transcend paradigms. http://donellameadows. org/archives/leverage-points-places-to-intervene-in-a-system/

assess how this work could effect fundamental change within the complex childcare systems. Under each area was a series of ideas that could support parents more effectively than the current system. These included:

- Making Time – implementation of Universal Basic Income, paid parental leave for a year, flexible schooling where you could mix time in traditional settings with learning in community venues, three-day weekends, mindfulness and meditation for thirty minutes every day in classrooms and the workplace.
- A Right to Play – Children starting school at seven years old, building the infrastructure and capacity to enable infants, children and families to have the right to a playful life, funding for play, etc.
- Children's Agency – a children's government so they can have a say on issues that impact on their lives, a Capital of Children aimed at supporting the creative citizenship of kids, greater diversification of books in educational establishments.
- Alternative Learning Models – ending mandatory testing and SATS and introducing micro (classroom-sized) schools, workplace childcare and creating more bespoke learning models.*

Some of these ideas were rooted in the survival ideas of immigrants upon arriving in England. For example, intergenerational

---

* For a full list of the Radical Childcare investment areas, go to: https://www.radicalchild.care/10-investment-areas

care where young people benefit from the wisdom of older people while the elderly benefit from the company of youth. Local savings groups to help people get accommodation when landlords wouldn't rent to people with turbans, no food waste, not using plastic bags, reusing resources.

More than anything, the Hub's work was liberating the potential of people. This is in stark contrast to how many of our institutions operate. Indy Johar, co-founder of Project 00 and Dark Matter Labs, questions whether we as a society are unlocking the true capabilities of humans or merely obsessed with realising the economic aspirations of a few.

The Hub closed its doors in 2019 to make way for CIVIC SQUARE, aiming to reimagine the public square. There's a quote from *New York Times* columnist David Brooks on its website, 'It could be that the neighbourhood, not the individual, is the fundamental unit of social change. If you're trying to improve lives, maybe you have to think about changing many elements of a single neighbourhood, in a systematic way, at a steady pace.'[4]

CIVIC SQUARE is building a place where the community bonds through genuine connection and creativity and not through complaints, crisis, convenience or capital. They have moved away from Birmingham's city centre to be close to more marginalised communities who will drive CIVIC SQUARE's culture and content. This development aims to be an extraordinary place for people to work, eat, raise their children and play as a community. It is a collective vision, neighbourhood activism and mobilisation but tied to a bigger idea of change.

Kaur told me:

There is a trio of things that I think about, which is inter-dependence, equity, liberation in a way that the western industrial philanthropic complex and our economy has individualised everything. It's individualised risk. It's individualised economic units. It's created the myth of the nuclear family, the individual, homo economicus as the rational economic man. Therefore, very slowly, deliberately through our language, through the way we design systems, and we organise, we have moved to that without realising.

I think about that in my own culture because the word for aunty in Punjabi is Massi, which means 'like your mum'. As I understood this more and more as I grew up, I started to realise that the way we construct ourselves in every way is to separate us. At which point you start to lose this idea that we are interdependent, that progress in my liberation is bounded in how well I am and how my life is connected to yours. There are no separate parts, we're just all part of this web.

There were moments during the COVID-19 pandemic where you suddenly realise it's just tons better being part of a helpful, supportive, caring, rainbows-on-the-window community. The problem is when your systems around you are wrapped up in a different goal, then very quickly you have to revert to 'how do we survive?'

I think the start is about interdependence and under-standing that our liberation, our progress, and our ability to move forward is deeply wrapped up with each other, whether we like it or not.

We all are prone to discouragement due to the size of the problems we face in the world. As Kaur pointed out, though, when she was a guest on my podcast, *Just Cause*, 'you know it's not enough. But if, for example, your playgroup, run by a parent, enabling other parents to have time for themselves, feeds into greater resource for play from the local council, then they will embrace their part in individual as well as systemic change.'

CIVIC SQUARE is still in development. But it will feature a climate-resilient design, it will operate a circular economic model, focusing on environmental and health benefits, not consumption and waste. This public square will highlight shared ownership, community housing concepts like Fairhold,[5] designed by Open Systems Lab as part of their Affordable Land work, and a decentralised model. It is a vision that will build people's spirit to resist destructive social policies and prepare for an environmentally hostile future. In this collective community vision, a beautiful image, everybody thrives.

* * * * *

Across the globe, there are many movements, non-profits and cooperatives that create bold ideas based on collective, localised visions of care that have led to transformative change. Amahra Spence pointed me towards Project Row Houses in Third Ward, Houston, Texas, where a coalition of seven African American artists purchased and refurbished twenty-two shotgun houses. Shotgun houses are narrow and rectangular with doors at each end and single rooms placed one after the other, with no hallways. They used the houses to support artists, small businesses and single mothers.

The idea is that once they had supported people, they too would contribute to helping others. 'They weren't trying to ideate on some future community who are going to come in and beautify the place,' says Spence.

> It was very much about who's here now, how can we make this the dopest it can be, the most just place for those that are here now? They saw that there were a lot of single mothers, so it's like, 'we need to invest in provisions for these single mothers.'
>
> It's a really low-income ward, so all of the things we can do to support people to run their own businesses (we know we have a lot of hustlers), how can we take those skills and invest in those people who can do things that might be a bit more legit? I think it's very much about investing in people who are here now and letting that influence the way neighbourhood change can happen at scale everywhere else.

Harlem Children's Zone is another place-based project which is hugely ambitious in its quest to enhance residents' educational prospects. Educator Geoffrey Canada founded it in 1997. I am sure he had seen the cycle of state responses to crisis many times before. The high percentage of kids caught doing something wrong, deemed 'at risk' of doing something wrong, accused of doing something wrong, one of the three. It could be about knife crime, school exclusion, gang membership. The problem makes the news, moral panic ensues. A common problem, permanent glitch, temporary fixes, never fixed.

A common question that the state, the authorities, the

powers that be are embarrassed about. A problem they or a previous administration had likely created or previously ignored. So the authorities want to be seen to be doing something about it. Throw some money at it, a little pot, perhaps two, three years' worth. Loads of charities apply. Demand outweighs supply, they say. Other funders follow. They need visibility, too; they need to be seen to be doing something.

Maybe a thousand kids are engaged. Some find work, some gain qualifications and some are 'saved'. Everybody pats each other on the back, the 'superhero' practitioners, the funders, the authorities. Money runs out. Priorities change. Interest wanes. Everything stays the same, except more charities are created, more young people are dependent, but the money has run out. Demand outweighs supply, they say. The problem is not fixed. It did not stem the flow of blood, it was just a temporary remedy. A few years later, the problem is back in vogue; a moral panic ensues, the authorities are embarrassed again, you get the picture.

So, when Geoffrey Canada started working at the Rheedlen Centers for Children and Families as Education Director in 1983, he probably faced this dilemma. He worked with young people at risk of exclusion and truants. Canada knew that this approach was not addressing the core of their problems. Furthermore, short-term funding meant he could not build a sustainable model to tackle the root causes of young people's issues.

Canada had been 'superman' operating in an area blighted by high numbers of children born into poverty, to single parenthood, with increased rates of obesity. He didn't just want to address school exclusion; he knew young people needed more. They needed more than just superman. Canada wanted to change the game. Disrupt the pattern. Wanted to develop a long-term intervention that would reverse the cycle of poverty resulting from years of discrimination and decay.

Working with young people was just a start. He wanted to alter the conditions and systems surrounding them to influence young people's peers, parents, teachers, wider community and services. If he was going to improve young people's life chances through education by improving attainment, he knew he had to link educational inequality to social inequality. As Rasuli Lewis, Director of the Harlem Children's Zone's Practitioners Institute told me when I interviewed him in 2014, what happens outside the classroom affects what happens in the classroom.[6] Developing the character of the community would be just as important as developing the character of young people.

Canada wanted to address why poor people were poor. The evidence he discovered suggested that it was largely due to a lack of specific skills.[7] That being the case, what then are the key problems faced by impoverished children and their families, and what skills, information and services would be required to address these problems?

So, in collaboration with experts, Canada created a whole-system approach to narrowing the Black–white achievement gap in education. It was designed specifically for the Harlem community, taking history and the racial demographics into consideration and recognising the need for a long-term, comprehensive, place-based approach. Canada wasn't so much changing the system as creating a whole new one.

By 2002, Rheedlen had changed its name to the Harlem Children's Zone (HCZ). HCZ developed a coordinated educational, social and medical services programme, serving children and young people from birth right through to adulthood. Cradle to career. 'To bring about widespread change it is necessary to work on a scale large enough to create a tipping point in a community's cultural norms, a threshold beyond which a shift occurs away from destructive patterns and toward constructive goals.'[8]

HCZ was built on four core principles. First, it wanted to build and rebuild communities. Second, it wanted to create a pipeline of high-quality services, 'to meet children wherever they were, whenever they needed us. Getting in early, very early and supporting them through their whole lives,' said Lewis.

Third, scale. HCZ has slowly built up to working in-depth with over 12,000 children and young people. Suddenly, youth problems once believed to be too big now appear to be solvable because of the scale. Fourth, data which HCZ used to inform its practice, its reporting, how it improves, ensuring it can reach every possible child.

By 2017, HCZ served over 13,000 youth (aged from birth to twenty-three) and over 14,000 adults in ninety-seven blocks in Harlem through twenty-four educational, support and health services. This includes the Promise Academy Charter School – a school that serves only water and food with no sugar or salt, using local produce – a food policy teachers also adhere to.

In addition, there's Harlem Gems Head Start (for children

aged three to five), the Community Pride community-building programme, tenant associations, one-to-one counselling, computer literacy and a foster care service. There is a coordinated approach to identifying any child, young person or family facing problems, and providing services to help them.

As of 2018, there were 861 HCZ students in university, with a 97 per cent acceptance rate,[9] over 9,000 youth participating in its health and nutrition programme,[10] and over 1,200 families had remained stable and avoided foster care. In addition, it helped almost 3,000 families gain nearly $5 million in refunds through its free tax preparation programme.

It currently has an endowment of between $145 and $175 million (HCZ has been heavily supported by the likes of former hedge fund manager Stanley Druckenmiller) and has become a thought leader in place-based, whole-system approaches to educational inequality. Indeed, HCZ has played a fundamental role in shifting the non-profit sector's paradigm away from singular interventions. The *New York Times Sunday Magazine* described HCZ as 'one of the most ambitious social experiments of our time.'[11] HCZ is potentially a model that could be replicated in many local communities globally to break the cycle of poverty.

In 2010 the Obama Administration initiated the Promise Neighbourhood Program [sic] to replicate HCZ's cradle-to-college-to-career approach in twenty cities. The United States Department of Education pledged $150 million towards replication. While it is true that a charismatic leader drove HCZ, it was clear in speaking to Lewis that the vision is to build a community of leaders and not to wait for another superman like Geoffrey Canada to emerge.

* * * * *

'Charisma won't save us,' warns Amahra Spence. We exist in a society that highlights the individual, not the collective. History tells us more stories about heroic or charismatic leaders, whether good or bad for this world, than about community resilience and uprisings. My son knows as much about Henry VIII as he does his favourite footballer, the Argentinean striker Sergio Agüero. He is fed history through a lens of predominantly white male leaders, their courage or tyranny based on winning or losing.

It stands to reason that this model remains the norm about who and what we trust. We often hear about the presidents or the kings who are praised for creating change, but we do not hear much about the people who forced these so-called leaders to act. Lost are the many movements and collectives that generate change without having a single lead. We also tend to think about name-brand charities, those with the most visibility.

What if we invested in or created more local cooperative or collaborative approaches to change? What if we donated time, money or ideas to work that represents the whole community, serves its needs, but crucially is fully reflective, in governance, of the community it serves while seeking to prioritise those furthest away from resource?

In the sixties, the civil rights group, the Student Nonviolent Coordinating Committee (SNCC), spoke of building a beloved community. In her review of the book *Hands on the Freedom Plow*, author Cheryl Greenberg described the structure of the book as an embodiment of the SNCC, which envisioned a society that 'based itself on radical egalitarianism, mutual respect, and unconditional support for every person's unique gifts and contributions'.[12] The SNCC tried to build its organisation around such principles. Supporting collectives constructed on such values of community leadership should be the archetype we seek instead of waiting for 'Superman'.

21

Radical solidarity

Recognise that we are interdependent by radically listening to and standing with communities on the front line of harm

Around the time I was learning to drive, soon after I'd graduated in 1994, Nigerian writer and activist Ken Saro-Wiwa was executed for demanding the right to clean air and water. Once a week, my driving instructor, a portly Mediterranean man with thinning dark hair and permanent beard stubble, picked me up for lessons I had little interest in taking.

He always told jokes, always took my driving faults personally, always stopped at petrol stations to fill the tank mid-way through the lesson. I had my concerns. Why am I learning to drive when I don't have and can't find a job? Where would I be going to? Why have a car when I have no destination? It's a waste of money, of resources, of time. I didn't realise it was also wasting lives. I didn't realise that my lifestyle, my livelihood, was being fed at the expense of other people's lives.

*

Shell started extracting petroleum oil in the Niger Delta in 1958. According to the arts-activism charity Platform, by the early seventies, Ogoni chiefs had begun petitioning, charging the company with 'seriously threatening the well-being and even the very lives' of local people.[1] Oil spillages covered farmland; the air was polluted, water contaminated, nature corrupted. The Ogoni and Iko people's peaceful demonstrations were met with death, rape, torture and destroyed homes. Shell allegedly paid off the constabularies to maintain control with force and bribed local people while failing to meet international environmental safety standards. Shell has always denied that it was involved in human rights violations.

The Movement for the Survival of the Ogoni People (MOSOP) launched in 1990. Soon after, Ken Saro-Wiwa started to seek support from the international community through his speeches and literature. In one speech, he accused the Nigerian government of genocide and Shell and Chevron of racism.[2] On 4 January 1993, around 300,000 Ogoni people held a peaceful demonstration against Shell, while celebrating the Year of Indigenous Peoples. The 4 January is now known as Ogoni Day.

The Nigerian military increased its presence locally, however, continuing to serve and protect the interests of international businesses. They also started to intentionally exacerbate existing tensions between local tribes on top of bullying and intimidating Ogoni activists. Saro-Wiwa was denied travel, arrested and often refused medical treatment for his heart problem while incarcerated.[3] But Ogoni campaigners sustained their non-violent protests. It came at a cost. Some 2,000 locals were killed, twenty-seven villages destroyed and 80,000 people displaced.[4] But Ogoni campaigners wouldn't shut up. They wouldn't bow.

On 21 May 1994, four conservative Ogoni leaders were beaten and hacked to death. The police authorities suggested that their own people may have killed these leaders because they opposed the Ogoni campaigners' protests against Shell. This appeared to be a ploy to destabilise protesters – typical divide and rule tactics. Armed forces raided local villages, violating people's human rights, and arrested Saro-Wiwa and other suspects.[5] The international community, including Amnesty International, condemned the arrest.

Over the following year, others, from Andrew Rowell's book *Green Backlash* to Channel 4's film *Delta Force*, would cast further doubt on the circumstances surrounding the Ogoni elders' deaths.[6] In addition, Shell was accused in a New York Federal Court of bribing prosecution witnesses to implicate Saro-Wiwa and the other Ogoni activists. They denied the claims and the proceedings are ongoing. In a report into the trial of Ken Saro-Wiwa and others, Michael Birnbaum QC said, 'It is my view that the breaches of fundamental rights are so serious as to arouse grave concern that any trial before this tribunal will be fundamentally flawed and unfair.'[7]

Saro-Wiwa, Saturday Dobee, Nordu Eawo, Daniel Gbooko, Paul Levera, Felix Nuate, Baribor Bera, Barinem Kiobel and John Kpuine were sentenced to death in late October 1995. On 10 November, they were executed by hanging by the Nigerian military regime. They became known as the Ogoni Nine. The execution prompted the then UK Prime Minister John Major to criticise the unjust nature of the trial, verdict, sentence and murder. For many years afterwards, violence against locals continued, as did the extraction of oil at the expense of indigenous people's livelihoods.[8]

* * * * *

I didn't find out about the Ogoni Nine until some fourteen years after I'd failed my driving test, around 2009. I was soon to leave the Stephen Lawrence Charitable Trust, where I had directed education programmes for three years. Ben Amunwa, a campaigner from the environmental justice group Platform, launched the 'Remember Saro-Wiwa' campaign. British-Nigerian artist Sokari Douglas Camp had designed *Battle Bus: Living Memorial for Ken Saro-Wiwa* in 2006, calling attention to ecological violence faced by the Ogoni people.

Amunwa approached the Trust about situating the bus temporarily on the Stephen Lawrence Centre's site and launching an education programme to engage young people in environmental justice.

Platform, founded by Jane Trowell and James Marriott, had always been clear that climate justice was more than just science: it was about people's lives. They acted with urgency. They wanted to tackle the systems that perpetuate violence. Platform had campaigned for many years against some of London's major arts institutions. The British Museum and Tate exhibited goods from colonised countries or continued to receive funding from the fossil fuel companies damaging our environment. These arts institutions also had a poor record of community engagement.

Platform wanted to make the public aware of the web of complicity and interconnectedness between the fossil-fuel companies and seemingly unrelated entities, like the British Museum. Only a handful of these arts organisations control the sector, with no accountability to communities, only their trustees and donors. They were beneficiaries of millions of pounds of public money and fossil-fuel sponsorship, while peddling pilfered commodities, serving a privileged few but with the power to wield unhealthy levels of influence.

At the beginning, Black and brown environmental activists were not a significant part of Platform. Amunwa wanted to change that. He wanted to take Platform out of its comfort zone and bring in more young people who were not white, middle-class, Oxbridge types.[9]

The choice of the Stephen Lawrence Centre as a host for the Battle Bus and the education programme was deliberate. Amunwa connected the systems of oppression that link Lawrence's and Saro-Wiwa's deaths and the universality of police corruption, state violence, and institutional and structural racism. 'The underlying premise was the disposability of Black and brown lives and the mechanisms that maintain that and also benefit from it,' said writer and activist Sai Murray on my *Just Cause* podcast in 2019. It was also a way of reconnecting young Brits to 'the land we [Britain] despoiled' while profiling 'those people who have been most oppressed, [those] whose land has been destroyed'.[10]

I left the Trust before Platform piloted a five-day course at the centre in 2010 called Shake! (later called Voices that Shake!). Created by Murray and poet Zena Edwards, with DJ Eric Soul, Ana Tovey of Chocolate Films, political educator Ed Lewis, Amunwa and Trowell, fourteen 16–25-year-olds attended the pilot that intersected arts, activism, and racial and environmental justice.

I came across Platform again in 2012, when I was working at the Esmée Fairbairn Foundation. Shake! had recruited Farzana Khan to develop and lead the programme, and the course piqued my interest. When I met Farzana and Jane, it was clear that their work did not fit into any of the boxes that people working in philanthropy construct around what constitutes a quality 'so-called' youth provision.

The course technically lasted five days (although it catalysed longer term collaborative work), so my first thought was *what can they achieve in such a limited time?* There were no identifiable outcomes, no exit points to employment, education or training, which I had been institutionalised to believe were the only 'hard' outcomes for youth education projects. Shake! was not a NEET-to-'EET' initiative. This was generally the framing of young people at the time; young people were defined by what they supposedly couldn't do and what they didn't have, more so than their attributes, talents or potential.

By 2012, I had been in philanthropy for three years. Most of the youth programmes shuffled young people into boxes: 'gang affected', 'NEET'. Most did not consider the trauma faced by beneficiaries. Many were race-neutral and not gendered. Most were not legitimately reaching young people with the most need or on the verge of crisis. It was common for these programmes to reform young people by discarding their culture and lived experiences.

Many were formulaic, more concerned with making young people what employers wanted them to be. Those organisations claiming to run leadership programmes were often delivering employability projects, and many were paying young people to participate, replacing genuine relationships with a transactional approach to engagement.

Shake! was led by young people of colour. They were unapologetically political. The Stephen Lawrence and Ken Saro-Wiwa campaigns' spirit seemed to set the tone for their work in seeking systemic change while standing in solidarity with Black, brown, and indigenous activism globally. Shake!'s work was intersectional before the term started trending in the UK's social sector.

They mixed young people from different backgrounds, and it was heavily relational. When environmental issues were not as fashionable as they are today, and even when they became so, there was an over-emphasis on climate change, not climate justice; Shake! was talking about the environment's interconnectedness with social issues from a global perspective. It centred young people with lived experience and used the arts and media platforms to create visions of change.

I didn't see much of this through my first few years working in philanthropy. I am not claiming that I knew of every youth organisation across the UK. Still, I sat in enough meetings to know that the type of issues Shake! was addressing and how they were doing it was not common among most youth programmes and any of the mainstream ones I had come across.

They were not steering young people towards what employers or Russell Group universities wanted them to be. They didn't bow to 'Tony Blair speak'. At this time, most applications from youth organisations started to sound the same, the NEETs, ASBO narrative of negativity, slickly written, with young people defined solely by outcomes with language akin to a government consultation document.

It was bullshit. And I knew it, often because project workers within these major organisations told me what it was really like working within these rigid hierarchal structures. At the time, the philanthropic sector did not come down hard enough on these organisations. Bad practices and ethics were endemic. As a grant-maker, I turned down the blatant. Tried to reform the marginally bad, often with little success.

Voices that Shake! and other social enterprises, like Ruth Ibegbuna's RECLAIM and Whitney Iles's Project 507 shifted the paradigm for youth programmes. RECLAIM reinvigorated campaigning in the social sector and championed working-class youth's voices, particularly those from northern England.

At the same time, 507 was a pioneer of taking a trauma-informed approach to supporting young people. In their own ways, Shake!, RECLAIM and Project 507 each redefined and reimagined youth work. They created the future. Between 2012 and 2018, while Voices that Shake! continued delivering its courses, more campaign-oriented charities emerged. Some were great, and others jumped on the bandwagon. After Obama's first election, in the 2010s, 'community organising' became a buzzword. Social action became an ill-defined must-have for young people. Funders started jumping on it too. However, a common pattern emerged. The larger charities and those with more privileges misappropriated and monetised the work of Shake!, RECLAIM and 507, often without crediting the originators, often by diluting the practice, often by taking away the soul.

Led by Khan, Murray, Edwards, Paula Serafini and Dhelia

Snoussi, Voices that Shake! worked globally, creating and curating many campaigns and events. For example, in its ten-year research report, 'Voices that Shake! – Shake! the System', it points to how its pillars of practice – being trauma-informed, prioritising self-care, connecting the physical to the emotional, race to mental health, using spiritual, movement-based and non-Eurocentric tools to centre the body in the process of healing – were core to supporting a generation of artists and activists.

Some of the core principles included solidarity through shared lived experiences, radical connections to other movements and generations, and honouring ancestors' work, spirit and innovations. 'We would reiterate [that] climate justice and social justice can't be separated in any way,' said Murray on my podcast:

Climate justice, the front line in the UK, is gentrification, it's food deserts in east London, it's lack of access to clean air, it's lack of access to public health or public health being violent spaces for us. So all the infrastructures that make not just life worth living but also dignify us are things that are deeply racialised disproportionately and they mirror a global structuring and then it also comes back to points of resource allocation and extractivism. We have all of this oil and all of these different ways in which we see the same dynamics of this rich country or this rich corporation [it] has all of the resources and that imbalances the rest of the world.

If radical solidarity in charities was rare, in funding it was non-existent. The only philanthropic organisation I came across in the UK at this time that demonstrated radical solidarity anywhere close to Voices that Shake! was Edge Fund. Soon after meeting Farzana, I met Rose Longhurst, a social justice activist and member of the Fund. When I interviewed her for this book, she explained how Edge Fund emerged and influenced giving internationally.

In 2012, a few Network for Social Change members (a group of 'radical philanthropists', which included Patrick Boase) worked with activists and Sophie Pritchard, who had previously managed the Lush Charity Pot, to set up Edge Fund. Edge Fund was established to fund groups fighting injustice and inequality in the UK and Ireland using a power-sharing model of decision-making. As well as attracting attention due to the grassroots campaigns we fund (such as supporting Sisters Uncut, Black Lives Matter UK and Disabled People Against the Cuts in their very early stages), Edge's funding model offers an alternative to normal modes of philanthropic funding.

Edge Fund was designed as a participatory grant-maker before the term was in use. All decisions, from the staffing and communications to the strategy and grant-making, are made by members: people who are actively fighting injustice in their communities. Proposals are received from grassroots groups before being reviewed and decided upon by members and grantees – firstly those with direct experience of the specific issue, then the broader community – upending the notion of 'philanthropist' and 'recipient' and building solidarity amongst diverse communities. One of the aims of Edge Fund was to challenge traditional philanthropic models that are undemocratic, unaccountable and untransparent. As such, an 'Influencing Funders' working group was set up in 2013. When the network for progressive philanthropy, EDGE Funders Alliance, began outreach in Europe in 2015, Edge Fund was invited to participate, and used the space to spread awareness of Edge Fund's alternative funding model.

Several members of EDGE Funders Alliance heard a presentation about Edge Fund's 'democratised funding' model at the same time as they were hearing similar calls for shared decision-making from their grantees. In response, four European foundation members of EDGE Funders Alliance went on to convene a community of activists (including folks from Edge Fund) who went on to found FundAction in 2017 through an elaborate co-design process. Using similar principles and practices to Edge, FundAction is a participatory fund and platform for-and-by European social movements.

The inaugural round of grants that the FundAction community collectively agreed on included FemFund, the first feminist fund in Poland. Established in 2018 to strengthen grassroots activism in a moment of skyrocketing backlash against feminism in the country, the founders, one of whom is a member of FundAction, connected with Edge Fund (amongst others) to inform their grant-making process. Since then, FemFund have evolved the practice of radical philanthropy further, using their approach to build funding practices that promote resilience, solidarity and intersectionality.

FundAction's inaugural round of grants supported

several groups who are not eligible for (or would not seek) funding from elsewhere, a commonality amongst all the organisations highlighted here. For example, one of FundAction's inaugural grants went to Magacin, a social and cultural space in Serbia, that – despite serving a wide range of community members with activities including dance classes – has an informal status that barred it from accessing traditional funding sources. Another grant went to Mwasi Collectif Afroféministe, an association that hosted a summer school for Black womxn in France, where the notion of organising around an Afro-feminist community is sadly considered highly controversial.

Edge Fund supports grassroots organisations often excluded from mainstream philanthropic funding opportunities because they are unregistered or deemed too political. Its funding has supported projects addressing everything from abolishing immigration detention and improving EU migrant rights to initiatives addressing rape culture and land ownership in Scotland. It was also an early supporter of Ubele Initiative, which was at the forefront of resourcing Black charities in the UK after George Floyd's killing, and Sisters Uncut, who led many of the 'Kill the Bill' protests.

Like Edge Fund, Voices that Shake! to me was a feeling, a process, a practice, a way of being, not just an outcome. I didn't understand this back in 2012. I was more concerned about the destinations. But the destination of young participants of Voices that Shake!, as defined by the charity sector, did not define them. It wasn't about jobs, leadership styles, placements. It was about young people's well-being, self-management, their ability to be themselves, true to themselves, and make bold life choices.

This was never a youth programme; its practices extended beyond the confines of a sector. 'You can also start building alternative ecologies outside of the charity system that are much more mutual, that are solidarity economies and actually down to practice equity,' says Khan:

> For example, it might be your housing situation. It might be how you eat. I know a lot of folks, and I'm not just talking about cooperatives and communing, but like if you are rejecting that dynamic, and you are choosing to be in equitable relationships, you're choosing to be in a community, then you have to practise all of this stuff around accountability, loving differently, listening differently. I think it invites us into a radical space. I do see it happening. I do see people wanting to practise that.

While many of its young people went on to achieve impressive outcomes in the arts, in politics, as researchers, as activists and social sector leaders, Voices that Shake! has always resisted attributing participants' success to the course or using their names as a platform to elevate its 'brand'. It did not do the fashionable things to gain funding. In the spirit of Ella Baker, its practitioners made a life, not a career.

* * * * *

During the Interdependence Festival in 2019, academic and writer Luke de Noronha talked about state violence through hostile immigration policies. De Noronha emphasised how you couldn't divorce this issue from the climate crisis:

> [Borders] fix people in space and in law so that they cannot move freely to where wages and conditions are better.
>
> Borders, therefore, are fundamental to capitalism and global order. While companies move their operations freely across borders seeking the cheapest labour and new resources to extract, people are forced to live in the wastelands produced by the destructive forms of development and they are then prevented from moving across international borders to seek better conditions.[11]

The law discriminates against people of colour through immigration policies without considering how Britain damaged their countries of origin. More sinister is how right-wing politicians and press have impressed upon the public that immigration drains public resources, takes jobs away from the British, threatens community cohesion and undermines 'British values'.

The social sector has mirrored the approach taken by the government as described above. You may expect this allegedly more left-leaning sector to do better. But, like the UK government, it fails to recognise the interdependence of our struggles. Many do not operate through a solidarity lens. This is an inherent trait of large arts institutions and heritage organisations too. They are complicit in preserving power, dictating what constitutes valid art, creating narrow Eurocentric standards.

The Global Majority are always visitors. Even if these organisations wanted to be radical, their donors and sponsors would likely try to prevent them from breaking free. This is not a story of being political. It is about equity; it is about being fair, being representative; it is about choice.

If social sector work or the arts are genuine about serving the public, they must cede power. These national institutions, often run by the elite, will never suit everyone's needs if they cannot at the very least show solidarity. The government's approach of single-issue frames is precisely why the social sector needs to be more radical and intersectional. Still, it falls short, with Voices that Shake! and Edge being anomalies rather than the norm.

The organisation Platform aimed to redistribute power. Part of its process was to stand in solidarity with the Saro-Wiwa campaign and cede power to Voices that Shake! Platform's operations, governance and campaigns look different now than they did fifteen years ago. Standing in solidarity is also about our decisions; our power lies in our choices: the newspapers we buy, the institutions we visit, the organisations we donate to and the products we consume.

At the Interdependence Festival, environmental lawyer Tessa Khan said, 'Whether we're fighting for climate justice or economic justice, food sovereignty, people's sovereignty – all of these crises are being driven or underpinned by global institutions, global mobility of capital, global military cooperation, global trade and investment arrangements, and so on.' Khan emphasised the power of international solidarity as a lever of change. She mentioned the Anti-Apartheid Movement and how the international community responded to the calls of the African National Congress (ANC) to impose economic sanctions on South Africa. This of course played a significant part in ending apartheid.[12]

* * * * *

After the Ogoni Nine's deaths, violence from the military and extraction from the multinational corporations continued. In 2009, Shell paid $15.5 million to the victims' families in an out-of-court settlement from legal action brought by Saro-Wiwa's son.[13] But the company denied any responsibility for the deaths of the Ogoni Nine. Years later, key witnesses said that Shell had allegedly bribed them to supply a false testimony that Saro-Wiwa had been involved in the murders of the elders.[14] Shell said such claims were false and without merit.

At the time of the payment, Shell had around ninety oil fields in Nigeria. The company developed some community initiatives in Ogoni, but this was little more than a mask for the devastation it had caused. The plight of Saro-Wiwa is indicative of what had been occurring in many nations across the globe. Our world. One where we are dependent on the labour and struggles of others to lead our lifestyles.

We cannot divorce ourselves from global issues. 'In 2017, 56 upper middle-income countries contributed to 46 per cent of global emissions, while 34 low-income countries, most of them in sub-Sahara Africa, contributed to only 1 per cent of the total. Despite the fact that the latter group hardly contributes to global warming, its countries are likely to be the ones most severely affected by extreme weather events.'[15]

As Luke de Noronha concluded during his speech at the Interdependence Festival:

[The] struggle for a different world, one without borders and walls, would also be one where we learn to respect our environment and to recognise our interdependence with all humans and non-humans. The biosphere is not determined by national borders, and neither should our politics be.

The struggle against the hostile environment is about more than Theresa May's flagship immigration policy or Tory bashing. It's also about the struggle for less hostile environments for all life. Within environmental movements, struggling for a world with no borders really is the only option we have if our goal is to secure the means of life for all of us on this fragile planet – the only one we have.[16]

Maybe, near the start of the new year, we should all pledge our commitment to rebalancing our world by supporting those organisations, individuals or movements who fight for a world beyond borders and recognise that we are interdependent. They realise that what is happening to them will eventually happen to you.

22

Self-determination

Trust in the most impacted communities to determine their own destiny

Bobby is staring, concern written all over his face. The creases in his brows suggest that hope is impossible. But there is something resolute about the way he looks too. His Afro is a near-perfect disc, beard and moustache – like former athlete and activist John Carlos – form a ring the shape of a crown around his pursed lips. Bobby is wearing a dark-coloured long-sleeved shirt with leather trimmings on the collars, breast pockets and shoulder patches.

The shirt is buttoned part way down his chest to reveal what looks like a black string vest. I cannot see the full contours of his face. While his body faces me, at this moment, his head is turned slightly to his left, although not enough to form a complete profile. But I cannot stop staring at him. I am not sure if this is his default look, a brooding expression permanently etched on his face because he'd been through a few things in his thirty-four or so years: jail, shoot-outs, movement building, betrayal, protest, accusations of murder. But his troubled look makes it seem as if he's about to embrace, cry or explode.

Huey is sitting next to Bobby, staring back at him. His gaze not as intense. But his is an almost perfect profile. Huey's Afro is taller and wavier than Bobby's, almost as if it has been blow-dried. Huey's skin is smooth, cheeks puffy, chin sagging, like he has an marshmallow resting in the visible side of his mouth. But his face exudes calm. Somehow, Huey conveys a cross between being traumatised, indifferent, and on the verge of smiling. Like Bobby, his eyebrows are thick, long, deep; they write an unpredictable narrative as they sit above eyes that look like they've been touched with eyeliner.

Like Bobby, he wears a stylish shirt, light in tone, a hint of blue or grey. Like Bobby, I don't know what Huey's thinking, as I catch them at this moment. They don't know what is going to happen next. But I wonder if, in such moments, the two of them are looking at each other in the knowledge that a horrible fate or an enduring legacy is the only possible path in which their relationship will end.

I've never held a stare with anyone quite in that way before. A look of depths. Into depths. In pivotal moments, yes. In 2012, my son had to go into hospital for a procedure to plug a hole that had been leaking excessive blood into his heart two months after his second birthday. The doctors told us it wasn't severe but could cause serious problems later in his life. Better we do something about it now. They call it a heart murmur, which sounds kind of trivial when you think about the term. Heart murmur, not a phrase that terrorises, a phrase that strikes fear.

They wheeled him to the theatre and gave him an anaesthetic. My partner and I watched as, within seconds, his tiny body became limp and he expired temporarily in front of our eyes. The sequence of events is blurry. But it involved, I believe, someone reading us the last rites and a waiver form we had to sign, I guess, absolving the hospital of any blame if anything were to go wrong. I had that stare then. Had that stare through the time he spent in surgery. I was thankful that I didn't lead a life where that stare was an everyday thing, where every moment felt pivotal, life-altering.

None of us can escape it. We all have trauma, some more than others. If you're lucky, you'll have someone who will stare back at you. If you're lucky, this will not be an everyday gaze. But for many, they do not have a choice; joy may not be an emotion they trust. Bobby and Huey had options. They could have walked away. But they chose to confront; it was the only way they felt they could respond to a society where the accumulation of discrimination was traumatising them and their community. Like I could not from my son, they could not look away.

I sit here feeling mildly nervous writing this story because there are many people far better qualified to tell it than me. The pressure mounts. How can I make this story different to what has been said in the past; can I find a new way of telling Bobby's and Huey's story? Not sure I can do it. Can't climb that mountain. But the reality is, I can't stop staring at them. This picture. Was it staged? Are there archives with more pictures of them looking at each other this way? I keep wondering what their stares mean, what it means to me, what it means to all of us.

To some, I'm sure, their story is one of a horrible fate. But, in my eyes, their story is one of an enduring legacy. A legacy enhanced further after the events of 2020.

Bobby Seale and Huey P. Newton co-founded the Black Panther Party in October 1966. They were responding to wide-scale discrimination faced by Black people in America. Seale and Newton started by monitoring police actions. They understood the Californian gun laws and knew they had every right to carry arms to protect their community. So the Panthers patrolled the streets of Oakland to safeguard African American citizens. Whenever they saw the police stopping or harassing a person of colour, they would watch, at times dressed in black leather jackets and berets, armed with twelve-gauge shotguns to ensure that officers were not abusing their powers.

They were overseeing the overseers. It was a direct and visual act of defiance and one that exercised Black people's right to defend themselves on the streets because of the danger posed by the police. The Panthers were unambiguous in their intentions and efforts. As authors Joshua Bloom and Waldo Martin wrote in the book *Black Against Empire*, 'The Panthers' politics of armed self-defence gave them political leverage, forcibly contesting the legitimacy of the American political regime.'[1] A wave of bills and regulations were swiftly passed to tighten gun usage in 1967 and 1968. Imagine, even the National Rifle Association (NRA) was backing gun control.

Although there were shootouts between the Panthers and the police, it was not Huey's or Bobby's intention for these encounters to end in bloodshed. For a country like America, which celebrates war and understands combat and violence as the primary means of order, this Black army was startling, a threat, particularly compared to the peaceful protests of the civil rights movement.

The Panthers recognised the role policing played in reinforcing political power, physically and psychologically, and how they undermined state control by dismantling this. 'Politics is war without bloodshed' and 'war is politics with bloodshed.'[2] But they also understood how policing undermined Black people's power to determine the destiny of the Black community.[3]

While the Panthers' patrols remain a prevailing image and its swift demise persists as a central feature of the mainstream media narrative, the Party's legacy of self-determination extends much further than these accounts.

Influenced by Malcolm X, the Panthers outlined a 'Ten-Point Platform and Program' in October 1966, stating their beliefs and what they wanted for Black communities.[4] These points were deliberately simple and accessible; they wanted freedom, decent housing, an end to police brutality and capitalism, and full employment for Black people, among other things. The Panthers set about tackling these issues by understanding their role as the vanguard of a revolution. They were clear that it will be the people who will initiate the revolution.[5]

Alongside the patrols, Seale and Newton developed sixty-eight community survival programmes. The services included a 'Free Breakfast for Children' programme to prevent malnourishment in school children, understanding that hunger was a significant barrier to kids' learning. They successfully campaigned to get traffic lights installed at a busy intersection in Oakland where children had been run over.[6]

The Panthers developed 'People's Free Food', giving away groceries for those in need. Other programmes included a volunteer bureau, Liberation schools, free clothing, dental care, youth training, nutrition classes, legal advice, employability training, drug/alcohol awareness, disabled people's services, teen council, sports, martial arts, music and dance, free plumbing, and tutoring. All of its services had been grounded in the communities it served.

Seale and Newton designed these services as a political tool to meet the community's immediate needs but not create dependence.

All these programs satisfy the deep needs of the community but they are not solutions to our problems. That is why we call them survival programs, meaning survival pending revolution. We say that the survival program of the Black Panther Party is like the survival kit of a sailor stranded on a raft.

It helps him to sustain himself until he can get completely out of that situation. So the survival programs are not answers or solutions, but they will help us to organize the community around a true analysis and understanding of their situation. When consciousness and understanding is raised to a high level then the community will seize the time and deliver themselves from the boot of their oppressors.[7]

By catering to its communities' immediate needs, the Panthers mobilised political support and will, its survival programmes posing more of a threat to American authorities than the patrols. In 1969, J. Edgar Hoover, Director of the Federal Bureau of Investigation (FBI), said:

> The Breakfast for Children Program (BCP) has been instituted by the BPP (Black Panther Party) in several cities to provide a stable breakfast for ghetto children ... The program has met with some success and has resulted in considerable favorable publicity for BPP ... The resulting publicity tends to portray the BPP in a favorable light and clouds the violent nature of the group and its ultimate aim of insurrection ... and, what is more distressing, provides the BPP with a ready audience composed of highly impressionable youths ... Consequently, the BCP represents the best and most influential activity going for the BPP and, as such, is potentially the greatest threat to efforts by authorities ... to neutralize the BPP and destroy what it stands for.[8]

Hoover believed that the Panthers were the greatest threat to security within the United States.[9] The American authorities did everything they could to destroy the organisation. In 1959, under Hoover's directorship, the FBI created COINTELPRO (COunter INTELligence PROgram), which used illegal tactics to disrupt and destabilise activist groups such as the Black Power, communist, feminist, anti-war, environmental and American Indian movements. COINTELPRO assassinated and falsely imprisoned activists, planted spies, discredited groups, and strategically disrupted the judiciary system to obliterate these activities.

Among those assassinated was twenty-one-year-old Fred Hampton, head of the Illinois chapter of the Panthers. Hoover was determined to avert the rise of what he described as a messiah, someone who could unify and energise the Black Power movement. The FBI planned to carry out an armed raid of Hampton's premises in 1969. An informant drugged Hampton so he would be sedated when the FBI arrived.

The police raided the house after 4 a.m. while Hampton was asleep in his bedroom. They fired almost one hundred rounds of bullets into the house. Ballistics experts would later deduce that only one shot was fired in response by one of the Panthers in the house that night. Hampton and his girl-friend, Deborah Johnson, then almost nine months pregnant, were still alive when the police entered the bedroom. They removed Johnson from the room and shot Hampton twice in the head while he lay unconscious.

The Panthers couldn't survive. Wasn't just state violence. State concessions also served to weaken the Panthers' mobili-sation of its community. In 1969, California poured $5 million into implementing a free school breakfasts programme, which led to twenty-eight other states implementing similar initia-tives. Philanthropists often speak of backing ideas that can scale.

While I won't get into any debates here about attribution or who came up with the idea first, there is some correlation between the Panthers initiating its breakfast programme in 1968 and, soon after, the state commencing a similar scheme. By 2012, free breakfast programmes fed over 13 million American children.[10]

By 1970, the Panthers had offices in over sixty cities. Their annual budget was $1.2 million. At its height, their breakfast programme regularly supported over 20,000 children by 1969, while their newspaper had a circulation of at least 150,000.[11] The *New York Times* published over 1,200 articles on the Panthers in 1970 alone.[12]

According to a top-secret report to US President Richard Nixon, around 43 per cent of young Black people in the United States had a 'great respect' for the Panthers.[13] It had also forged alliances with many non-Black groups, including anti-Vietnam War campaigns and the Young Lords, fighting for Puerto Rican and Latino people's human rights. While the Panthers were anti-colonial, they veered away from anti-white ideologies. Also, by 1968 almost two-thirds of its membership was female. Many Panthers would go on to careers as artists, academics, politicians and non-profit leaders. The Panthers' influence spread globally too.

In July 1967, Stokely Carmichael, leader of the Student Nonviolent Coordinating Committee (SNCC) and, for a brief time, a member of the Panthers, spoke at the Dialectics of Liberation Conference at the Roundhouse in London. Carmichael, known for coining the phrases 'Black Power' and 'institutional racism', preached self-determination instead of legal reform as the means for social change. His presence added impetus to an already active and growing generation of Black activists in England. The British Black Panthers emerged in 1968. Writer Obi Egbuna, Darcus Howe, Linton Kwesi Johnson and Olive Morris led the UK version. Later, Altheia Jones-LeCointe, Farrukh Dhondy and Mala Sen were among the leaders of the Party. The British Panthers classified

Black as a political label to encompass all people of colour facing racial discrimination, not only African diaspora people.

Guided by Jones-LeCointe, the movement grew to 3,000 members while campaigning against policing and racism.[14] In 2020, artist and filmmaker Steve McQueen captured some of the Party's legacy in the film *Mangrove*, which tells the story of the Panthers' role in protesting against the frequent police harassment and raids on Frank Critchlow's Mangrove restaurant in Notting Hill. Members of the Party organised a peaceful protest that erupted into a violent confrontation with and instigated by the police. Nine protestors, known as the Mangrove Nine, were charged.

Some decided to represent themselves, while others sought representation from barrister Ian Macdonald. The accused requested an all-Black jury for the trial and situated the hearing back onto racism within the police. The Mangrove Nine were found not guilty, and it was the first time there had been some admittance of racism in policing, recorded in the judgement. Howe turned the trial against the Mangrove Nine into a trial against the police and won. The Metropolitan Police's assistant commissioner tried to have the judge's statement struck from the record. But it was never withdrawn.

The British Black Panthers disbanded in 1972. But members of the Party created social change in countless spheres. The *Race Today* journal (1973–1988) and the Black People's Day of Action (2 March 1981), when close to 20,000 people marched for justice for the victims and survivors of the New Cross Fire, are both part of the Panthers' legacy. Members of the Party created the International Book Fair of Radical, Black and Third World Books (1982–95). Morris co-founded the Brixton Black Women's Group, the Manchester Black Women's Co-operative, the Black Women's Mutual Aid Group and the Organisation of Women of African and Asian Descent (OWAAD).

Linton Kwesi Johnson's poetry (*Dread Beat An' Blood, Inglan is a Bitch*) documented the Black-British experience while the media work of Dhondy (Commissioning Editor of Channel 4 from 1984 to 1997) opened doors for future generations of Black people.

The US Black Panther Party also inspired the Dalit Panthers, combating caste discrimination in India, and the Brown Berets, a pro-Chicano movement campaigning for farm workers' rights in the US.

Bobby and Huey didn't always agree. When they first met in the early sixties, they allegedly quarrelled over the US government's actions during the Cuban Missile Crisis. They argued again in 1974, allegedly, over the production of a movie about the Panthers. This dispute followed a turbulent period for the Party. Bobby and Huey had spent time behind bars.

Huey was convicted of killing a police officer in 1968, only for the authorities to reverse this decision in 1970. Huey was shot during the altercation. Bobby was imprisoned on slim conspiracy charges to incite a riot at the Democratic National Convention in 1968. He was eventually charged with sixteen counts of contempt of court for frequent outbursts. While in jail, he was also accused of ordering the murders of two Panther members.

In 1973, after his release, Seale unsuccessfully ran for Mayor of Oakland. By this point the Panther leadership, fraught with paranoia and internal conflict, primarily caused by COINTELPRO tactics, had limited its effectiveness. Seale left in 1974, the same year Newton was accused of killing a seventeen-year-old sex worker, Kathleen Smith. Huey went into hiding in Cuba until 1977.

On Newton's return, he stood trial for Smith's murder. After two trials and two deadlocked juries, he won his retrial. But, by this point, the Panthers were no longer a force and the Party finally collapsed in 1982.

In 2020, after the police killed George Floyd, we witnessed the largest anti-racism demonstrations in my adult life. As I spoke to many activists, campaigners, charity leaders and artists for this book, the Black Panthers came up frequently. It had been clear that Black Lives Matter had 'seized the political imagination' at a global level like no Black-led movement since the Panthers. Indeed, it was primarily due to Black Lives Matter and the protests that George Floyd's murderer, Derek Chauvin, was found guilty and anti-racism was so high up on the agenda for the new Biden administration.

The Panthers always advocated for self-determination for Black people as a way of tackling racial injustice. It was attacking white supremacy and capitalism, but it was not trying to harm people.

Self-determination led to the Panthers creating their survival programmes because the state was not meeting Black people's needs. During the COVID-19 outbreak, we witnessed the Panthers' approach to supporting vulnerable young people in footballer Marcus Rashford's campaign to extend free school meals to holidays.

Rashford's advocacy led the government to overturn their policy to halt free food to vulnerable families during holiday periods, resulting in almost £400 million in funding to resolve holiday hunger for pupils.[15] During the early days of the pandemic, we saw many groups mobilise local people to deliver nutritious food to their communities, from Made Up Kitchen in east London to NYC Shut It Down in New York.

In Britain, we witnessed the rise of over 4,000 mutual aid groups. This way of supporting people pre-dates the Panthers but is rooted in Black communities. Many years before the Panthers, the West African tradition called susu, from the Yoruban word 'esusu', was a savings cooperative that enabled close circles of people to pool resources and tend to the sick.

In Jamaica and Trinidad, these savings circles are called 'pardners'; it's called 'sociedad' in the Dominican Republic.[16] Across the globe, poor and immigrant communities have historically found ways to support each other when oppressed or disenfranchised by those in power. Indeed, Black people pioneered credit unions in the UK. The Hornsey Co-operative Credit Union, based initially on the pardner scheme, supported Black people struggling to gain financial support. By 2013, the Hornsey Co-operative's fiftieth anniversary, 371 credit unions had benefited some 1.3 million people.[17]

On 5 June 2020, Eshe Kiama Zuri wrote an article for *Gal-Dem* about mutual aid's Black roots. In the piece, Zuri writes:

White people hate Black mutual aid. That's a fact. Pre-COVID-19, mutual aid was something to shun, something to ignore, something to attack and tear down, especially when run by Black people. UK Mutual Aid was one of the few mutual aid 'named' groups in the UK.

Conversations about it outside of our space always resulted in arguments. The idea of sharing with others, especially when suggested by Black people, came as an attack to people's precious privilege and security. We don't have to think hard to find the reasons why white people dislike seeing Black people organise – not just together, but for the benefit of all groups affected by white (straight, cisgender, non-disabled, middle-class, financially secure, etc.) supremacist society. Nor to see how this dynamic is equally upheld in white activist spaces that thrive on protecting whiteness and pushing academic, theory-heavy, exclusionary politics.[18]

Zuri signed off their Gal-Dem article by saying, 'This one is for the Black women and non-binary people who have carried our communities on their backs with no appreciation. Mutual aid came from you.'[19]

* * * * *

It has been around forty years since the Panthers disbanded. And Black people are still dying in the street at the hands of the state. Did the Panthers contribute to their own downfall? Yes. Internal fighting, ideological differences and patriarchy were among the many problems within the Party. But the right to self-determination remains crucial for groups marginalised by an unfair system. And the system has been significantly more damaging to the oppressed than the Panthers had been to white people.

America has the highest prison population in the world, with over 2.2 million people incarcerated. Thirty-four per cent are Black men. The War on Drugs policies of former US presidents Richard Nixon and Ronald Reagan, the police's stop and search tactics, and the rise of privately owned prisons are among the significant causes of this increase in Black male incarceration.

It is a system that incentivises imprisonment for profit by over-policing Black and brown communities and punishing them for minor offences. Michelle Alexander's seminal text, *The New Jim Crow*, noted that, if trends continue, 'one in three young African American men will serve time in prison.'[20] 'The United States imprisons a larger percentage of its Black population than South Africa did at the height of apartheid.'[21]

As Alexander says in *The New Jim Crow*:

Communities are poor and have failing schools and broken homes not because of their personal failings, but because we've declared war on them, spent billions on building prisons while allowing schools to fail, targeted children in these communities, stopping, searching, frisking them – and the first arrest is typically for some nonviolent minor drug offense, which occurs with equal frequency in middle class white neighbourhoods, but typically goes ignored. We saddle them with criminal records, jail them, then release them to a parallel universe where they are discriminated against for the rest of their lives, locked into permanent second-class status.[22]

Self-determination has always felt so natural to me. Couldn't understand why people were so fearful. Well, I could. Politicians and the mainstream media interpret marginalised communities' right to self-determination as segregationist. Yet racist, homophobic, ableist, and transphobic policies, media coverage and policing produce division in reality. The debate around self-determination in Britain often comes back to, *What about the white working class?*

For many years, the debate has been going on and it recently re-emerged when grime artist Stormzy decided to start a scholarship scheme for Black Cambridge University students, recognising how historically under-represented Black pupils were at Oxbridge and how this was related to race and class.

Sir Bryan Thwaites offered to pay £1 million in tuition fees to disadvantaged white male pupils at Dulwich College and Winchester College. Thwaites cited Stormzy's Cambridge University scholarship as a comparison. However, there was a fundamental difference. The pupils to which Thwaites refers were losing out due to class, not race. By donating strictly to white pupils, he would be rejecting Black working-class pupils due to race.

Am I anything less as a result of any dispossessed community exercising its right to self-determination? Am I anything less if people and communities facing the most disadvantage receive support first? The answer to both questions, for me, is no. In his tribute to the Black Panthers in the *Guardian*, academic Kehinde Andrews said that it's difficult to maintain an organisation through such prominent confrontations, particularly with legal costs continually draining resources.[23] The demise of the Black Panthers taught us this harsh lesson. There can be more peaceful means. But the Panthers also taught us that self-determination is not something to fear.

Self-determination comes in many different forms. Luam Kidane, a researcher, curator and the Director of Movement Partnerships for funder Thousand Currents, explores movement building at the intersections of indigenous governance models, cultural production and articulations of self-determination.

When I interviewed her for this book, she said, 'It's our grandmothers, it's our farmers, our cultural producers, it is us, Africans, who know what the solutions are. The liberation of African peoples and the self-determination of African peoples is the vision and that should be guiding any engagement we have or that we seek.'

Kidane's activism has taken her across the globe, from Africa to Europe, and North America, where she has been an organiser on issues of Black liberation, immigration, economic justice and power building. I was interested to hear what inspires her activism and drives her belief in an alternative to current systems that oppress Black, brown and indigenous people.

She advocates for 'building power from below', centralising decision-making through the community and their experiences and building consensus through dialogue. She emphasises the importance of not over-structuring dialogue but enhancing it; this way, it will always respond to people's needs. Kidane mentioned the Eritrean People's Liberation

Front (EPLF) and its collective vision and practice as an example.

While there was a leadership structure, the community informed this. But she also warned that this shifted once the EPLF, and all other revolutionary movements in Africa who fought for independence, had to translate their movement practices into a state context. Mainstreaming this work into existing state practices meant reducing power-sharing and relying on state-selected individuals to hold power. As a result, across Africa, the monopoly of violence and coercion, the key features of state politics, have overshadowed the revolutionary possibilities that were present during some of the independence movements.

Kidane also mentioned the Abahlali baseMjondolo (AbM) movement of shack-dwellers that started with actions in Durban, South Africa. AbM first occupied land at Kennedy Road. A shack settlement was promised to them by the eThekwini Metropolitan Municipality but was sold to a private buyer in 2005. AbM's protests halted evictions from the site, improved basic services and influenced redevelopment.

The movement has, however, been subject to state violence. Despite this, AbM has expanded from 750 members in 2005 to 100,000 today while leading land occupations and protests in Pietermaritzburg, Cape Town and other localities across South Africa.[24] The movement is led by visions of participatory democracy; the community guides all decisions; it's a non-registered body with leadership that is accountable to each member. Cultural production and song inform its educational work.

'The predominant structures that we have in place,

including the state, and the mechanisms that the state uses to make decisions do not work for the liberation of African peoples,' says Kidane.

So, my interest in indigenous governance models, anti-authoritarian thought and practice is centralised around how can we as African peoples create different mechanisms of building community and accountability that are not punitive or coercive, that don't rely on violence.

So, for that reason, I am particularly interested in the ways in which we've managed both historically but also contemporarily to build these structures as Africans even if they're flawed and only work for a small amount of time and don't work later on, how we're managing to create systems in which horizontalism, in which cooperation, reciprocity and stewardship of the land are the principles that then build the ways in which we interact with each other as people in the community and between communities as well. That is the vision that guides my work. How can we take from what is and continue to build and nurture other ways of being with each other so that we can get out of this cycle of violence, of exploitation, of oppression as African peoples?

The self-determination of local communities across the globe and how they ground their work within their community's experiences, meeting their most immediate needs, shone through some of the best relief efforts during the pandemic in 2020. But the best of these efforts, the ones providing prompt services but not divorcing these efforts from the need to tackle structural issues, resonated most with the Panthers' approach. These were movements and collectives that were providing services pending structural reform.

The Black Panthers are no longer with us. Nor is Huey. Nor are some of the Panthers who remain incarcerated for crimes they likely did not commit. Yet police across the globe continue to kill and criminalise Black people unlawfully and lawfully. How can anyone fear the principles of non-violent self-determination in the face of a state that murders and, more often than not, gets away with it? Moreover, it raises the question about who society commonly defines as criminals.

23

Root causes

*Support campaigns and alliances that safeguard
people and planet by challenging, transforming or
dismantling extractive systems*

'Charity runs out of money. Justice with
systemic change does not.'[1]

STEVE BALLMER,
former CEO, Microsoft

In the 1967 movie *The President's Analyst*, Don Masters –
dark-skinned and stocky, with a silky Afro and a grey,
sleeveless T-shirt with 'Dizzy Gillespie for President' printed
on it – pushes a stacked clothes rail through a busy (what looks
like) New York street. He moves swiftly, burrowing through
the crowd purposefully like a rugby winger once he spots an
opening. Sweat glistening from his forehead and arms, he
is trying to escape from a crime he has just committed. He
had killed an Albanian man. But the crime is part of his job,
working for the United States Central Enquiries Agency.

It appears that Masters has not yet resolved, in his own mind, why he is in this profession. This makes him the perfect undercover agent to vet and recruit a psychiatrist, Dr Sidney Schaefer, to become the President of the United States' analyst.

Schaefer accepts the position, knowing that he will be at the president's call twenty-four hours a day. However, the psychiatrist cannot receive any supervision while in post, and so he quickly starts to unravel under the pressure. With no one to talk to, Schaefer eventually runs away.

Everyone, from the US agencies to the Soviets, is hunting him down. They all want to know the president's secrets. Schaefer is kidnapped and, a Soviet spy, Kropotkin,* and Masters team up to rescue him. To their surprise, The Phone Company (TPC) is Schaefer's abductor.

TPC wants the doctor to convince the president to support a new regulation. They want to inject every US citizen with a receiver and transmitter in their bloodstream so that they can make calls powered by their brains, without wires. TPC wants to substitute personal phone numbers for names, which would become the only form of legal identification. They want the US government to agree to pre-natal insertions of cerebrum communicators and advise that a communication tax levy is paid directly to TPC.

In the end, it turns out that robots are operating the company controlled, it would appear, by the White House.

*

* I wonder if the name is used as a reference to Peter Kropotkin, the Russian socialist, philosopher, anarchist and biologist, and proponent of an economic system based on mutual aid and cooperation.

Bad accents aside, *The President's Analyst* is a menacingly humorous, poignant, satirical gem. The movie speaks to some of the most pervasive systemic problems that exist in society today. These are real. The invasion of our privacy and the control technology has over us – from the way it can manipulate our actions to its ability to create echo chambers that reinforce our most extreme views – is not fiction.

Today, there's ambiguity over the ethical use of technology and the relationship between large tech firms and the government. This is particularly true when we consider the role tech firms play in surveillance and the privacy violations and human biases that infect machine programming.

Brittany Smith, previously Policy Director at research organisation Data & Society, champions diversity, anti-racism and inclusion in tech to build fairer technological systems and solutions. Smith introduced me to the work of Ruha Benjamin, professor of African American studies at Princeton University, founder of the Ida B. Wells Just Data Lab and author of *Race After Technology: Abolitionist Tools for the New Jim Code*.

Benjamin, an advocate for anti-racism in technology and science, explores, among other things, how algorithmic bias and discriminatory design can widen racial and social inequality. In her book *Race After Technology*, for example, Benjamin cites a beauty contest judged by deep-learning programmed robots in which all the winners were white, with only one visibly dark-skinned finalist. She also found that a gang database in the United States comprised 87 per cent Black and Latinx people, many of whom were babies under one.[2]

Smith also introduced me to the work of Joy Buolamwini,

a computer scientist who founded the Algorithmic Justice League (AJL), which works towards equitable and accountable AI. In 2018, Buolamwini worked with AI ethics researcher Timnit Gebru on the *Gender Shades* research, which exposed bias in IBM's and Microsoft's software. They exposed the prejudices prevalent in facial recognition technologies, many of which fail to detect dark-skinned faces.

AJL's work centres and elevates the voices of people most impacted by the harms of machine learning and AI. Gebru, some may remember, was allegedly fired by Google in December 2020 for her paper highlighting the risks of large language models, including environmental costs.* Buolamwini was the subject of the documentary *Coded Bias*, which follows her quest for legislation against algorithmic bias in the United States.

Away from tech, we have also seen the UK government introduce counter-terrorism strategies like Prevent, aimed at preventing, among other things, radicalisation. Unfortunately, this has seemingly forced workers in public bodies – such

---

* 'Large language models like OpenAI's GPT-3 and Google's GShard learn to write human-like text by internalizing billions of examples from the public web. Drawing on sources like ebooks, Wikipedia and social media platforms like Reddit, they make inferences to complete sentences and even whole paragraphs. But a new study jointly published by Google, Apple, Stanford University, OpenAI, the University of California, Berkeley and Northeastern University (https://ai.googleblog.com/2020/12/privacy-considerations-in-large.html) demonstrates the pitfall of this training approach. In it, the co-authors show that large language models can be prompted to show sensitive, private information when fed certain words and phrases.' Source: https://venturebeat.com/2020/12/16/google-apple-and-others-show-large-language-models-trained-on-public-data-expose-personal-information/#:~:text=Large%20language%20models%20like%20OpenAI's,sentences%20and%20even%20whole%20paragraphs.

as schools, health-care providers and social services – into becoming rabid informants, rather than citizens who safeguard those vulnerable to extreme behaviour. Countless innocent people have been wrongly accused of extremist behaviour. According to human rights charity Liberty, in 2017/18, nine out of ten Prevent referrals did not require de-radicalisation action.[3]

The policy has also been accused of racial profiling and turning our society into one that polices each other more than protecting everyone. The efficacy of Prevent is patchy, at best. Moral panics, propaganda and fake news (perpetuated by governments) fuel legislation that increases surveillance and control, promotes distrust and divisions and often diverts us from where the real problems may lie.

For me, in its quirky, slightly disorderly way, *The President's Analyst* spoke more to me about 'tackling root causes' and 'systems change' than the many conversations I've had about these terms over the years working in the social sector. They are two of the most misunderstood and overused phrases. In part, the poor articulation of these terms is why most people are not invested in them as a fundamental part of their giving. The power and wealth and lack of regulation of the Big Tech firms and our government's increased authority to surveil and in doing so avert protest or challenge are two of the biggest threats to democracy. Yet we do not have many, if any, large social sector organisations with the power or independence to provide a combative voice on these issues.

We know that the social sector tends to tackle individual incidences, the immediacy of supporting people in crisis tugs at our hearts. Funding and commissioning also tend to focus on helping individuals or changing their behaviour more than challenging systems; it is a services-led industry, intervening after crisis more than trying to prevent tragedy. This dynamic has been shifting, but not swiftly enough. While journalists and academics have attempted to provide arguments to funders and the public about donating to uncommon social causes, in different ways or at earlier intervention points, our giving hasn't changed radically in years.

The problem is, while you may feel good about helping someone in need, this does not solve the problem long term. To move towards a society that no longer overly relies on crisis services, we need to tackle the root cause of the problem. But this is not as instantly impactful or rewarding as helping an individual with immediate needs. Root cause and systems change have an identity crisis, generally not supported by those tasked with convincing the public to invest in this way.

* * * * *

Too often, when people make a case for systems-change work, they fall into two camps: the over-theorisers and those labelled as conspiracy theorists.

The over-theorisers tend to use a lot of jargon. Most have not faced the sharp end of inadequate systems. They speak in a language more concerned with gaining credibility from the academic community or government than speaking to the masses. They will commission inquiries and papers and host countless round tables to get policymakers to think differently.

These attempts tend to seek ownership through authorship and often exclude people at the edge of our systems.

It's questionable how much change they've made with their work, but they occupy space at events and in places of influence with these theories. They have closer proximity to wealth than the community and position themselves to sway opinions on behalf of ordinary people.

The over-theorisers also tend to suck the life out of these issues, depersonalising them, like a banking experience. This is not only true of systems-change conversations. It is a trait of the social sector more broadly. I remember sitting in a meeting soon after the EU referendum in 2016 discussing the implications of Brexit on the social sector. The discussion had no colour, no candour. I sat silently. Wanted to get out.

I felt like Issa Dee in the TV series *Insecure*. Every time she'd look around while working at the non-profit We Got Y'all, she'd see a sea of careerist faces. She looked around, wondering why everyone lacked passion or had no personal investment in the issues they were attempting to tackle. Why has everyone left their souls at the door? I couldn't understand why these discussions were as routine as filing taxes, as bland as the call-centre-like duck-egg coloured walls surrounding me.

Anyone who's worked in the social sector long enough will have been through these meetings many times. Few offer exact solutions. Actions tend to be more discussion. Meaningless metrics equal success. Evidence is carefully selected to reinforce a position. There's lots of jargon and endless nodding, although you suspect no one is listening. Practically everyone has a fixed ideological position but pretends as if they don't.

In this EU meeting, after sitting silently for a while, I offered that many Black and brown elders also voted to leave, that they were scared too, that this was not just a Black and white, north and south, 'white working class' issue. More nods. But no one shifted their views or their position. They had come in with a fixed agenda and actions, and nothing was going to move them from this. One of the most significant crimes in the social sector lies in its inefficiency, hours of actionless meetings and position(less) papers and reports that go nowhere. It was at times like spending hours burning incense with no scent.

After a while, I started to lose patience and deliberately shouted or barked in these meetings. I had spent many years being compliant, sticking to the rules, waiting my turn, listening. I was sitting around the table with super-smart people who were not honest enough to admit that they were ideologically uncomfortable with these conversations, insecure about their positions, angling for money, didn't like or underestimated me. After a while, I didn't care.

Being friendly, being liked, making others feel comfortable rarely moved the agenda on sufficiently. I spent too much time trying to make others in the room feel comfortable. Their inertia, defensiveness, passive-aggressiveness and use of exclusive language made me uncomfortable. Reality was always on my side. It was personal. And I couldn't sit in those rooms listening to those in power who were wholly divorced from my reality. I'm not sure either method worked. Those blank faces staring at me across these tables – I believe – already had a perception of me, what I was capable of doing and to what degree they would be friendly with me. In the end, it didn't matter. I felt better dropping the facade and, after a while, that was all that mattered.

*

The other camp is more experiential and viewed as emotional, irrational even; they understand the system because they have endured the stern end. Their approach is more anecdotal than based on the extensive stats or elaborate data that the mainstream values as evidence (even though their experiences are valid forms of evidence). They speak in a slightly different tone from the hierarchy in the social sector, with a bit more of an edge, and this sometimes undermines their credibility.

They are easily dismissed by mainstream institutions and, at worst, considered extreme or conspiracy theorists. I could see the dynamics play out in every meeting. I wished those with more emotion had more power. I hoped that those with technical expertise could humble themselves long enough to know that their positions were not under threat. The technical and the emotional are required, but the power balance between the two needed to be addressed.

The technical versus experiential sits at the heart of the battle for the social sector's soul. The technical rejects the experiential; it doesn't value it. In truth, significant social change requires both. But there's distrust on both sides. The technical, over-theorisers, are either ignorant to the possibility that there may be another way of achieving change, in part fuelled by a Eurocentric world-view or the threat that their status will be compromised. They cannot envisage a world where their expertise is decentred. So they co-opt, misappropriate, stay proximate, to hold on to power. The experiential fear exploitation and misappropriation, which, historically, has defined their relationship with power. So, what is the core purpose of the social sector? A remedy for symptoms or a catalyst for tackling root causes? Social services or social transformation? Or both?

After delivering projects, moving from the Stephen Lawrence Charitable Trust to Esmée Fairbairn Foundation in 2009, I accepted the trade-off when I entered philanthropy. At the Trust, the work was satisfying. I worked directly with young people or one step removed from them, still seeing the impact of my work daily. It might be smiles, tears, fear, confusion, joy or apprehension, but young people's emotions were vivid; I understood I was opening doors, enabling young people to learn things far earlier than I had. Every day was different. It could be primary school kids learning literacy through gaming design or university students assembling their portfolios. Yet, by the end of each day, I knew what I had contributed to society. I was happy, sad, exhilarated, exhausted, fulfilled.

In funding, I was further removed from frontline work and issues. I'd go home at 5 p.m. or 5.30 p.m., I didn't deliver work to benefit anyone directly, and there's lots of paperwork. Endless reading. It wasn't easy to tell what I'd done at the end of each day, the impact I might have had. But the potential to influence beyond the few, to alter the flow of funding towards social policy areas or issues neglected by the government, was compelling. I was able to fund work that influenced government policy. Ideas that may not have seen the light of day emerged due to independent funding. I was funding work that tested new approaches to tackling entrenched social issues, nudging the government in a quieter way than direct protest, but with the potential to achieve impact. While delivering projects, I was helping hundreds of young people. But, too often, I was under-resourced and too far away from influencers to shift or disrupt policy. There was resource in funding; there was space, and there was enough independence to influence whole systems, potentially impacting millions of young people. But I couldn't get over why so much of the philanthropic sector resembled a government department and why meetings were inconclusive, why there appeared to be a lack of ambition. No one makes decisions. I just couldn't get over the fact that the two worlds (service delivery and funding), so dependent on each other, were so divorced.

Despite the rhetoric, it felt as if there was no desire to tackle root causes in philanthropy and the mainstream social sector. Everyone appeared uncomfortable addressing their organisational complicity in upholding a system that marginalised so many communities. They somehow wanted to acknowledge problems in the system without looking in the mirror, therefore pointing the finger at other industries while protecting their positions of power. Without looking at the origins of these disparities, and the historical role of the social sector and philanthropy, you will never tackle the roots of the problem.

'At present. the extraction of *real value* from people, communities, nature and the planet is the driving force in our society,' says Nikki Clegg, Director of Operations and Grants at Thirty Percy Foundation. 'Extracting resources, labour, relationships and intelligence for financial gains (for the few) is the dominant purpose of the systems we live in and all of us, our organisations and sectors are intertwined in these systems. This is the underlying root cause that needs to be radically transformed for the future.'

* * * * *

When I went to New York in 2014, I met Rashad Robinson, President of Color of Change, which strengthens Black America's political voice through online organising. Co-founded by CNN host, author, lawyer and serial social entrepreneur Van Jones in September 2005 after Hurricane Katrina, it supported its near 1.1 million members to make the government more accountable and responsive to issues of concern to Black America.

'There lacked an organisation that could quickly capture the energy of these racial justice moments,' Robinson told me at the time. 'We are effective at telling stories, identifying what's happening and being quick enough not to gripe about it three months after the fact. We're in real-time, trying to channel people's anger and frustration into something that is a movement'.

Color of Change recognises that younger people tend to respond on social media, sharing a link, tweeting, and debating online. But they quickly move on. They've done their bit, let it out, shown their frustration to friends, family and the world. What does this achieve? Another issue emerges, and the cycle begins again, another re-tweet, another quote sent. Achieves what? No solution. No sustained action. More vexed people were having vexed conversations. Feelings expressed, but to what end? Color of Change turns this energy into action.

It is perhaps best known for its campaign against the

American Legislative Exchange Council (ALEC). It started campaigning against ALEC in 2011 for what it viewed as ALEC's role in suppressing the African American vote. Early in 2012, seventeen-year-old Trayvon Martin was pursued and shot dead by George Zimmerman. Martin, a Black teen, wearing a hoodie and armed with a packet of Skittles, iced tea and a mobile phone, was perceived as a threat by Zimmerman.

'In a culture that inundates us with images of Black men as criminals, we are continually reminded that something as simple as walking home from the corner store can draw unwanted attention that puts our very lives in danger. Black Americans face racial hatred every day, and far too often that animosity turns violent,' says Robinson.

Zimmerman was eventually found not guilty of second-degree murder and manslaughter. However, the case exposed Florida's Stand Your Ground law, a position that ALEC was fundamental in pushing. In practice, white people who kill Blacks are more likely to be vindicated for their actions under the Stand Your Ground law.[4] As a result, Color of Change ramped up its campaign for ALEC's corporate investors to divest from the organisation.

Color of Change highlighted ALEC's historical involvement in policies that disadvantaged Black and Latino people. It also shifted the emphasis from the individual act (Zimmerman shooting the unarmed Martin) to the policy (Stand Your Ground). Color of Change targeted ALEC's fifteen most recognisable corporate partners and gathered 500,000 signatures to back its campaign.

Several corporates divested, including Coca-Cola, Amazon, Kraft Foods, McDonald's, and Wendy's. The *Guardian* (3 December 2012) reported that ALEC lost close to four hundred state legislators from its membership and over sixty corporations, while its income took a significant tumble.[5] Equally important, the campaign alerted the public to ALEC's actions, which now means it is under constant scrutiny.

Since 2014, Color of Change has grown to over seven million members, exponential growth occurring after George Floyd's death in May 2020. It has campaigned against Facebook, Nike, Hollywood and McDonald's, among other industries and name-brand American products. Color of Change has continued to campaign against the systems and structures that oppress Black people, which can often seem opaque, by clearly identifying and targeting the organisations and policies that cause harm.

* * * * *

I had been in denial for many years. The social sector's bureaucratic tendencies consumed me at the expense of my instincts and emotions. Every breath I took was social justice; it was political, personal, a passion, which was not the case the higher up you went in philanthropy.

If the sector primarily provides services that are an extension of government services, why isn't it funded centrally, like the NHS or the education system? What if the money we gave and independent funding were directed towards more systemic issues? Why are we not gearing all our efforts towards creating the conditions for funding initiatives that tackle root causes?

For a time, I carried around a print-out of an article titled 'Audacious Philanthropy',[6] which appeared in the September/October 2017 edition of the *Harvard Business Review*. I found the article inspiring. The piece explored the critical ingredients required for philanthropists to support transformational change. The authors, Susan Wolf Ditkoff and Abe Grindle, examined fifteen inventions, initiatives, campaigns, developments and movements to find these common components for investments.

Among the case studies were the Anti-Apartheid Movement, 9/11, seat belts, and the fight for marriage equality. The authors found that it generally took over twenty years before these inventions or activities were fully established and mainstreamed. They also discovered that it was important that such innovations or demands could work at scale. The changes arising from these examples may not have been immediate or instantly rewarding, yet they saved millions of lives, mainly by changing systems, the law, policies or power.

This, for me, was the art of philanthropy, a phrase I first read in William Upski Wimsatt's book *No More Prisons*, even though I define it differently from the American author. How can you support work deemed radical today that may become the norm in the future? How can you spot these ideas early enough before they are polluted or diluted for political means while providing long-term, sustained, unrestricted support?

I would always think to myself, what social movement or social innovation would I have wanted to fund? What's the bigger picture? Is it doing any harm? Does it take an intersectional lens? Is it rooted in the most marginalised communities? Will it address the root cause of an issue by tackling systemic problems? Does it offer a vision of hope? It was emotional. Political. But the games I'd have to play to see these ideas funded told me that the thirst for real change in philanthropy was not really there.

We do not think twice about seat belts or public libraries being part of our everyday lives. We probably take them for granted. But, at one point, they were untested, unproven ideas, visions from visionaries. Yet the funding industry (yeah, you know, created by dudes in shiny suits with access to insights from funders; those who re-brand what grassroots organisations deliver, who tell everyone what they're doing wrong, who create a language of exclusion, who create their own markets but are rarely held accountable) is such that theories of change, 'validated', dated conceptions of evaluation and inappropriate uses of randomised controlled trials* become 'must-haves' when assessing applications, at the expense of meaningful risk, systems change, people's lived experiences, their stories, their passion, their understanding of a system that has failed them. Tools are important. But secondary. The idea, the quality of the work should come first. First thought, *Can it make a meaningful difference?* If so, *to what degree can it truly shift the status quo? Can these practices truly lead to institutional changes in policy, behaviours or practice?*

---

* 'The randomised control trial (RCT) is a trial in which subjects are randomly assigned to one of two groups: one (the experimental group) receiving the intervention that is being tested, and the other (the comparison group or control) receiving an alternative (conventional) treatment.' Source: https://emj.bmj.com/content/20/2/164. RCTs are considered the highest standard of effective evaluation of research.

While most of the energy in the social sector comes from grassroots organisations, I met many in grant-making who made it fun and thirsted for structural change; they lived it and breathed it. People like Jenny Oppenheimer, Shane Ryan, Dan Paskins, Rowena Estwick, Mthoko Madonda and others. I love them all because they would get irate, vexed, ill at the status quo and, in their unique ways, were dogged in their beliefs that change could happen.

They cared. Felt guilty if they couldn't do their utmost. Of course, we didn't always agree. I'm sure there were many occasions where they didn't like me or the things I said or did. I'm not doing this as some kind of rap-tune dedication, but I didn't want to leave it to the end of the acknowledgements section because this sits at the heart of the book. For all the criticisms, there are many good people who are trying to change the system from within or move towards a more progressive agenda. As is always the case, however, they are operating in a system that profits from preservation.

* * * * *

I didn't see the point of doing this work if you were not trying to use your privilege to change the system. To accomplish this is complex but not impossible. And rigorous research has been conducted to look at how we achieve long-term systemic change.

'This *can* be achieved through a change in culturally accepted narratives and values, changes to policies, legislations and regulations (or – and arguably much less likely – by the fundamental re-direction of a system's "purpose"),' says Nikki Clegg:

I believe the first two of these are the best leverage points to bringing about the changes we need. Either one can happen before the other and they can often catalyse changes in each other. For example, Ruth Bader Ginsburg [who] recognised that cultural views about gender equality had changed in mainstream narratives and values of American society but that the law had not been amended to reflect these changes. This was a large part of her life's work, working to amend the law to reflect this change in social opinion/values – solidifying the feeling of the time into the rules and structures of the American system – changing it for the long term.

Clegg referred to some of the key ingredients required for transformational change, which include: a shift in power dynamics, key individuals/leadership, viable alternatives to the status quo, crisis points, political and social pressures, social movements or trends, a shift in the mindset of the 'elite' (those with power) and an evidence base of the need/ demand for change and the effectiveness of these potential changes. 'Not one of these things alone will bring about transformational change,' she says, 'it comes from a groundswell of lots of different factors combining to create a tipping point.'

There is no question that if more resources went into systemic solutions, this would make for more effective giving. The problem is, rarely will donating time or resources to systemic change, which could take over twenty years to realise any substantial impact, yield the instant gratification that, for many, plays a significant role in our generosity. If you are far from a social issue, it is the highly emotional moments of injustice and cruelty that may disarm you into action, change your mind, alter your perspective.

Even though many of us can see the logic behind putting more money and resource into systems change, the complexity and time frames related to this approach can be off-putting. So what is the way forward? How best can we communicate the effectiveness of tackling root causes through systems change?

We know that direct action, protests, strikes and die-ins tend to disrupt with greater immediacy than typical charitable work but often put demonstrators in harm's way with the authorities. We also know that divesting from extractive companies and governments will affect their financial bottom lines. Nevertheless, these are non-violent tactics we can all engage in that have proven effective in changing systems. In his book *Counterpower: Making Change Happen*, author Tim Gee analysed various movements worldwide, from the Anti-Apartheid Movement in South Africa to the Arab Spring, from Indian independence to environmental activism.

Gee discovered that the concept of counterpower was vital, with three core pillars underpinning these movements' success:

The first is Idea Counterpower, which can be exercised by challenging accepted truths, refusing to obey and finding new channels of communication. The second is Economic Counterpower, exercised through strikes, boycotts, democratic regulation and ethical consumption. The third is

Physical Counterpower, which can occasionally mean literally fighting back, or, alternatively, nonviolently placing our bodies in the way of injustice.

The classic definition of power is 'the ability for A to get B to do something that B would not otherwise have done.'
Counterpower is the ability of B to remove the power of A ... every government requires people to obey its orders. If enough people refuse to obey those orders, the government cannot govern ... Power is when the few control the many; Counterpower is when the many resist the control of the few.[7]

Some studies suggest that a critical mass of around 25 per cent is enough to tip the balance for what may once have been a minority view.[8] Other studies show the tipping point could be as low as 10 per cent.[9] Either way, it is not in a government's interest for a critical mass of people to share the same views about any element of a failing system because that fundamentally ruptures an economic structure, which inevitably benefits the rich, who tend to be buddies with public officials with power.

We saw this with the poll tax uprisings in 1990. Thatcher's 'Community Charge', which could have had those of low socio-economic status paying as much in tax as a millionaire, sparked protests across the UK. As Gee says in *Counterpower*, 'activists worked out that if just 1 in every 37 people eligible to pay refused to do so, the court system would be clogged up for 17 years.'[10] The protests and non-payments combined with the Conservatives losing seats in the by-election led to the removal of Thatcher and the tax.

At the tail end of 2020, we observed the government's attempt to discredit the racial and climate justice movements, which had started to challenge culturally accepted narratives and values in the UK. The government doubled-down on its efforts to discredit anti-capitalism, the Black Lives Matter movement, critical race theory, the decolonising movement, climate justice activism and social sector campaigning. These various struggles against an unjust economic, social and political system had started to converge.

In short, people began to recognise how our problems were linked. No UK government wants a conflict like the poll tax uprising, where so many people voiced their opinions, disobeyed the law and forced political change. But, in 2020, we started to see embers of protest that shifted from more passive acts of giving towards, at least, a greater drive towards direct action. Counterpower challenges the narrative and disrupts the economy.

While *Counterpower* focuses on movements and campaigns that challenge the system outside of our established institutions, some organisations or collectives try to effect profound change within our systems. This is where a scalable solution is created, involving a cast of characters within and outside the system, to change policies, practices or behaviours.

One such example is contextual safeguarding, pioneered by Professor Carlene Firmin. At present, our child-protection systems tend to recognise abuse through the prism of a parent or guardian's relationship to the child. However, the system fails to protect children and young people in the broader context, such as their environment, peers, movement outside the home, social media or bullying outside the school gates. As Firmin told me when she appeared on my *Just Cause* podcast in 2019, much of what happens in these spaces is out of parents' control. These are the places where young people could be subject to abuse and exploitation. In this context, there may be no problems between a parent and child.

However, an older sibling may be the carer of that child. The older sibling could have been groomed into selling drugs due to an abusive relationship with a dealer. The system will not tend to intervene until a point where it's likely too late because it doesn't account for this context. Under Firmin's model, the local authorities would understand the broader framework to prevent children and young people from getting into trouble in the first place.

The spaces that young people occupy where they are potentially at risk of abuse are often policed. Young people receive little protection and are often perceived as anti-social, gang members, a threat. The general public may not view them as vulnerable children, Firmin said to me.

Firmin works through existing systems and agencies, local authorities and charities to create a contextual safeguarding model that enables services to move from interventions to prevention. Her model moves from an existing system that almost solely assesses parents' capacity to protect their children towards a community's capacity to safeguard children. It's a shift away from people within communities informing on young people to one that enhances everyone's ability to protect them.

Firmin's work was initially informed by the experiences of gang-affected girls and the fact that many of the services working with 'at risk' young people did not take a gendered approach. In working with, interviewing and studying these young women's real-life stories, Firmin started to understand the complexity of a system that wasn't protecting them. She also understood that a single organisation could not deliver contextual safeguarding and that it would take multiple agencies working collectively and effectively to implement at scale.

Firmin told me many stories that illustrated how easy it is for vulnerable young people to fall through the cracks in our current system, yet how contextual safeguarding could be an effective alternative. She told me about a mother with physical and learning disabilities whose son brought girls back to her house. The mother was being threatened with eviction because it was suspected that the girls were sexually exploited. Instead of evicting her, as is often the case in similar scenarios, the local partnership installed CCTV and lighting near her property to identify the perpetrators of the alleged exploitation.

The partnership worked with local schools to determine who the leaders and followers were. They provided diversionary activities for the followers during the times they usually went to the house. The abuse stopped occurring; the mother retained her home, the survivors found support, and the key assailants were identified.

It wasn't a case where the authorities shifted the mother and, likely, the problems to another area. It's all about dealing with risk outside of the home and other places young people may occupy and creating conditions that 'make the environment more hostile to abuse, and what we've got at the moment is environments that are hostile to our young people'.

Firmin is currently implementing contextual safeguarding in ten local authorities, with many more on the waiting list. She also supports over 8,000 practitioners across the UK. Her work is 'rewriting the rules of child protection', offering a solution to many of the problems we see on our newspapers' front pages, from county lines to knife crime, from peer-to-peer abuse to paedophile rackets. The work, which is not direct service delivery, may not be as touching as reading about child abuse. Still, it has the potential to create systemic change that means we will not see as many of those heart-wrenching headlines about abused children on our front pages.

Firmin's work offers a vision of a better, more effective system. One that, like seat belts, will save many lives. For me, her work moves us towards a more harmonious, inter-generational, community-based and culturally aligned society. She is creating a highly implementable and realistic alternative that recognises and harnesses the good that lies within people and the care we have for our communities. I am absolutely convinced that child protection will, eventually, be delivered through a contextual safeguarding lens, nationally.

Whether it is campaigning from the outside in, trying to get a critical mass to overturn bad policies or an organisation operating from the inside out, transforming systems is one of the strongest characteristics of good giving.

* * * * *

When *The President's Analyst* came out in 1967, it was a flop. The movie became a cult classic many years later. Systems change is similar. Because it fundamentally ruptures what we think is the truth, it can appear to be scary. But this type of giving tends to leave a longer legacy. Sometimes these things take time to marinate, like the difference between the soft texture my mum achieves with her rice 'n' peas by letting the kidney beans soak overnight to my dampened version using tinned rice and beans. Investing in ideas that challenge convention and confront some of our truths is an art. The art of philanthropy. But it may also be the difference between instant gratification and a legacy of giving that endures beyond our lives.

24

Abundance

Heed the ideas, innovations and joy generated in under-served communities

'Our communities are abundant.'

Immy Kaur, 2020

Before there was philanthropy, there was reggae. During my time as a reggae journalist, I was only a few yards away from a fatal shooting; I once had to go into hiding, I survived threats, police harassment, and hearing about many people I'd interviewed dying prematurely. Most of the items I wrote were features and reviews, not scandalous news items. But in reggae, with more drama per minute than a soap opera, many of these artists personified Jamaica's ghetto truths: the good, the bad and the ugly, the expansive, the creative, the boundless and the joy. Later, I realised that there were similarities between community innovation and reggae music. I also realised that both are still largely misunderstood.

*

I started writing about reggae, well, primarily dancehall music, in 1995. It wasn't a good time for the genre. A few years earlier, dancehall, the spoken word version of reggae, looked set to follow hip-hop into the mainstream. 'Big, dutty, stinkin'' Shabba Ranks was a major star, taking his gruff voice and wild, thrusting hips near the top of the Billboard charts. It was the first time that reggae had had a global superstar since Bob Marley died in 1981.

But Shabba was the antithesis of Marley. Where Marley sang with sweet tones, Shabba's voice was coarse like a revved-up Harley Davidson. Marley spoke about unity, Shabba chatted about sex. Marley was pretty. Shabba was, well, Shabba. Marley's talent was evident, from the clarity of his verses and politics to melodies that enchanted the world. Shabba's tended to be all show, with outrageously baggy and extravagant costumes. Marley's music has stood the test of time, while Shabba's tended to hit the spot for a particular moment.

Shabba couldn't compete. But his rise was remarkable nonetheless because, on paper, he had none of the hallmarks for international pop success. But he understood his strengths. He understood that he wasn't the prettiest, so he dared to boast about his sexual prowess. His voice was deep but dextrous, but he didn't shift away from his comfort zone by trying to sing more than chat.

And he knew how to make a memorable tune. If you're not Jamaican, you may not understand every line, but you'd remember the hook, you'd get the point, you'd marvel at how he'd ride the rhythm. Shabba and dancehall's world came tumbling down when he defended Buju Banton's homophobic track 'Boom Bye Bye' on popular culture programme *The Word* in 1992.* The incident exposed the prevalence of homophobia in dancehall; the genre expired and, with it, any hope it had of growing into a popular art form.

By 1995, dancehall was trying to heal, its recovery led by – in part – underground rivals Bounty Killer and Beenie Man. Over the years, I would interview them on multiple occasions. I admired their work ethic, ceaseless creativity, and willingness to go on stage and battle each other with no concern for reputation, safety or defeat. During the first lockdown, the two came together in a staged sound clash as part of music producers Swizz Beatz's and Timbaland's Verzuz series.

Beenie Man, with his broad, cheeky grin, sunken nose and innocent eyes, still had the look of a mischievous child at forty-six, the type that could cheat in an exam and get away with it, the kind you couldn't catch when you played 'it' in the playground. Bounty Killer was the opposite. He never looked like the type who would indulge in any tomfoolery. His face was full of creases and menace. Permanently vexed.

For just over an hour, DJs Richie D and Kurt Riley played bits of twenty tunes apiece, with Bounty and Beenie providing hilarious commentary, improvised freestyles and chatting over their hits to see who's the best. Bounty Killer, hair

---

* Buju Banton wrote 'Boom Bye Bye' as a sixteen-year-old and has since renounced it. While serving time in a US prison, he said: 'I recognise that the song has caused much pain ... I am determined to put this song in the past and continue moving forward as an artist and as a man. I affirm once and for all that everyone has the right to live as they so choose.' Source: https://www.theguardian.com/music/2020/jul/02/every-black-man-have-to-fight-buju-banton-on-prison-and-liberation.

cane-rowed, wearing a tight black and gold Fendi suit jacket, convulsed throughout, arms, elbows, head flashing manically in different directions; even in happiness, he looked strained. Beenie Man wore shiny Gucci trousers and a 'Team Beenie #oneking' T-shirt. Almost half a million people tuned in, including Rihanna, rapper Busta Rhymes, cricketer Chris Gayle, Jamaican Prime Minister Andrew Holness and model Jourdan Dunn.

They watched Bounty's adlibs, Beenie chase the police away ('We have five hundred thousand people watching, do you wanna be that guy?'). Dancehall music was trending again – a timely reminder of the joy and innovation that emerges from the streets of Jamaica. Dancehall exposes the truths of society and how art and real-life intersect. But it is also a tale of how the livelihoods of Black, brown and indigenous people are often misunderstood, maligned, dismissed, spoken for, silenced.

Dancehall is an expression of the abundance that lies in low-or-no-income communities across the globe. A key characteristic of giving should be to heed the abundance that lies in these communities, more so than the images of pain and dependency and negativity perpetuated by large, mainstream institutions.

* * * * *

The first known DJ was Count Matchuki. He started as a 'selector' (Jamaican term for a disc jockey or someone who selects records on radio or in clubs) on Tom Wong's Tom the Great Sebastian sound system in 1950. Duke Vin, the man who introduced sound system culture to Britain in 1954, was also a selector for Tom.

Matchuki, heavily influenced by American R&B DJs, introduced each track with jive-talking before playing a tune. He added quips, adlibs, rhymes and 'peps' (clicking sounds close to the mic, a bit like beatboxing). His rhythmical spoken word kept the crowd joyous if a record wasn't eliciting much of a response.[1]

In Jamaica, rappers or emcees are known as DJs because they served the dual function of selecting the records and entertaining the crowd with rhymes. King Stitt was the next pioneering DJ who started toasting (another Jamaican term for DJing) for Coxsone Dodd in 1957.

U-Roy was the first star DJ. By 1969, DJs had started to appear on records. U-Roy was 'voicing' and chatting over old productions by Jamaican producer Duke Reid. Unlike Matchuki and Stitt, U-Roy, among others, shifted away from US-styled chatting, his voice reflecting the cadence and language of the Jamaican ghettos.[2] Listening to his tracks, like those of his peer Dennis Alcapone, was like overhearing stories from locals chatting on the street about everyday life, personal issues and local politics.

Fans of more melodic forms of reggae, like rocksteady and ska, turned their noses up at DJ music. They thought it was a fad and did not value it as much as the records with vocalists. DJ music's relationship to reggae was akin to draughts' affiliation to chess.

Sound system operator, engineer and producer King Tubby created the ideal rhythmical backdrop for DJs. Tubby transformed old Duke Reid tunes by fading out the vocals and radicalising these instrumentals by echoing guitar segments on the tracks and amplifying the drum and the bass, creating a remodelled but harder version. Tubby may have invented the remix. Soon, practically every track released in Jamaica by the early seventies featured a dubbed-up instrumental 'version' on its B-side.

These outlandish instrumentals proved popular in the clubs and dancehalls. It was also cost-effective. Producers created two tunes for the price of one; the original recorded with the artist and a band, and a remixed version by the studio engineer. The 'versions', complete with rimshots, slide faders, delay echoes, phasing, outrageous drum and basslines, rippling guitar stabs, haunting horn riffs, and throbbing organs, proved ripe for the DJs too – the altered, harsher sound providing ample space for a DJ to toast over. A selector could play a dub version for a lengthy period in the dancehalls while a DJ created many rhymes over the one 'riddim'.

The genre evolved further during the seventies. This was a period when political warfare between Michael Manley's lefty People's National Party and Edward Seaga's right-wing Jamaica Labour Party came to a head. The two leaders employed local 'dons' (gangsters) and their posses to carry out violent acts against each other.

The 1980 election resulted in 844 deaths in a country with just over two million people.[3] Throughout this time, reggae music, notably roots, was a voice of unity. With his bejewelled red, gold and green teeth and extravagant attire, Big Youth was the dancehall star, using his sing-jaying (singing combined with DJing or rapping) style while chanting his Rastafarian beliefs. DJ music flirted with international success in the late seventies but never took off.

By the early eighties, things changed again. Marley died, Jamaica's economy was catastrophic, the local 'dons' – once empowered but now discarded by politicians after the 1980 elections – started trading crack cocaine, the major record labels lost interest in reggae, and the continued hangover from the political violence forced many musicians to flee the country.

DJ music evolved into dancehall around the late seventies and early eighties. If roots had global appeal, dancehall was local. Artists were not talking about the trials and tribulations of ghetto life much any more. Instead, dancehall became pure escapism, reflecting the need for locals to get away from their everyday struggles. Slackness came into vogue. With little money available, producers continued recycling old songs, with a steady stream of DJ tunes about sex, weed and guns.

In England, Saxon Studio, a south-east London-based sound system, unleashed a squad of artists who influenced contemporary Black and urban music in the UK. Peter King popularised the fast-style DJing, Papa Levi revived conscious lyrics in dancehall with 'Mi God Mi King', Tippa Irie hit the national charts with 'Hello Darling', Smiley Culture reflected the experiences of Black people with the Met in 'Police Officer' while Maxi Priest would go on to become one of the biggest reggae stars globally.

In Jamaica, slackness continued to dominate and dancehall remained an outcast until late 1984. Then, Wayne Smith produced a riddim based on a pattern on a Casio MT-40 keyboard, allegedly based on David Bowie's 'Hang on to Yourself'. Smith approached producer King Jammy, who slowed the riddim down, added a piano and some claps, and in 1985 unleashed the song 'Under Mi Sleng Teng'.

The track became the first digital dancehall track. Ragga was born. Jammy's method for producing tracks proved cost-effective. It was far cheaper for a producer to create music using this method or recreate old tracks digitally than it was to hire a band. Jammy and the many producers that followed knocked out hundreds of tunes, bringing in loads of artists to record different versions on the same riddim.

The digital sound was ideal for DJs. The sound was synthetic, unfussy and abrupt. DJs had to work hard on these stripped-down instrumentals to create palatable tunes. But the DJs – what they said, how they said it, how creative they could be – became stars, more popular than the singers. Unlike the DJs who were only famous for brief periods in the past, the new DJs carved longer careers.

Moreover, the digital development enabled producers to create multiple tunes from one riddim. For example, the pummelling 'Sleng Teng' riddim produced over 450 tracks. The 'Stalag' riddim (named after the World War II movie *Stalag 17*), originally produced by Winston Riley in 1973, generated close to three hundred tracks. Among them, classic dancehall hits like Sister Nancy's 'Bam Bam' and Tenor Saw's 'Ring the Alarm' and tracks by Jay-Z and Lauryn Hill.

Ragga peaked commercially in the early nineties. Shabba Ranks, as mentioned, became the most prominent international reggae star since Marley, winning two Grammy awards. Major labels raided Jamaica of its leading dancehall artists, but what followed was a severe dilution of the genre.

We saw countless collaborations with rappers, plenty of dancehall tunes over R&B beats and some artists marketed as the new Marley; the major labels did everything but present dancehall in its original form. A shame. After Shabba's appearance on *The Word*, the labels abandoned dancehall as quickly as the Jamaican politicians ditched the local 'dons'.

Ragga wasn't dead and buried, though. Through the early to mid-nineties, artists such as Tony Rebel and Garnett Silk brought roots back to dancehall. Buju Banton converted to Rastafarianism and dancehall shifted from a *for-the-moment* genre to one that legitimately produced enduring classics. Dancehall mirrored the shift in hip-hop almost a decade earlier, when Public Enemy and Rakim brought greater depth and skill to rap music, altering it from a singles market to one with high-quality albums that stood the test of time. Similarly, Buju, Sizzla and others released albums that gave dancehall a level of credibility and permanence in the pantheon of classic reggae we had not seen previously.

Further commercial success followed, with Beenie Man and Sean Paul showing that a harder dancehall sound could transcend Jamaica. Then, Damian Marley took the roots and dancehall (R&D) sound to its commercially credible apex with *Welcome to Jamrock* in 2005. More recently, we see dancehall's influence on Afrobeats and grime, and impersonations from pop artists like Beyoncé and Drake.

* * * * *

I've fast-tracked dancehall's piece of history somewhat. There's more to say, more detail, more nuance than I can give space to here. But it is a vital history that tells a story of ghetto people's lives, with songs that are often misconstrued. This is so true when it comes to innovation and social justice too.

Dancehall emerged from a unique set of circumstances – poverty driven by colonisation, political violence, drugs, American political interference – and a spirit of resistance to these episodes that inspired its creation. It started from wanting to have fun, escape and speak to local people's lifestyles without the resource or money to do so. Even when it carved a space for itself commercially, it was denigrated, manipulated, reduced, neglected, diluted, mimicked. But while the impact of dancehall is now global, the circumstances that produced it have not gone away. DJs tend to be loyal to their local fanbase. When these artists face criticism for their lyrics or supposedly 'selling out', they rarely take a commercial pathway. For better or worse, the reputation of their peers on the ground is more important than fame. This has been a gift and a curse. These artists are the personification of poor people's struggles, speak truth to power and for many, how they represent their communities is more important than global recognition.

The music comes from pain and poverty, but it is abundant and does not pathologise despite its faults. Unlike many rappers who use their wealth to escape the ghetto and the danger it brings, often at the expense of their artistry, dancehall artists stay relevant because they remain in the same circles.

The curse, of course, is that they continue to place themselves in danger, which, for many, has led to fatal consequences. That aside, dancehall's story symbolically provides many lessons about the abundance and innovation that emerge from poverty.

*

Regenerative. One need only look to the history of slavery to know that Black people invented their languages and used poetry, storytelling and lyricism as a way of surviving, educating, entertaining, communicating and preserving their well-being. Spoken word – the DJs' language – is part of a tradition that goes back further than the 1950s, when Count Matchuki first adlibbed and 'pepped' in smoky dancehalls.

These artists were channelling the heart of Jamaican culture, making something from nothing. When you think of community innovators, their work is rooted in the experience of their neighbours and peers. Like dancehall, they never inherited any money to initiate their work. Like dancehall, at their core, they recycle, recreate and regenerate with what little resource they have. This is not a story of expensive PowerPoints or studios, innovators or artists with the luxury of time to create or record, staff recruited or musicians imported from across the globe, or sizeable grants or financial advances.

This is a story of DJs chatting over old tunes, building on the past. It's a story of engineers and producers remixing old songs but creating versions for different audiences. It was about taking a tune, creating two anchor versions, a DJ side and an instrumental and then getting an army of singers and DJs to record their versions. For every riddim produced, there were usually ten or more other versions on the market. This ethos of being regenerative sits at the heart of community innovation but is all too often misunderstood by those with the power to decide whether they 'deserve' resourcing or not.

*

Curb Cut Effect. In dancehall, you have a genre that emerged from a tiny plantation nation and set the foundation for rap music and much of what we see in dance music today. Like a lot of community innovation, it may not – on the surface – appear relevant to the masses, but creativity that emerges from the grassroots often forecasts everyone's future.

DJ Kool Herc is acknowledged by many as the founder of rap. As a twelve-year-old, he emigrated with his parents from Jamaica to New York. In 1973, he set up a sound system, which took many of the elements from dancehall.[4] Herc isolated the music breaks on tracks and prolonged the beats and percussion. He also hired an emcee, Coke La Rock, to rhyme during these breaks.

Rap music and hip-hop have become among the most significant cultural developments globally in the last fifty years. King Tubby's 'versions' pre-date remixing and much of what became known as dance music. Peter King's fast-style chatting is a precursor to jungle, UK garage and grime emceeing. Dancehall and dub innovators very much shaped the climate of contemporary electronic and spoken word music. One need only read about the civil rights movement and its influence on feminism, LGBTQ+ activism and migrant rights to know that some of the inventions that emerge from the grassroots, which we may not understand or indeed may fear, can influence and have a positive impact across the globe.

FUBU. I must thank curator and writer Aliyah Hasinah for this. While in discussion with Immy Kaur at the Department of Dreams festival in 2020, I spoke about the link between

dancehall and philanthropy. Aliyah referred to the key principle of dancehall as FUBU (For Us, By Us), referring to a
US Black-owned clothing company founded in the nineties.

Aliyah was correct. Dancehall was a product of and produced for its environment. It didn't have an international
audience in mind. It wasn't trying to be politically correct.
The artists created music for local people, for the dancehalls,
for money, for survival. They wanted local people living
in challenging times to go wild, have fun, forget, refuel,
'shock-out', 'bruk wine'. It wasn't seeking validity from the
middle classes. It was brash, confident, unburdened by the
white gaze.

The artists took everything that was going outside their
yards, at work, incidents with neighbours, encounters with
strangers, the language, the stories. Some of it was raw. Some
of it was harsh. Some of it too X-rated. Some of it violent,
sexist and homophobic. It wasn't all good. It wasn't all bad.

When activists speak of the atrocities caused by the British
in the past, people with power, often those that create the
culture wars to divide and rule, say it was the sign of those
times. When it happens now, those same people will say it's
a few rotten apples. Dancehall, often criticised, was also of
its time, of its place, and a lot less dangerous than the history
our government is so eager to protect.

Our systems of oppression are complex. The solutions are
too. Community innovation will be messy; it takes time,
cohesion, consensus, conflict, inter-generationality, failure,
different methods, lived experiences, persistence, mourn-
ing. It's not a simple process, so we shouldn't view it in
narrow terms.

Imagination. Tudor Rose nightclub in Southall was always a bit of a fabled venue. I went to see Beenie Man there some time in the late nineties. There were rumours that the 'King of Dancehall' would not get his full performance fee. I was getting calls throughout much of the day about it. I went anyway, half expecting Beenie Man not to show. But late into the night, Beenie emerged on stage with a DJ.

Allegedly Beenie was being pressured into performing. Beenie was not his usual animated self. But he knocked out a forty-five-minute show. However, what I found remarkable was that his DJ used only about half a dozen riddim tracks (instrumentals) all night. This performance was not your usual staged set, with a band or a DJ lining up Beenie's hit records. Beenie essentially sang his hits and created several tunes out of each riddim.

I saw Capleton do the same thing at a club in north London. Again, there were rumours that he might not show up. It wasn't until after midnight that he finally took to the stage, like Beenie, with no band, just a DJ. Capleton ran through his hits backed by a handful of riddims. He concocted numerous tunes from the riddims and put on one of the best shows I have ever seen. A friend of mine fainted, such was Capleton's ability to excite a crowd with little or no resource. I will forever remember these shows because they demonstrated how these artists could improvise and create something from nothing.

In my time working in the social sector, it has never failed to amaze me how brilliant community organisers are, particularly youth workers, at creating something from nothing.

Their work and often the dire circumstances in which they have to operate dictates that they have to think instinctively, operating between experience, intelligence and intuition to thrive.

Ideas creators as the ideas selectors.* If you want to harness these ideas, it's best to support those closest to the designs of the ideas. On multiple occasions, we saw how major record labels tried to invest in dancehall to change it. They tried to shift the genre's conception into something they felt an international audience could understand without having faith in what the music could achieve in its raw form.

The intermediaries didn't understand it; they interpreted it so that they felt it would be comprehensible to others and, ultimately, faced little or no consequence for mismanaging many artists' careers. I think Adam Grant in the book *Originals* said that the best idea selectors are the idea generators. This is the case with dancehall.

Take Bounty Killer as an example. He was a master of reinvention. While he remained a hardcore DJ, maintaining his standing as the 'Poor People's Governor', he also enjoyed international success with No Doubt (Grammy award-winning 'Hey Baby') and The Fugees ('Hip-Hopera'). His album *My Xperience* purportedly shifted over 250,000 copies.

Yet his legacy remains as much about the many artists he has discovered or nurtured. This includes Cham ('Ghetto Story' with Alicia Keys was a Hot-100 hit in America),

---

* This was one of the key takeaways from Adam Grant's book *Originals: How Non-Conformists Move the World* (WH Allen, 2017).

Elephant Man (two Hot-100 hits), Mavado (he has recorded with Nicki Minaj, DJ Khaled among others) and Vybz Kartel (the leading dancehall DJ of the last decade). I mentioned earlier Saxon Studio and the artists they produced. Through much of Jamaica, you will find artists and producers who have achieved similar levels of talent generation. You need to invest in the ideas creators as ideas selectors. What if we were to do the same in the social sector?

* * * * *

We don't know how much damage mainstream philanthropy has caused by failing to invest in the innovation, creativity and best ideas within communities – the visions that could have been manifested had they been visible, trusted and nurtured. In music, the major labels continue to profit, while the dancehall scene has been perishing. In philanthropy, the impact is opaque. It's easier for me to quantify that damage in music because there is evidence for us to see. This is more difficult to measure in philanthropy without trawling through the rejections by funders of work that would later prove prophetic.

There are so many ideas that lie within communities that could change the world. Dub poet Mutabaruka once said to me that the big labels separate culture from music. This is often the case in philanthropy, reducing and institutionalising community innovation into a language it seeks to own and monetise.

Often, richness and innovation are lost in translation because those tasked with translating it fail to understand it. 'You can only give agency to innovation if you understand who the innovators are,' says Baljeet Sandhu. 'You can only understand that they are innovators if you respect that they are knowledge producers.'

Jamaican-British sociologist Stuart Hall suggested that people's identities will be a complex hybridity and the Caribbean is the home of it. That may be why dancehall could morph into anything it damn well pleased. It achieved success in spite of the system, not because of it. Imagine if it had had the right backing from commercial partners.

Imagine if community innovation had appropriate support from business or philanthropy too. Imagine if investors recognised our culture's richness and solutions and put aside their desire to create dependency from pain? Community innovation at its best can be, like dancehall, an example of the beauty of hybridity. You may not fully understand it, but only judge after you hear all sides of the story, not solely through the prism of the media or your close network of friends. Find out more. Get closer. Listen intently to those making the music. Why? Because the people in under-served communities are not a genre or a sub-genre. They are the music.

25

Outsider within

*Centre the anti-racist and intersectional approaches
of Black womxn*

'If we're building from the place of the most
acute marginalisation, and I know it sounds
fluffy, but if they win, we win. If I build it around
me, even though I'm subjected to so many
intersecting oppressions, I am not going to
automatically attend to the needs of someone
who is trans because I never had my right to be
in this gendered body questioned. If I have it
embedded in my own needs, I don't have to think
about access in the same way, as someone for
whom mobility, the way our systems are set up is
a physical barrier. If we start to build from that
place, we think about accountability differently,
we resource differently, we think about how
we do our business differently. We think about
how we construct relationships differently. We
start to think about transformation not just as
individual benefit, but as individual labour, then
as collective labour.'

MARAI LARASI, 2020

The silencing continues. Erasure continues. I thought about this a lot as the fortieth anniversary of the Black People's Day of Action approached on 2 March 2021. The Day of Action was a demonstration of 20,000 people over the New Cross Fire, which caused the deaths of thirteen young Black people on 18 January 1981. I kept thinking about Yvonne Ruddock, celebrating her sixteenth birthday that night, who perished, and that she was six months younger than Prime Minister Boris Johnson.

I thought about how the fire, allegedly deliberately started and considered a racist attack by the local community, attracted little to no attention from the mainstream press. How the police swiftly dismissed and ruled out foul play, how disposable these Black bodies had been to Britain and how haunting it was for many Black kids growing up at the time feeling that this country did not have your back.

Then I thought about Boris Johnson and how he had risen to become the Mayor of London and then Prime Minister despite a history of what could be considered racist, sexist, homophobic, anti-working-class and Islamophobic remarks. How he peddled lies to get a Brexit deal done, and how he had somehow risen to lead Britain poorly during the worst public health crisis since World War II.

The way Britain is centred is wrong. A white, patriarchal, elite, hetero-positioned Britain will not benefit many people; it will only create rules and conditions to serve what it sees in the mirror. This isn't fake news. They have created a facade about preserving British identity to mask their cold-blooded desire to protect their wealth. By doing so, the elite upholds a society that does not benefit Black or brown or disabled people, women, the working classes, the middle-classes from working-class backgrounds, LGBTQ+ communities, young people or older people.

I start writing, trying to find the right tone, but my cramped stomach cannot leave my mind alone. I think about Yvonne Ruddock and Boris Johnson. And how, in years to come, Britain will attempt to erase one while erecting a statue to honour the other. A knot in my stomach persists as I think that the erasure of one and the celebration of the other prevent Britain from being comfortable with itself. It is vital to break any cycle of repetition that creates behaviours that keep us collectively broken.

Erasure was a critical concept that sat at the heart of the Combahee River Collective's work. The Black feminist lesbian socialist group started in Boston in 1974, and its members included author and scholar Barbara Smith, iconic poet Audre Lorde and former Black Panther, Demita Frazier. They named the collective after Harriet Tubman's Combahee River Raid, which aimed to free 750 slaves in South Carolina. The collective responded to the exclusion of Black women's voices and experiences from the primarily white, middle-class-led feminist movement and patriarchal Black Power and civil rights movements.

Black women face greater societal barriers than either of these groups because they experience racism and sexism simultaneously. In addition, many experience further inter-secting oppressions, especially classism, but also ableism and homophobia among other things. By centring Black women's experiences, the collective believed that 'If Black women were free, it would mean that everyone else would have to be free since our freedom would necessitate the destruction of all systems of oppression.'[1]

They are perhaps best known for the Combahee River Collective Statement, released in April 1977, which coined the term 'identity politics':

> We realize that the only people who care enough about us to work consistently for our liberation are us. Our politics evolve from a healthy love for ourselves, our sisters and our community which allows us to continue our struggle and work. This focusing upon our own oppression is embodied in the concept of identity politics. We believe that the most profound and potentially most radical politics come directly out of our own identity, as opposed to working to end somebody else's oppression.[2]

Within the statement, you will find the roots of the term intersectionality, coined by Kimberlé Crenshaw in 1989. As Crenshaw recently explained, 'It's basically a lens, a prism, for seeing the way in which various forms of inequality often operate together and exacerbate each other. We tend to talk about race inequality as separate from inequality based on gender, class, sexuality or immigrant status. What's often missing is how some people are subject to all of these, and the experience is not just the sum of its parts.'[3]

The statement, which exposed the racism of white feminism and the sexism in Black nationalism, inspired the Black Lives Matter movement, which was founded by Patrisse

Cullors, Alicia Garza and Opal Tometi. This collective of intersectional feminists didn't exclude other groups or undermine other movements with their activism. Instead, they aspired to depose capitalism, liberate Black women and find an alternative to white-hetero-patriarchal norms.

This idea of creating an alternative system that did not reproduce the harms of capitalism came through powerfully in my conversations with Fania Noël, a Haitian French Afro-feminist organiser and writer, and former member of the French-based Afro-feminist collective Mwasi. She is the co-founder of the political journal on intersectionality *Revue AssiégéEs*, a board member of Black Feminist Future and the author of *Afro-communautaire: Appartenir à nous-mêmes* and *Et maintenant le pouvoir. Un horizon politique afroféministe*. Mwasi, formed in 2015, provides a safe space for Black, mixed-heritage women and femmes while advocating for Black liberation and challenging police violence and state racism. Its membership features women from over twenty nations, so migrant rights and experiences are central to its positioning. In 2017, Mwasi organised the Nyansapo Festival, the first Afro-feminist festival in France. The Mayor of Paris and white feminists opposed the festival because Mwasi had organised some workshops solely for Black women.

Despite threats to cancel the event, the Nyansapo Festival went ahead. A year later, they organised a two-day event as part of International Women's Day at La Générale Nord-Est arts centre called *'Déjouer le silence'* ('Thwarting Silence').[4] Noël was clear that liberation will not arise through replication of current oppressive systems.

'This is the measure for groups with predominantly white feminist or predominantly Black men activists because those two groups are in competition to be as powerful as white men and as we know we can never do that, we have to do something else,' says Noël. When she spoke about a vision for a better society, she talked about wellness and everyone having the right to food and a roof over their heads. She spoke of health and ancestry, not dehumanising people by saying they were perfect and not being afraid to unbuild harms from the past. She spoke about the free will of the body and how patriarchy wants to control women's bodies and that women do not have to be one way or fixed.

Noël called solidarity the 'verb of action' and warned that money was not solidarity, but building common political goals was vital. She spoke about being non-extractive too. But she also highlighted faith, hope and love for humans as crucial characteristics. Noël's words echoed many of the values espoused by the Combahee River Collective, with liberatory principles that would benefit everyone in society.

The silencing was apparent after George Floyd's death on 25 May 2020. We witnessed the many statements from business, sport and charities claiming solidarity with Black Lives Matter. Floyd's lynching followed Breonna Taylor's killing on 13 March 2020, shot six times by police during a raid on her apartment. Three plain-clothed officers entered her premises, searching for Taylor's ex-boyfriend, Jamarcus Glover, a suspected drug dealer.

Glover wasn't there. Taylor was in bed with her boyfriend Kenneth Walker. Upon hearing the officers enter the apartment using a battering ram, Walker fired a shot, hitting policeman Jonathan Mattingly in the leg. The officers opened fire, discharging thirty-two rounds, six of which hit Taylor. There were many errors in the subsequent police reports and officer Brett Hankison was sacked because he 'wantonly and blindly fired 10 rounds'.[5] On 23 September 2020, Hankison was charged with endangering Taylor's neighbours, but none of the officers stood trial for Breonna's death.

There did not appear to be as much outrage at Breonna Taylor's killing as Floyd's at a global level. Unlike Floyd, we did not witness Taylor's death, which may have contributed to why her killing did not emit the same visceral emotions. But her case, a failure of policing and the judicial system, like the demise of many Black women, seemed lost. I am not comparing the two. But the *invisibilisation* of Black women speaks to a story, her story, that's often erased.

The same is true in funding. In an article for *Inside Philanthropy* titled 'The Dire State of Funding for Black Feminist Movements – And What Donors Can Do About It', Hakima Abbas, co-founder of the Black Feminist Fund and Kellea Miller, deputy director of Human Rights Funders Network, found that between 0.1 per cent to 0.35 per cent of foundation funding goes to Black feminist movements. The research findings drew from an analysis of over 27,000 human rights grants awarded in 2018 totalling $3.7 billion.[6]

We have witnessed some breakthroughs in 2020 and 2021. Yvonne Field, founder of the Ubele Initiative, was fundamental in catalysing the Phoenix Way Partnership, alongside the National Lottery Community Fund's then deputy director

Shane Ryan, delivery and learning partners Global Fund for Children and brap, and over thirty racially minoritised groups and individuals across England.

The partnership originally began in April 2020 with the launch of the Phoenix Fund, which distributed around £2 million in small emergency grants to Black and brown-led groups in response to the disproportionate impact the pandemic was having on racially minoritised communities. The Fund was, in part, prompted by Ubele's report 'Impact of COVID-19 on BAME community and Voluntary Organisations' in April 2020, which suggested that nine out of ten BAME micro and small organisations were set to close if the crisis continued beyond three months.[7]

The success of the Fund led to the Community Fund, in June 2021, announcing a £50 million collaboration with the Phoenix Way Partnership, comprising Black and brown-led social purpose groups across England.

Yvonne and Ubele facilitated radical listening and community dialogue sessions with groups across the UK, which led to an approach that fully involved the most affected communities in design, delivery and decision-making. The approach was transparent and did not erase anyone's experiences. It is often the case, in the social sector, that many leaders create frameworks to keep themselves in the frame. They centralise themselves and monetise other people's expertise when, in fact, the best thing they should do is step aside. They should be an ally and understand that they are not the authors of change or best equipped to translate other people's experience.

The Phoenix Fund was authentic and urgent, humble and

fluent, ambitious and, at points, messy. Social change work is messy. But at no point did it lose sight of its core principles and Yvonne was central to that. While Ubele was the lead facilitator, the Phoenix Way Partnership emphasised community leadership. While many within the social sector wanted to laud Yvonne's work, and rightfully so, she resisted the temptation of being cast as the figurehead of the Fund. It was never about ownership or credit. It was about action, impact and collective giving.

A few things struck me as I observed the Phoenix Way Partnership up close. Yvonne would always speak about justice as a reality, not just a dream. It starts with belief. Belief born from experience. Belief born from her ancestors, her elders, her desire to pass on to others, and ensure that we are not erased. Belief when I, and I'm sure others, didn't believe. I remember Yvonne telling me what she'd learned from her experiences as part of the Anti-Apartheid Movement. She said there was a long-term strategy; she spoke of the internal struggles, the messiness of it; she said there was strong community-based leadership and foot soldiers, people prepared to lay down their lives. There was a shared history and, 'alongside that, there was laughter, and singing and people making life,' she said. Most importantly, she told me, 'I never met a Black South African who said, "we're not going to win this battle."'

Yvonne's grounding in activism emerged from observing and standing on the shoulders of her elders. She learned a lot from Sybil Phoenix OBE, who helped unwanted children, and founded a supported-housing scheme for young single mums and the Moonshot youth club in Lewisham. Yvonne also learned from Mavis Best, who, in 1981, started the Scrap

Sus Campaign, opposing the police's discriminatory stop and search tactics. Best led a group of Black women to police stations to rescue young people from the clutches of the Met and she campaigned to abolish the sus law.

The law, which disproportionately targeted young Black men, was scrapped after three years due, in part, to Best's constant lobbying. Yvonne would follow them to meetings, 'hang on to their coat tails' and hope that 'some of their wisdom and knowledge and skills would rub off on me'. Of Sybil Phoenix, she says, 'She's got this spirit that was just like, no was not an option. No was never an option with Sybil. You would say no and she would come back to you with a question with a slightly different frame but you knew in the end, you knew that you had to say yes to her, to give her what she wanted.'

Ubele embarked on over three years of community dialogue before developing its approach to building sustainable infrastructure for African diaspora communities. Yvonne describes herself as a 'nomad entrepreneur'. Her mission is to intervene in the public, private, and social systems, but she never closely aligns herself with these systems for long. She never stays long enough to stagnate, to be co-opted, to be institutionalised.

So much of her spirit ran through the bloodstreams of the Phoenix Way Partnership. Even though most of us who formed the wider partnership didn't know or had never met each other, there was deep trust. There was humility, as Yvonne was never afraid to say she didn't know or bring in others with greater expertise. Ownership or individualism were never factors. There was listening and transparency.

And there was that unyielding belief. I am sure there are other models of fund development globally that have had similar qualities. But, in being closer to this fund than others, I saw a glimpse of philanthropy the way it should be.

The Phoenix Way Partnership reminded me of the importance of simultaneity, the Combahee River Collective and why the perspectives of the outsider within should be central to any social change movement. In August 2020, Michelle Daley, director of ALLFIE, launched a new pressure group called Disabled Black Lives Matter (DBLM), highlighting the absence of the experiences of Black disabled people in the disability rights movement in the UK.

ALLFIE campaigns for a more inclusive society, particularly in education. However, the experiences of Black disabled women are often excluded from disability rights campaigning. Erasure of these experiences is real and the failure to recognise intersectional discrimination marginalises and ignores Black disabled women.

But the DBLM campaign is not only relevant to the disability rights sector. DBLM offers an approach where the experiences of those at the hard edge of intersectional oppression inform our solutions to society's social problems whilst creating a healthier culture.

'I think all movements need to address intersectional barriers,' says Daley. 'I think they must. I think Black movements, disabled people's movements, LGBTQ movements, whatever movement, needs to address the intersectional issue.'

The approach is born from a place of being an outsider within and her ancestry, which inform her practices:

We know the journey of being a Caribbean and we know the pain. We carry the name of our slave masters, we bear their names and we know our slave masters' blood runs through us. We have to be honest about that. As I started to learn stuff, ableism and racism sit together closely because, in order to have any form of freedom after the end of the transatlantic slave trade and enslavement, it was based on ableism. So these things really connect tightly.

My practice, the way I think, although I work in the disabled people's movement, that is not just my practice. I draw a lot to Black civil rights movements and struggles and I draw a lot to Caribbean struggle. You'll see that in my thinking.

* * * * *

For Kimberlé Crenshaw, Breonna Taylor's death should catalyse a change in the Black liberation movement. In December 2014, the African American Policy Forum (AAPF) and the Center for Intersectionality and Social Policy Studies (CISPS) at Columbia Law School founded the #SayHerName campaign to highlight the fatalities of Black women at the police's hands.[8]

In her essay as part of the Abolition for the People series for Kaepernick Publishing and LEVEL, Crenshaw pointed out that the absolution of the police officers in the Taylor case occurred sixty-five years to the day that twelve white jury members acquitted two white men of the killing of fourteen-year-old Emmett Till.[9]

Till was tortured, beaten close to death, then shot in the head, with an eye extracted, barbed wire had been wrapped around his neck and his body thrown in the river for saying 'bye, baby' to a white woman, Carolyn Bryant. According to Bryant's testimony, Till grabbed and verbally assaulted her. In 2007, she confessed that she fabricated her testimony. Emmett's mother, Mamie Till, held an open-casket funeral so the world could see Emmett's decapitated face and 'let people see what they did to my boy.'[10]

Emmett Till's murder and the subsequent verdict roused Black activism in the fifties. For Crenshaw, the Breonna Taylor case should do the same, but with a different emphasis. 'If Breonna's story serves as the cornerstone for a generation of activism, like Emmett's did, it will foreground something new in the Black freedom struggle, something that the #SayHerName campaign has been fighting for since 2014. It will make all Black women central to any analysis of and challenge to anti-Blackness.'

Black female activism comes in many forms. After dubiously losing the race to become Georgia's statehouse governor in 2018, a marginal defeat many attributed to voter suppression, American politician and lawyer Stacey Abrams founded Fair Fight Action. This promotes fair elections, tackles voter suppression, particularly of people of colour, and increases participation in democracy, among other things.

Abrams didn't gripe about her loss. Instead, she grinded, helping to register over 800,000 people in Georgia. Through Abrams's efforts, in 2020, the state turned from red (Donald Trump) to blue (Democratic candidate Joe Biden) in the presidential election for the first time since 1992, and elected two Democratic senators: a Black man and a Jewish man. It was a selfless act, altering power in Georgia. Often, we view power through the lens of wealth, political clout or media influence. Abrams's mobilising provided an example that people-power can defeat these conceptions of influence, even within the confines of a capitalist and white supremacist system.

But this is a global struggle. Further examples of the importance of valuing the lived experiences of Black women across the globe include the Green Belt Movement, founded by environmentalist, feminist and activist Dr Wangari Maathai in 1977. The movement aims to plant trees across Kenya to combat soil erosion, generate income for women and create firewood for cooking. Maathai fought for women's rights, understanding how deforestation negatively affected the livelihoods of women living in rural Kenya. She built a movement based on community mobilisation, environmental conservation and justice. In building Green Belt, Maathai survived imprisonment, exile and physical violence to create a movement that, at the time of her death in 2011, had planted 30 million trees.[11] She became the first African woman to win the Nobel Peace Prize in 2004.

The Green Belt Movement has now planted over 51 million trees while supporting over 30,000 women to conserve land and earn an income.[12] 'She understood the politics of creating change,' says Maria Adebowale-Schwarte, founding director of Living Space and chief executive officer of Foundation for Future London. 'This woman was talking about keeping valuable land as public space as a right for local people to have spaces they can go to co-own public spaces. She was incredibly impactful as a movement builder because she was led by civil society and nurtured collective and collaborative leadership, she challenged legislation and she stood up to very powerful and quite often dangerous government departments and frameworks. She did something quite amazing because she was talking about human rights and environments together.'

* * * * *

Author Tyrone McKinley Freeman centred his book *Madam C. J. Walker's Gospel of Giving* on Walker's philanthropy, not her entrepreneurship. Walker's success in the cosmetics and hair care markets is well documented, where she became the first female self-made millionaire in America. Freeman dissects the principles behind Walker's giving and how this offered a purer, more bottom-up approach to philanthropy than her white male contemporaries, John D. Rockefeller and Andrew Carnegie.

The book opens with the following lines: 'Black. Female. Daughter of slaves. Orphan. Child laborer. Widowed young mother. Penniless migrant. Poor washerwoman. Philanthropist.'[13] Immediately, the book sets out how Walker's lived experiences informed her approach to giving, one that was not solely based on financial gifts and predicated on beliefs divorced from the lived realities of those to whom she gave money, time and resources.

As an African American woman in the late nineteenth and early twentieth century, her wealth could not fully incubate her from racism. Walker supported orphanages, many women's organisations, schools, retirement homes for the formerly enslaved; she spoke at political functions later in her life and even helped to pay off the mortgage on abolitionist Frederick Douglass's home.

In *Madam C. J. Walker's Gospel of Giving*, Freeman says, 'African Americans not only turned to philanthropy out of necessity for survival, they lived it as an expression of their identity and generosity in spite of all that was being done to them and that had been taken away from them. And black women led the way. If black women lead intersectional lives, it follows that their philanthropy will be intersectional as well, meaning not limited to one type of gift, institution, societal sector, or approach. Rather, it is diverse, multifaceted, overlapping, interactive, and reflective of their embodied identities.'[14]

The elements Freeman recognises, embodied identities and intersectional approaches are not typical characteristics in mainstream philanthropy. The Andrew Carnegie gospel of wealth and giving still rules. Freeman identified five key characteristics of Walker's giving:

- Proximity – Due to her experiences of racism and menial work, she identified with the people she was supporting; that proximity meant that she never questioned whether the beneficiaries of her giving were worthy or not.
- Resourcefulness – moving beyond just money as the sole source of giving towards the need to be creative and flexible to address people's needs.
- Collaboration – Walker mobilised between working-class and middle-class networks, finding this role as a translator between the two as an effective way of sharing resources to benefit those most in need.
- Incrementalism – 'willingness and obligation became the drivers of giving over ability'.[15]

- Joy – emerging from her church background, she saw giving as a duty and a joy, not a science, even though her philanthropy seemingly combined the two.[16]

These are good guiding characteristics for giving, present in many of the examples mentioned in this chapter. Black women are not a homogeneous group. But core principles behind the giving of so many Black womxn-led initiatives across the globe embrace complexity and difference. Things are looking up. Black feminist thought was the foundation of Marai Larasi's work in addressing violence against women and girls while she was the director of Imkaan. Larasi is bringing her experiences, thinking and practices to her work as part of a collective developing Project Tallawah, a fund led by Global Majority woman for Global Majority women.

The Black Feminist Fund (BFF), founded by Amina Doherty, Hakima Abbas and Tynesha McHarris, aims to raise $100 million to provide solidarity funding to Black feminist organisations and womxn in Africa, the Americas and Europe.

Its website states that, 'Black feminists have resisted multiple oppressions and planted seeds of a better world for centuries'.[17] This is also the first global fund aimed at mobilising more resources to and addressing issues faced by Black womxn. Project Tallawah and BFF both have the potential to radically re-centre philanthropy.

At its best, by centring Black womxn in resourcing social justice, it is an equitable approach that is unlikely to relegate other movements, that will embrace multiple truths and bring joy and challenge. This vision may sound romantic, but if we truly desire a more equitable future, then centring work around Black womxnhood, in all its different shades and guises, is perhaps one that could be the most liberating to all. As Rachel Muthoga said to me, 'The passage for increased space and voice for Black women carries along so many other people ... I think it's one where everyone rises.'

26

Liberatory visions

Support liberatory and alternative visions that are better than our capitalist world

'Remember to imagine and craft the worlds you cannot live without, just as you dismantle the ones you cannot live within.'[1]

RUHA BENJAMIN, professor of African American studies, Princeton University

Uruguayan writer Eduardo Galeano once described the 1974 Dutch football side as 'a team in which each one was all eleven'.[2] The Netherlands played the game without hierarchy. They countered standardised methods of playing football by making each team member position-less. Every outfield player could do everything – attack, defend and create.

It's like a work colleague who is equally adept at managing, administration, marketing and legal affairs. In attack, the Dutch exploited space, making the pitch wide by constantly interchanging positions. Three or four of them would press, suffocating opponents, daring them to do something breath-taking with the ball in minimal time. The players worked hard for each other, appearing and disappearing like glistening needle-eye raindrops on a window during a drizzly night.

The Dutch team's style of play at the 1974 World Cup was beautiful, unexpected and harmonious. The hippies in orange shirts created a system where the forward, primarily tasked with scoring goals, could drop into defence. Where a midfielder, charged with manufacturing opportunities, could assume the position of a scorer.

The structure stayed the same. If a defender became creative, a midfielder would occupy his defensive space. These interchanges transpired throughout the game, each player with the freedom to innovate, express themselves, and be more than what convention told them to be, as long as they were willing to work hard for the rest of the unit. It was expressive and strategic. 'You make space, you come into space. And if the ball doesn't come, you leave this space and another player will come into it,' commented Jonathan Wilson in 2008.[3]

The press called it 'Total Football'. The 1974 Dutch team was not the first to employ this approach. But the Netherlands epitomised it, building on the foundations laid by the Dutch club side Ajax of Amsterdam, managed by Rinus Michels and led by legendary players Johan Cruyff and Johan Neeskens.

The Netherlands team was a sporting example of a liberatory vision, something that veered far from convention and transcended its time; something that was beautiful, something that explored the possibilities of what could be. For Ajax, liberation on the pitch extended to how the team operated off the field.

As *FT* columnist and author Simon Kuper said in his book *Barça*, 'Michels and Cruyff invented the future.'[4] They influenced modern football, from the great Euro-winning Dutch side in 1988 to the great Barcelona and Spanish national teams between 2008 and 2012.

In his book *Brilliant Orange*, author David Winner said that Ajax was like a 'workers' cooperative';[5] the players often picked the team, devised the tactics, selected the captain, and scheduled their friendly matches. For a brief time, the unit functioned in a way that would seem ideal for society. It had connectivity and mutuality; it was democratic, horizontal in structure, and relational, recognising each player's considerable skills. There was trust in the system because the players were the system, and they had a voice, with no one limited by position. 'Within the Ajax model, players derived their meaning, their significance, from their interrelationships with other players.'[6]

These Dutch teams made the unthinkable seem conceivable. While it is easy to see a revolution in art or sport, it's not quite as visible in the field of social transformation. Perhaps a demonstration or protest has that power; a mass of people uniting over a cause can sway our views. *Can that many people, willing to put their bodies on the line, be wrong?*

A protest doesn't necessarily offer a vision of what needs to change, rather it is often more an objection to the status quo. When you couple protest and the will to dismantle a system, with a liberatory vision, you arrive at a feeling as enduring as any historical moment. And there are plenty of people across the globe who are breaking conventions.

* * * * *

A functional world would not operate with economic disparities, race inequality, violence against women and exploitation of our natural resources. It is all man-made, therefore it can be undone. But it is not enough to say what's wrong; you have to offer solutions or a vision of what can be.

The social sector refers to people who create novel ideas with a social purpose as social entrepreneurs. I see them more as social artists.

If we want to change our world radically, we cannot talk about abolishing the police or the criminal justice system; there must be a conception of what will replace them. This is where things get blurry, and politicians and the media are often unhelpful. These social artists have solutions, ideas, experimentations of what an alternative could look like.

This is often missing in mainstream commentary when we hear activists say they want to defund the police. You see these headlines and may think *that's ridiculous*. Credibility disintegrates. You see this pattern on television and in the press all the time. Mainstream, conservative views have plenty of bandwidth; anything resembling an alternative is swiftly demeaned as extreme, unfeasible, overemotional, woke, lacking in evidence.

But it's like watching a theatre performance that concludes at the interval; there is a half that is never told and, depending on who governs the performance, it's unlikely that the majority of us will ever find out.

When American activist, academic and former Black Panther Angela Davis spoke to poet and novelist Jackie Kay at the Manchester Literary Festival in October 2020, she talked about abolitionist imagination. I recall Davis talking about imagining security and safety in a more favourable way, one that involves employment, housing, education and health care, our basic needs, not armed human beings. She spoke about the need for new institutions, ones that do not tackle violence with violence, and new health-care systems. I remember her saying 'another world is possible'.[7]

Liberatory visions do not begin and end with abolishing the police or the prison system but invite us to imagine an alternative. One that fundamentally questions policing or imprisonment. We have been conditioned to think these violent measures are the only way to reprimand poor behaviour. It's like giving kids exams at school. We've come to accept it. But what is the efficacy of these approaches? Why do we have to accept these norms?

One role that institutional philanthropy could play is to resource the alternatives, enabling unorthodox ideas to flourish. Why not create platforms with independent funding for the general public to discover the other half of the play for themselves? Opportunities for communities to see it, feel it, participate in it and believe in it. The unwillingness of institutional philanthropy to commit to this task is perhaps one of its biggest failures.

Unlike art or sport, we rarely see liberatory visions elevated or exposed to the masses. There's not a high commercial appeal for them, which I don't understand. There are plenty of daytime or primetime television shows illustrating how we can renovate our houses or garages or the meals we can cook with the ingredients we have in our homes. There are shows about buying our dream homes in the countryside or in another country. These are highly relatable shows.

They enable you to place yourself in the lives of those ordinary folks seeking something new, looking for something better out of life. Their dreams do not appear out of reach. The general public who appear in these shows do not seem too different from you or your neighbours. I find it surprising that we do not have more television shows illustrating a more cohesive community. More shows that are aspirational in a broader social context than our circumstances. I am not suggesting for a moment that we would suddenly start watching a social transformation show over a football game or *A Place in the Sun*.

But I wonder whether we need greater exposure to social artists to donate more sustainably and equitably to their visions? What would happen if we gave social artists as much prime-time advertising as Go Compare? What if we could spread these social artists' ideas on social media as much as we circulate misinformation? What if funding bodies gave these artists substantial, long-term funding like the money given by the Arts Council to its National Portfolio Organisations?

It's likely that the people who stop such shows from being commissioned are the same types of people who prevent more resources from going to these artists and projects within the social sector. Too often, we dwell on the extremities, dreams or despair, with nothing in between to fill our desire for hope.

When I speak to Ruth Ibegbuna, I see hope. She has founded three social enterprises, the youth leadership charity RECLAIM, The Roots Programme, which bridges divides in the UK, and a supplementary school called Rekindle. This former teacher has been a CEO, a Clore and Ashoka Fellow, author of the book *On Youth* and one of the *Sunday Times'* five hundred most influential people.

RECLAIM was one of few youth organisations legitimately constructing its work through young people's experiences when I first entered philanthropy. It involved youth in local campaigns, developing leadership through activism and awareness, linking them to issues that concerned them and empowering them to do something about it.

It had a strong race and class analysis, and responsibly mixed young people from different backgrounds. RECLAIM didn't define young people as a problem but elevated and trusted their voices. Yet, Ibegbuna has always referred to herself as a teacher. So it shouldn't have come as a surprise when she launched Rekindle, a school that is 'educating with heart and soul'.

Young people from South Manchester aged from seventeen to twenty-four are governing this school. Rekindle uses education as an entry point to develop a greater sense of social purpose in young people's lives. It also creates strong networks, critical thinking skills and prioritises mental well-being. Ibegbuna is by no means the first or only person to envisage a more holistic, culturally appropriate and experiential way of educating young people.

But she's offering an alternative to a system that has failed working-class communities. Rekindle centres its work around young people's needs, prioritising family engagement, nutritious meals, community support and safeguarding young people. Her work moves beyond changes to the curriculum, beyond being more inclusive or diversifying school texts. Rekindle offers a shift that centres young people, particularly the working class, which means that the system has to compromise, not individuals.

Fundamentally, at the heart of Ibegbuna's work is young people's well-being and talent, not solely their grades. Their developmental and educational needs, preparation for the next stage of life, and understanding of how to build healthy relationships are paramount. Rekindle, imagined by young people, is not the type of school that could be initiated within the confines of Britain's current education system. But Ibegbuna is not a woman who operates within confines, which is why her work is 'Total Justice'.

Ibegbuna is not the only person I've come across creating visions of hope that are accessible. As mentioned earlier, Immy Kaur in Birmingham is working on CIVIC SQUARE, a collectively owned public square, for local people to connect, eat, play, share resources and work. Importantly, like Ibegbuna, it is being built by and through the lens of the most socially disenfranchised. It's beautiful, immersive, and scalable.

CIVIC SQUARE will use the doughnut economics model, pioneered by University of Oxford economist Kate Raworth as an alternative to economic growth models. This approach is regenerative and redistributive, where prosperity equals meeting people's social needs (food, water, social equity, gender equality, etc.) without damaging our planet (climate change, land conservation, air pollution). Doughnut economics offers an alternative to capitalism.

Also in Birmingham, cultural producer Amahra Spence has opened YARD, an art house run by artists, which offers a place for connection, a place for reinvestment into communities, an ideal intersection of the arts and community, creativity and social change, hospitality and a safe space.

Ruth Ibegbuna feels that we

'need to name what are we moving towards. What's this better thing. What kind of society are we working towards? Lockdown has shown me that there are elements of my life that are pretty toxic and I didn't like it. OK, that's fine. What do you want to keep? Where do you want to go? What kind of lives do you want our children to live? I think people need to feel that they are giving their time, their resources and their energy to something tangible. Something they can feel, see, and understand. I think that it's in [the] government's interest for us to never do that because we never talk about the future.

Martin Luther King was very big on talking about what the future looks like, so people could feel emotional and imagine it. Therefore, 'I want to give my time and energy to what that man is saying.' We don't talk about that. We talk about, 'This feels bad at the moment, so let's do something small to make us feel less bad.' We don't talk about what feeling good would feel like for everyone in the country and I think we need to start naming what good is.

At the end of the day, families will give their time to something that feels good. Something that will make their children's lives better. Because there's no big movement as to what that could be, they will do something that's within touching distance. That could be raising money for the local football club. If that could be worked out, a kind of simple and structural: this is what we're working towards in ten years, this is the kind of society we're building, look at what good looks like in ten years. It would make people look at that and think, 'Geez, I want to buy into that. I want my kids to be part of that. OK, I can enter this here.'

Ibegbuna's work, alongside that of Whitney Iles, Immy Kaur and Amahra Spence, and others, enables people to dare to dream, to realise the impossible. But their practices are also rooted in reality, which means that the dreams they are manifesting are tangible.

* * * * *

We have witnessed mass change worldwide, where liberatory visions have become a reality, where systems have been dismantled and replaced by new structures. The 'fourth world war', for example, began on 1 January 1994 in Mexico. The Ejército Zapatista de Liberación Nacional (EZLN or Zapatista), comprising 5,000 Mayans, seized seven cities in Chiapas in southern Mexico, with the ultimate aim to overthrow the Mexican government.

The Zapatista peasant uprising strategically coincided with the North American Free Trade Agreement (NAFTA), which removed land reparations for indigenous groups from the Mexican constitution. As one of EZLN's leaders, Subcomandante Marcos, said, 'neoliberalism is a new war for the conquest of territory.'[8] This was an armed war against over five hundred years of racism, poverty, colonialism, exploitation and genocide[9] to build a system based on participatory democracy and, as author Alex Khasnabish says in the book *Zapatistas*, 'dialogue, inclusivity and the mutual recognition of dignity'.[10]

With their faces concealed, the Zapatistas took control of these cities, battling the federal army at every step. Around four hundred people were killed.[11] But an interesting dynamic occurred. People outside of Chiapas sympathised with the Zapatistas.[12]

Mexico demanded an end to the war and President Carlos Salinas de Gortari had to respond. On 12 January 1994, a ceasefire was declared. While the army took back some of the territories gained by the Zapatistas, the Mayans retained control of enough districts to create an alternative to capitalism. The Zapatistas are non-hierarchal, and indigenous communities lead this alternative vision. They run local cooperatives to ensure wealth and labour are equally distributed. They centre women in communal leadership. They are a vision of a different normal.

The Zapatistas did not defeat Salinas and the federal army. However, they created an alternative to capitalism. They devised the rightful role of the institutionalised part of the social sector by employing these organisations for technical support to help the oppressed. They operate in an environmentally sustainable manner.

Their schools emphasise women's rights; they address the impact of capitalism, remove grading systems and have their curriculum decided by the community. Health and education are free, young people participate in decision-making and the community owns the land. It's not perfect, but the Zapatistas dismantled exploitation, patriarchy, racism, classism and hierarchy, replacing them with a system in tune with their ancestry and, therefore, nature.

The Movimento dos Trabalhadores Sem Terra (Landless People's Movement or MST) is another example of a liberatory vision that became a reality. MST emerged in 1979 in Brazil, led by landless farm workers. They started by occupying some land in response to the increasing mechanisation of agriculture. MST has continued to grow and has settled more than 1.5 million people on 17 million acres of land.[13]

Like the Zapatistas, MST emphasises indigenous groups' autonomy in health, education, and food production while using a cooperative structure to ensure economic equity. 'The framework of circular economy right now, which is the buzzword of the climate folk, the funders, [is] what indigenous communities have long worked on,' says Baljeet Sandhu. 'It's their whole being of understanding themselves, planet earth, the universe, and their future. If you look at the frameworks of today, it is exactly what these communities have been teaching us. That's indigenous tribes, proper frameworks of the living world.'

I sometimes struggle to catch up with myself. My hopes, dreams, ambitions and aspirations spring to life often, but disappear as swiftly once my day starts, once life and bills and concern for my children eat into it. It's like being given two minutes to appreciate Jean-Michel Basquiat's *Tuxedo*. Not enough time. Too much to absorb so quickly. You see the melange of Malcolm X, olive oil, crosses, arrows, internal dialogue within the embodiment of words, ladders, the King of England, the sack of the goths and Gustavus Vassa all flashing in front of you.

But you don't have the time to absorb, appreciate, form an opinion or enjoy. The lockdown gave me time to think but not enough contact to act. The quest for hope is an ache that, over time, fights against a love I'm struggling to trust. Thoughts are overwhelming. Difficult to grasp. Quick fixes replace the chase. And through it all, I wonder whether I will ever catch up with myself before everything unravels, before I become undone. This sorrow, the distance it creates from those I love, rests between the cracks in my face, a stream forever dried between lines that never lied.

And yet this is where the art of giving, in its broadest term, lies; investing whatever you've got to give in things that very few of us can conceive. Ideas that reimagine with 'a sound understanding of interconnectedness, interdependence, mutuality'.[14] We invest our time watching Lionel Messi play football or sit, mouth agape, watching *Hamilton*; why not in social transformation? Some of the answers lie in the institutionalisation of the social sector, which suppresses marginalised voices.

But most of the solutions lie within us. We may not be at a point of embodying our giving. Our mindsets may still be in a transition towards this change. But we can start by altering our behaviour. Social artists are creating 'Total Justice' and inventing the future in communities across the globe. From CIVIC SQUARE to YARD, from Rekindle to Healing Justice London from Cooperation Jackson to Abahlali baseMjondolo (AbM) movement.

If you want to be a 'good ancestor', there may not be a better place to invest than in liberatory visions, because in these innovators and activists, freedom is invention.

Part 4

Just Cause

27

A common project

'In the course of history, there comes a time
when humanity is called to shift to a new level
of consciousness, to reach a higher moral
ground. A time when we have to shed our fear
and give hope to each other. That time is now.'[1]

WANGARI MAATHAI

In an age where, for many, wi-fi seems as essential as food,
clothing and water, I say this without a hint of irony, that
the revolution will be sketched, not streamed. The planet is
descending. Capitalism is killing it. None of us should think, for
a moment, that we are exempt from the terrors of a world where
wealth accumulation is our world's most valued individual goal.
But many people and communities are fighting back peacefully.
They are not extremists. Nor are they superheroes. They're
beautifully human; they care deeply, they love humanity.

Something Sebastian Ordoñez Muñoz said at the
Interdependence Festival has always stayed with me. He
spoke about the importance of teaching our children about
these occurrences of resistance. That's what I've tried to do

with this book. I've tried to flood this book with experiences of resistance and innovation. Some are big and historical; others are small and local. But they are remarkable and the remarkable is often near us, around the corner, within us.

This book, simple. These are the individuals and ideas I want my children to hear about and learn from; stories about what is possible, stories that reverse the toxic narratives commonly fed to us, seducing us into believing that change cannot happen. These conceptions pervade, consciously, unconsciously. Always there. Our capitalist system, one that has not been kind to Black, indigenous and people of colour, has embedded these concepts into our collective psyche.

I wrote about individuals and ideas who I believe are better than our capitalist world; individuals and ideas without any desire to create a world with losers. You don't need to agree with me nor with my politics. But what I present here are ideas that should be central, nuggets of a new way, the first way, a way that is not private, public or charitable, just a flood of good stuff with the potential to reimagine and redefine our lives and livelihoods positively. It will do you no harm.

Don't fall into the trap. One so many of us, irrespective of our background or beliefs, fall into. Call it the social sector theory of change: white supremacy (ignoring us or the issue), white fragility (defensiveness when challenged) and white saviour (trying to save us). This book is about awakening to the possibility that there can be another way, one that may be situated differently to you. And part of this change involves rewriting what has already been rewritten.

*

If Jamaican sprinter Nesta Carter can lose his 4 × 100 metres gold medal from the 2008 Beijing Olympics after his frozen blood and urine samples were retested in 2016, I see no reason why we can't 'retest' the canon. Why can't we check the historians, scientists and writers to determine the extent to which they 'doped' records, ecology, land, verbs and nouns? When my son received a school assignment about Carl Linnaeus, I wouldn't allow him to learn about the Swedish botanist's legacy as the father of modern taxonomy without letting him know he was also the godfather of racism.

If we want to rebalance our world, we need to decolonise these supposed 'standards'. We also need to highlight the brilliance of the obscured; the great works that didn't receive the awards, the plaudits. There's plenty out there, literature, inventions and ideologies that we don't have to excuse or caution for being racist, homophobic or 'of their times'. There are plenty of brilliant, non-discriminatory works that have been erased because they were beyond their present.

Many of these beyond-the-present 'authors' were experiencing these 'isms'. They came from a place that imagined a vastly different reality to the canon. Their realities, once deemed hostile and extreme, are now acknowledged as reasonable. But it shouldn't take the canon to decide what is reasonable and when it is 'safe' for mass consumption.

I recognise that decolonisation and 'retesting' are crucial to healing and alleviating us from the trauma of historical oppression. It is crucial to us developing a sense of belonging, being our whole selves, acknowledging difference as a norm, being complete. Still, throughout this book, I have deliberately focused on concepts that have or may transform and transcend.

These experiences risk erasure while our current profit-making power structures remain the framework for our world. Our world may be liberating for the 1–2 per cent that 'own' it, but it will not be for most of us. And, unfortunately, it is the 1–2 per cent that dictate much of how we view the world, how our relationships are mediated, influencing how we give and to whom.

So, this is a call – to use academic, writer and cultural studies pioneer Stuart Hall's words – for A Common Project.* To resource ideas and initiatives from the social artists and the outsiders within. This is a call for giving to be experiential and cultural, grounded in the practices of the most impacted communities, particularly Black, indigenous and people of colour. This is a call for reparations, tax justice and greater distribution of wealth to our most harmed communities. Some of the interconnected characteristics that should guide our giving in the future are:

- Reparatory justice: Adopt a reparative and regenerative frame, shifting from a lens of giving to one of giving back.

---

* 'I simply don't think, for example, that the current Labour leadership understands that its political fate depends on whether or not it can construct a politics, in the next 20 years, which is able to address itself, not to one, but to a diversity of different points of antagonism in society; unifying them, in their differences, within a common project. I don't think they have grasped that Labour's capacity to grow as a political force depends absolutely on its capacity to draw from the popular energies of very different movements; movements *outside* the party which it did not – could not – set in play, and which it cannot therefore 'administer'. It retains an entirely bureaucratic conception of politics.' – Stuart Hall, in James Martin (ed.), *Antonio Gramsci: Critical Assessments of Leading Political Philosophers*, 2002, Oxfordshire: Routledge, p.236.

- Knowledge equity: Value the wisdom and expertise of those with lived experiences of unfair and inequitable systems.
- Collective care: Support collectives that build the well-being, power and economic strength of marginalised communities.
- Radical solidarity: Recognise that we are interdependent by radically listening to and standing with those on the front line of harm.
- Self-determination: Trust in the most impacted communities to determine their own destiny.
- Root cause: Support campaigns and alliances that safeguard people and the planet by challenging, transforming or dismantling extractive systems.
- Abundance: Heed the ideas, innovations and joy generated in under-served communities.
- Outsider within: Centre the anti-racist and intersectional approaches of Black womxn.
- Liberatory visions: Support liberatory and alternative visions that are better than our capitalist world.

If COVID-19 taught us anything, it was that we are interdependent. We are not in a world where we can shut our borders and incubate ourselves away from other world problems. We are the other. We cannot extract from different communities to enhance our livelihoods and turn our backs to the damage we have caused as a result. Alas, it may take those problems landing on our doorsteps before we change. But if we want to be proactive, there are plenty of opportunities to contribute to change.

* * * * *

For the public, perhaps start by asking the organisations you'd like to give to questions related to the above characteristics. Is diversity only reflected in your pictures of need and not your leadership of change? In what ways are you accountable to the communities you serve? Does the demographics of your team mirror the people you serve? How close are you to the communities you serve? Do you value difference and take an equitable approach to deliver your work? Do you address the root cause of the issue by tackling the systemic problems instead of just trying to change the behaviour of individuals? Does your organisation take a pain or blame frame? How do you celebrate the self-determination and ideas of the communities you serve? Are you intersectional in your approach? What is your track record in tackling racism and commitment to anti-racism? It may not be the case that every organisation will answer all of these questions positively. But a critical starting point would be to determine the degree to which the organisation is led and governed by the people most impacted by the issue you are interested in donating to.

Try looking up some of the organisations featured this book or in the acknowledgements section at the back. It is not an exhaustive list, by any means. But if you want to enter a new web of giving, the organisations in this book offer a good starting point. So whenever you have a little time, explore, read and learn more. The wonderful thing is, each link will likely lead you to other relevant work and resources. It's a good way to start retesting and retraining yourself.

The final thing I'd say is that *we* have the power to change the world. We may not think so. But through the choices we make, the things we donate to or support, and, of course, through protesting, direct action and divesting, we can change our societies. For example, amid the tragedy and chaos of the pandemic in 2021, football fans rallied to oppose the implementation of the European Super League (ESL).

Real Madrid's president Florentino Perez tried to instigate an elite breakaway league, supported by the billionaire owners of twelve wealthy football teams. The ESL was a money grab, an exclusive club for selected members to soak up an even greater share of football's commercial revenue without any responsibility towards the sport's global wellbeing. In protest, supporters took to the streets, which – to a significant degree – led to the ESL disbanding and sanctions imposed on the 'rebel' clubs.

These protests also created a greater awareness of different models of 'ownership', namely in the German Bundesliga. There were no German clubs involved in the ESL because of their '50+1' rule, where club members have overall control of each team because they own 51 per cent of the shares. It's a trivial example, I know. But change was immediate. The ESL folded in less than a week. Social change rarely occurs so swiftly. But it occurs. And it usually starts with the efforts and labour of 'ordinary' people. However, these protests need to be sustained for true systemic change. The fans were victorious. But the ESL will not go away, not while those in power remain the same, and not until there's a definitive change in the law, for example, the Premier League adopting the German Bundesliga model.

*

Trusts and foundations must start interrogating and rethinking their wealth, listening to the communities they serve and repairing the harms caused by their financial growth. If institutional philanthropy is to have a significant impact on people and the planet, it must adopt a reparative and regenerative frame. Institutional philanthropy must look in the mirror, stop behaving as if it isn't transient, and stop acting as if it should be everlasting, like nature.

This conduct is the ultimate sign of arrogance. It needs humility and to commit more to its giving than its preserving. This will mean ceding power and enabling more of the creators of ideas from communities to become the ideas selectors, wealth distributors and organisational directors. It may also mean absorbing risk on behalf of the communities you serve or spending out your endowment. Any credible strategy in institutional philanthropy will offer a vision of sacrifice and transference of power. Neither business nor the public sector are equipped to take the lead here.

You have the independence and ability to do things differently. If it sounds too big, start first by committing to releasing some of your endowment. Create a twenty-year plan that cedes control of some of your assets. As indicated earlier, the top three hundred funders in the UK are worth £67 billion but distribute approximately £2.9 billion per annum. What if, to be blunt, each of the top three hundred funders distributes an additional 4 per cent of their endowments over the next twenty years directly into anti-racist, regenerative community asset-building efforts?

What if they invested in Black womxn-led intersectional approaches to social change? What if they based their giving on the knowledge, expertise and wisdom of the most impacted communities? During this period, what if they followed the lead of the Thirty Percy Foundation in resourcing the artists and activists from Black and brown communities to craft new models of giving? What if there was a concerted effort among these funders to support alternative economic models to capitalism? How about supporting work that makes a case for a universal basic income or tax justice, which would give the public more time to adopt giving as an everyday practice?

'If you want people to be really part of decision making, you have to think about how can they do this without being worried about their very basic needs about rooms, overheads, food, education for their children? You have to meet that,' says Maria Adebowale-Schwarte,

That's another thing that I like about this universal salary or income that some countries have – you have to have that. It can't be the minimum; it has to be in a way people can thrive.

So you have this system where someone will always have your back. But as part of that, we have a civil society where we expect people to help with some of that decision-making, creating social good, helping your neighbours, providing volunteer support to your local groups, your school. I think that is the only way you can really do it, otherwise you're going to try build a society on the bricks that are already crumbling. You're expecting people to be equally involved when they can't be.

*

Stephanie Brobbey, a former private wealth lawyer and founder of The Good Ancestor Movement, is challenging wealth advisors (lawyers, tax advisors, wealth planners, etc.) – who sit behind the scenes and sustain these extractive growth systems for a few – to change their ways. Brobbey aims to influence these advisors' behaviours and encourage the wealth holders to be more progressive than previous generations. Her more ethical approach will develop a new economic model that is more equitable, reparative and regenerative and, for high-net-worth individuals, foundations and wealth holders, negate social and environmental harms. She sees the greatest wealth transfer in history, from the baby boomers to next-generation high net-worth individuals, as a prime opportunity for philanthropists to do things differently.

For a new generation of wealth holders, there is an opportunity to shift away from philanthropy in its current form. I spoke to Lily Lewis, the founder and CEO of The Pocressi Initiative, which takes a trauma-informed approach to address the root causes of youth violence and works to deliver prevention, rehabilitation and abstinence addiction treatment.

'Everything I do strives to work through a racial equity lens,' she says. 'From the boards I join or the organisations I partner with. If they are white led, they must be willing to create an anti-racist action plan, work with external consultants, and complete a diversity and inclusivity audit that I made with The Social Investment Consultancy [led by Bonnie Chiu].'

I also spoke to Kristina Johansson, founder and director

of the Solberga Foundation, which supports transformative grassroots-led social change organisations, and co-founder of Resource Justice, which aids young wealth holders to redistribute their wealth, land and power.

'To sustain impact for the long term, impacted communities have to own, decide, shape, and lead philanthropy,' says Johansson. 'Philanthropy's current top-down approaches aren't working and if we want to see better results and actual systemic change, front-line and most impacted communities must lead the change as leaders and decision-makers. I believe philanthropy must democratise power in order to authentically and successfully support social movements.'

Many next-generation wealth holders are retesting and retraining themselves and thinking deeply about who they partner with, from advisers to supply chains. It's early stages. But these models appear to be less about legacy and more about efficacy.

'Where I have seen it effective, where I have seen people give, and really change their relationship towards giving, is [related to] their own personal relationship to power, provision and what they have,' says Farzana Khan. 'A lot of people don't want to unseat themselves because they can't imagine where else they will exist beyond what they have and how they give.

'The people that I find most unable to relinquish power, can't see themselves in any other way and aren't ready to even participate on the smallest thing, like having a meeting in a different way.'

* * * * *

One thing I can say conclusively, charity won't save us. Nor will institutional philanthropy. It may help. May ease suffering. But it has converted giving into a business, not a way of life. Institutional philanthropy thrives on the economics of pain. Radical change will not occur under current leadership. You cannot have systems and leadership that has upheld these extractive practices be responsible for our liberation.

The powers that be also know that if they were to truly embrace equity, charity and philanthropy as an institution would cease to exist. That doesn't mean that we should destroy the social sector. But the institution would be a tool that facilitates a shift towards giving being a fundamental part of our lifestyles.

In this vision, everyone would contribute to a society where we have equal access to good services, where we live in vibrant, connected communities, where we walk around free of envy, unburdened by social conditions that force us to compete and compare, to unconsciously groan and glare. I believe in the power of the original meaning of the word philanthropy to be transformative, even if its institutions may need to become extinct to do so.

'I think it starts with getting rid of the charitable sector,' says Ruth Ibegbuna. 'Getting rid of the idea of the charitable sector ... Something that's about us being better, getting to a better place and it not being about fixing problems but about finding solutions, visionary solutions and working towards them.'

'The thing that guides the work that I do is, "will this create the end of philanthropy?" And if the answer is no and I have the power to change that, then I don't do it. A real clarity. I have no illusion that there will ever be a world and a vision, a place where there's liberated Africans where philanthropy still exists,' says Luam Kidane.

'You need foundations and philanthropists to be uncomfortable with themselves and be willing to say "actually, if we've done good, we won't be around in five years!"' says Maria Adebowale-Schwarte.

'You can also start building alternative ecologies outside of the charity system that are much more mutual, that is a solidarity economy and actually down to practice equity,' says Farzana Khan. 'For example, it might be your housing situation. It might be how you eat. I know a lot of folks, and I'm not just talking about cooperatives and communing, but like, if you are rejecting that dynamic, and you are choosing to be in equitable relationships, you're choosing to be in community, then you have to practise all of this stuff around accountability, loving differently, listening differently. I think it invites us into a radical space.'

Traditional charity and philanthropy do not offer that radical space. We cannot expect a system focused on preserving wealth and power to liberate us. We need to get to a place where we can contribute to a fair and just world where we can all live our values.

Nikki Clegg says:

In this world we value the things that truly matter to us, things that bring us happiness and quality of life – family, friends, community (both locally and in a global sense), feeling safe and secure, having a place to call home, connection with nature, land, food and sustenance, health, well-being, education and continuous learning, having personal and collective purpose in our lives.

A world where we're in harmony with each other and with nature. Where we live much more humble and dematerialised lives. In this future the roles that are valued and required in our communities are those that are often hidden/unaccounted for in our current economy ... If you can, imagine a world where you woke up every day, feeling safe, happy and valued equally. Where you have time to enjoy the relationships in your life and to build new relationships with people around you, where you have the time, access and opportunity to spend time in nature. A life where you're not driven by financial security/gains but instead by what your body and your instincts tell you are important.'

'Imagine what [a] more circular, more connected, more equal, more anti-racist, more beautiful neighbourhoods could look like,' says Immy Kaur, 'where we're growing locally, where we're living inter-generationally ... where there's fewer cars, where things are more just for disabled people, more dementia-friendly. That could be a stunning vision.'

For every individual, initiative or idea mentioned in this book, there are hundreds of thousands of others out there creating significant changes in their communities. They may not be part of a registered organisation or have a website. There are lawyers, writers, social artists, and cultural producers with similar visions of radical change that we just don't know about. Governments do not approach them, and you will probably not see them on television. But they are out there, transforming lives, saving our planet and challenging oppressive systems.

It's not just Greta. Or Malala. There are more. There will be more. Amahra Spence once said to me that she felt as if the Black community in England are going through a revival akin to the Harlem Renaissance. 'Our 20s (2020) in relation to the former [Harlem Renaissance] 20s (1920s),' she said, 'the time rooted in Black expression, freedom and analysis of the structural manifested in a revival of culture, arts, scholarship, discovery, etc.'

In many ways, this book is not about giving at all. It's not about the social sector either. It's about, to use Marai Larasi's point, revolutionary love. Human kindness. It's about a love of humanity. But we must first start by listening. Radically listening to the voices of those from the most impacted communities. And we must take a reparative and generative approach and to trust, resource and stand by their solutions, by any means necessary. It may get a little messy and uncomfortable, and we may not see a change in our lifetime. But it is one way, a tangible way of breaking a system that disadvantages most of us, particularly Black, indigenous and people of colour. It doesn't have to be this way.

But there needs to be a common project. One in which we flood the system from a multitude of different directions, from the arts to academia, from politics to education, from science to the media, in a common cause.

Marai Larasi says:

It can't be one thing. You need those people that are going to be willing to contaminate themselves through engagement with the state and you're going to need those people who are like 'I'm not going anywhere near [the] state – my job is to agitate externally.' Whatever the actual structure looks like, in terms of how we connect those spaces, we do need to be more organised. We do need to be more strategic and we do also need to engage with care with each other.

I think so much has rested on us being individual champions, us trying to get on with it on our own, us trying to carry the weight of entire racialised communities on our shoulders, ancestral burdens, future burden, everything. Organising, connecting, building beloved community to do it, across disciplines.

We have to have a broad enough constituency of those of us that will do the various things. We can't afford to be judging each other and damaging each other because we happened to be the one in that space versus that space. We have to be able to see the connection between the person whose primary thing is going to be 'We need more black businesses' and the person who is going to be like 'Screw business, burn capitalism.'

We need to be able to have those people speak about the fact that liberation never occurs on one front. It has to be a multi-pronged approach. They didn't come for us in one way. They came to us with the Bible. They came to us with the ships. They came to us with the chains. They came to us with taking away language. They came to us with rape.

They came to us with physical assault. They came for us with all of it.

It can't be the one homogenous entity. I don't believe that that's possible.

The UK government's response to COVID-19 and the variants taught us that high-income countries' hoarding of wealth, power, and resources does not protect the masses but endangers us. The pandemic also highlighted that our systems are not fit for purpose, damaging our most marginalised communities and countries. Without a collective effort to dismantle or disrupt existing power structures, we will remain in a state where 'the old is dying and the new cannot be born'.[2]

According to a survey by Bath University and five other universities, young people across 10 countries are anxious about climate change,[3] while in the UK over 80 per cent of employees want more positive action from their workplaces on climate.[4] We are worried. We care. But we also spend too much time fearing difference more so than actively addressing those who actually do harm.

Throughout this book, we have met people redefining and reimagining our systems. They are creating change in the context of a world governed by a wealthy few and their gatekeepers who tell us that an alternative to these extractive systems is either not possible or can only be discovered by them. An alternative is possible. And discovery of new ways by the wealthy – that benefit everyone equitably – are rarely sustainable unless those in control are legitimately ceding power.

Collectively, we need to unlock our imaginations, reframe our frameworks and start giving back to those with visions of what an abundant future might look like. We need to say farewell to philanthropy as an institution and embody radical giving, within our daily lives.

For change to occur, we will need to invalidate some of our truths, educate ourselves and our children by taking heed of the realities and solutions of the most impacted communities. Radical philanthropy starts at a point when we have the courage to challenge our truths. I hope people will find themselves, and their visions for a better world by giving back, and not waiting for another crisis like COVID-19 before we act.

Together, we will shift philanthropy towards being a life not a living, rooted in the practices and traditions of communities on the front line of harm. While we are doing so, we will be singing I-Wayne's 'Living in Love' and playing our part in sparking a quiet revolution.

Liberation and justice need not be a dream. But they need resourcing. There may be no better place to start than investing in the visions of social artists and the outsiders within. Their dreams of utopia offer hope for us all.

Acknowledgements

This book is livicated to my family, Meadow and Marlowe, Keith and Elle Bardowell, Diana Evans, Paula B. Stanic and Karen Bardowell, Mya Goessl and Fedja Stanic.

This book would not have been possible without the editorial support from Mitali Sen, and assistance from Cobi-Jane Akinrele (founder of Aké Collective – https://www.ake.com.ng/), Safi Yamin-Yule and the Churchill Fellowship. Thanks also to The Weeklings, the Centre for Knowledge Equity and Helen Williams from HWSS.

This book is also livicated to the artists and activists, innovators and changemakers, some of whom are featured in this book. Special thanks to Farzana Khan, Amahra Spence, Whitney Iles, Ruth Ibegbuna, Yvonne Field, Marai Larasi, Luam Kidane, Baljeet Sandhu, Professor Carlene Firmin, Sai Murray, Immy Kaur, Harpreet Kaur Paul, Natalie Creary, Kiran Chahal, Stephanie Brobbey, and Maria Adebowale-Schwarte. *Giving Back* is also a product of the many interviews and conversations I've had with colleagues and associates, friends and fam over the years. Thanks to Shane Ryan, Shivanti Lowton, Darren Crosdale, Bonnie Chiu, Rachel Muthoga, Sade Banks, Jaden Osei-Bonsu, Michelle Daley, Nikki Clegg, Fania Noël, Jenny Oppenheimer (the philanthropy whisperer), Jake Hayman, Brittany Smith,

Darshan Sanghrajka, Nusrat Faizullah, Dan Paskins, Fozia Irfan, Ben Lindsay, Lily Lewis, Dr Debbie Weekes-Bernard, Rebekah Delsol, Anna de Pulford, Kamna Muralidharan, Alison Holdom, Professor Nicola Rollock, Zara Todd, Rinku Sen, Eric Dawson, Stephen Bediako, Kristina Johansson, Rose Longhurst, Fatima Iftikhar, Jacqui Dyer, Hannah Paterson, Baljit Banga, Tokunbo Ajasa-Oluwa, Asma Shah, Professor Gus John, Tara Flood, Julia Parnaby, Angela Saini, Michelle Moore, Dawn Plimmer, Chris Grant, Sidney Hargro, Sufina Ahmad, Rowena Estwick, Nani Jansen Reventlow, Shasta Ali and many more.

A massive respect goes out to Sharmaine Lovegrove and Maisie Lawrence and everyone at Dialogue Books for your faith in this book and unbelievable guidance and belief, and to my agent Oli Munson.

And finally, please check out some of these great organisations that exemplify many of the principles and characteristics outlined in this book. Among them, Black Thrive Global – https://blackthrive.org/, Rekindle – https://www.rekindleschool.org/, Ubele Initiative – https://www.ubele.org/, YARD Art House – https://www.yardarthouse.co/, Civic Square – https://civicsquare.cc/, Centre for Knowledge Equity – https://knowledgeequity.org/, Baobab Foundation – https://www.baobabfoundation.org.uk/, Contextual Safeguarding Network – https://contextualsafeguarding.org.uk/, Edge Fund – https://www.edgefund.org.uk/team, Healing Justice London – https://healingjusticeldn.org/, Good Ancestors Movement – https://www.goodancestormovement.com/, Super Being Labs – https://superbeinglabs.org/, Imkaan – https://www.imkaan.org.uk/, Project 507 – https://

project507.org/, You Make It! – https://www.you-make-it.org/, Communities Empowerment Network – http://cenlive.org/, Sisters Uncut – https://www.sistersuncut.org/, Alliance for Inclusive Education (ALLFIE) – https://www.allfie.org.uk/, Voices that Shake! – https://voicesthatshake.org/, Tipping Point – https://tippingpointuk.org/, Racial Justice Network – https://racialjusticenetwork.co.uk/, brap – https://www.brap.org.uk/ and Charity So White – https://charitysowhite.org/, Future Foundations UK – https://www.futurefoundationsuk.org/, Black Funding Network – https://www.blackfundingnetwork.org/, Granville Community Kitchen – https://granvillecommunitykitchen.org.uk/about/, Glitch – https://glitchcharity.co.uk/, The Black Curriculum – https://theblackcurriculum.com/, to name a few.

If you want to be kept up to date with the latest developments in philanthropy, please go to: http://www.tenyearstime.com.

References

1. During the Baobab Foundation's *Wealth Redistribution: Advancing Racial Justice* event, one of the speakers mentioned Cornell West's line, 'Justice is what love looks like in public'. One of the panellists, Vanessa Thomas from the Decolonizing Wealth Project, went on to say that 'reparations is love in public'. The epigraph is an adaptation of the two lines.
2. Whitney Iles, [@Whitney_Iles], (7 January 2022), [Tweet], Twitter, https://twitter.com/Whitney_Iles/status/1479589157106339841'

Introduction: Beyond the reserve's line

1. Derek A. Bardowell, 'They Just Don't Know: New and Pioneering Approaches to Tackling Racial Injustice in the Education System', Winston Churchill Memorial Trust, https://media.churchillfellowship.org/documents/Bardowell_D_Report_2014_Final.pdf.
2. Smitha Mundasad, 'Black people "twice as likely to catch coronavirus"', BBC News, https://www.bbc.co.uk/news/health-54907473.
3. Julie Unwin, Foreword, 'Civil Society in England: its current state and future opportunity', Civil Society Futures, https://civilsocietyfutures.org/wp-content/uploads/sites/6/2018/11/Civil-Society-Futures__Civil-Society-in-England__small-1.pdf, p.4.
4. 'UK Civil Society Almanac 2021', NCVO, https://beta.ncvo.org.uk/ncvo-publications/uk-civil-society-almanac-2021/profile/what-do-voluntary-organisations-do/.
5. Larry Elliott, 'World's 26 richest people own as much as poorest 50%, says Oxfam', *Guardian*, 21 Jan 2019, https://www.theguardian.com/business/2019/jan/21/world-26-richest-people-own-as-much-as-poorest-50-per-cent-oxfam-report.
6. Jason Hickel, Dylan Sullivan, Huzaifa Zoomkawala, 'Rich countries drained $152tn from the global South since 1960', Al Jazeera, 6 May 2021, https://www.aljazeera.com/opinions/2021/5/6/rich-countries-drained-152tn-from-the-global-south-since-1960. Haseeb Shabbir from the University of Hull mentioned this when I sat on a panel with him during the BAME Fundraising Conference on 28 July 2021.
7. Eoin McSweeney and Adam Pourahmadi, '2% of Elon Musk's wealth could help solve world hunger, says director of UN food scarcity organization', CNN Business, 1 November 2021, https://edition.cnn.com/2021/10/26/economy/musk-world-hunger-wfp-intl/index.html.
8. Kirsty Weakley, 'Public trust in charities has improved but there's more to do, says Commission', Civil Society News, 16 June 2020, https://www.civilsociety.co.uk/news/public-trust-in-charities-improves-but-there-s-more-to-do-says-commission.html.

9. 'UK Civil Society Almanac 2021', https://data.ncvo.org.uk/impact/.
10. ibid.; 'CAF UK Giving 2019: An overview of charitable giving in the UK', CAF, https://www.cafonline.org/docs/default-source/about-us-publications/caf-uk-giving-2019-report-an-overview-of-charitable-giving-in-the-uk.pdf?sfvrsn=c4a29a40_4.
11. Steven Dilworth, 'Why are the poor more generous than the wealthy?', Civil Society, 12 June 2013, https://www.civilsociety.co.uk/voices/why-are-the-poor-more-generous-than-the-wealthy-.html.
12. Patricia Hill Collins, *Black Feminist Thought: Knowledge, Consciousness, and the Politics of Empowerment*, Oxfordshire: Routledge, 2009. p. 12.
13. Leslie Lenkowsky, 'A Crucial Complement, Not a Replacement', *New York Times*, 27 November 2012, https://www.nytimes.com/roomfordebate/2012/11/27/are-charities-more-effective-than-government/a-crucial-complement-not-a-replacement.

Smirks and fever

1. Arundhati Roy, 'The pandemic is a portal', *Financial Times*, 4 April 2020, https://www.ft.com/content/10d8f5e8-74eb-11ea-95fe-fcd274e920ca.
2. Busra Nur Bilgic Cakmak, 'Virus death toll in hard-hit Europe passes 80,000', Anadolu Agency, 17 April 2020, https://www.aa.com.tr/en/europe/virus-death-toll-in-hard-hit-europe-passes-80-000/1808288.
3. John Johnston, 'Patrick Vallance says keeping coronavirus death toll below 20,000 would be "good outcome"', Politics Home, 17 March 2020, https://www.politicshome.com/news/article/uks-chief-scientific-adviser-says-20000-coronavirus-deaths-would-be-good-outcome.
4. Toby Helm, 'UK can keep COVID-19 deaths below 20,000, says medical director', *Guardian*, 28 March 2020, https://www.theguardian.com/world/2020/mar/28/uk-can-keep-COVID-19-deaths-below-20000-says-medical-director.
5. Boris Johnson on *This Morning*, 5 March 2020, https://www.youtube.com/watch?v=vOHiaPwtGl4&feature=youtu.be.
6. https://www.theguardian.com/law/2020/jul/08/one-in-10-of-londons-young-black-males-stopped-by-police-in-may.
7. Robert Booth, 'Britons feeling far less satisfied with life, official data shows', *Guardian*, 6 February 2020, https://www.theguardian.com/world/2020/feb/06/britons-feeling-far-less-satisfied-life-official-data-shows.'
8. W. E. B. Du Bois, *The Souls of Black Folk*, New York: New American Library, Inc, 1903, pp.10, 29.
9. This phrase came from an interview I conducted with multidisciplinary artist and creative producer Amahra Spence.
10. Robert Booth, 'BAME groups hit harder by COVID-19 than white people, UK study suggests', *Guardian*, 7 April 2020, https://www.theguardian.com/world/2020/apr/07/bame-groups-hit-harder-COVID-19-than-white-people-uk.
11. 'UK lockdown: Calls to domestic abuse helpline jump by half', BBC News, 27 April 2020, https://www.bbc.co.uk/news/uk-52433520.
12. Alastair Parvin, 'A New Land Contract', Medium, 21 June 2020, https://alastairparvin.medium.com/a-new-land-contract-684c3ba1f1b3.
13. Sarah-Marie Hall, Kimberly McIntosh, Eva Neitzert, Laura Pottinger, Kalwinder Sandhu, Mary-Ann Stephenson, Howard Reed and Leonie

Taylor. 'Intersecting Inequalities: the impact of austerity on Black and Minority Ethnic women in the UK', Runnymede Trust, https://www.runnymedetrust.org/uploads/PressReleases/Correct%20WBG%20report%20for%20Microsite.pdf, p.33.

14. Amelia Hill, '"Hostile environment": the hardline Home Office policy tearing families apart', *Guardian*, 28 November 2017, https://www.theguardian.com/uk-news/2017/nov/28/hostile-environment-the-hardline-home-office-policy-tearing-families-apart.

15. Sonia Sodha, 'NHS heroes … and targets of racists', *Guardian*, 5 April 2020, https://www.theguardian.com/world/2020/apr/05/nhs-heroes-and-targets-of-racists.

16. Sonia Sodha, Tweet, 2 April 2020, https://twitter.com/soniasodha/status/1245383818867064835?lang=en.

17. Afua Hirsch, 'If coronavirus doesn't discriminate, how come black people are bearing the brunt?', *Guardian*, 8 April 2020, https://www.theguardian.com/commentisfree/2020/apr/08/coronavirus-black-people-ethnic-minority-deaths-pandemic-inequality-afua-hirsch.

18. Aamna Mohdin, Glenn Swann, Caroline Bannock, 'How George Floyd's death sparked a wave of UK anti-racism protests', *Guardian*, 29 July 2020, https://www.theguardian.com/uk-news/2020/jul/29/george-floyd-death-fuelled-anti-racism-protests-britain.

19. Nadie White, 'Black Lives Matter Sparks "Largest Racial Justice Movement In UK History"', Huffington Post, 13 November 2020, https://www.huffingtonpost.co.uk/entry/black-lives-matter-petitions-protests-racial-justice_uk_5fa12dc2c5b6c588dc9561f2.

20. Munira Mirza, 'Lammy review: the myth of institutional racism', Spiked, 11 September 2017, https://www.spiked-online.com/2017/09/11/lammy-review-the-myth-of-institutional-racism/.

21. Tony Sewell, 'Master class in victimhood', *Prospect*, 22 September 2010, https://www.prospectmagazine.co.uk/magazine/black-boys-victimhood-school.

22. Cressida Dick, Home Affairs Committee Oral Evidence, House of Commons, 8 July 2020, https://committees.parliament.uk/oralevidence/668/pdf/, p.9.

23. Mattha Busby, 'Schools in England told not to use material from anti-capitalist groups', *Guardian*, 27 September 2020, https://www.theguardian.com/education/2020/sep/27/uk-schools-told-not-to-use-anti-capitalist-material-in-teaching.

24. The Rt Hon Elizabeth Trusts MP, 'Fight For Fairness', speech, 17 December 2020, https://capx.co/the-new-fight-for-fairness-liz-truss-speech-at-the-centre-for-policy-studies/.

25. Anti Racism Steering Group, 'The Sewell Report: an example of institutional racism', blog, Shelter, 7 April 2021, https://blog.shelter.org.uk/2021/04/the-sewell-report-an-example-of-institutional-racism/.

26. 'Runnymede Trust "disturbed" at Sewell report failings', Ekklesia, 2 April 2021, https://www.ekklesia.co.uk/2021/04/02/runnymede-trust-responds-to-sewell-report/.

27. ibid.

28. Nazia Parveen and Aamna Mohdin, 'Tory MPs demand inquiry into equality thinktank over race report criticism', *Guardian*, 20 April 2021, https://www.theguardian.com/world/2021/apr/20/

tory-mps-demand-inquiry-runnymede-trust-thinktank-race-report-criticism-charity-commission.
29. Toni Morrison, 'Racism and fascism', *The Journal of Negro Education*; Washington, Vol. 64, Iss. 3 (Summer 1995).
30. Haroon Siddique, 'Marcus Rashford forces Boris Johnson into second U-turn on child food poverty', *Guardian*, 8 November 2020, https://www.theguardian.com/education/2020/nov/08/marcus-rashford-forces-boris-johnson-into-second-u-turn-on-child-food-poverty.

My space, my city, my world

1. Rhodri Davies, *Public Good By Private Means: How Philanthropy Shapes Britain*, London: Alliance Publishing Trust, 2015, p.8.
2. Frank Prochaska, *Women and Philanthropy in 19th Century England*, Oxford: Oxford University Press, p.358.

The way, by charities

1. Rose Longhurst, 'Plurocratic philanthropy: Elite influence in philanthropic foundations and participatory grantmakers', https://participatorygrantmaking.issuelab.org/resource/plutocratic-philanthropy-elite-influence-in-philanthropic-foundations-and-participatory-grantmakers.html, p.11.
2. Kirsty Weakley, '99 per cent of trustees at charitable foundations are white', Civil Society News, 28 June 2018, https://www.civilsociety.co.uk/news/99-per-cent-of-trustees-at-charity-foundations-are-white.html.
3. Paul Vallely, 'How philanthropy benefits the super-rich', *Guardian*, 8 September 2020, https://www.theguardian.com/society/2020/sep/08/how-philanthropy-benefits-the-super-rich.
4. Jane Mayer, *Dark Money, The Hidden History of the Billionaires Behind the Rise of the Radical Right*, New York: Anchor Books, 2017, p.3.
5. 'Charity Income Spotlight Report', Charity Financials, https://www.charityfinancials.com/insights/reports/charity-financials-income-spotlight-report-2020.
6. Darren Walker, *From Generosity to Justice: A New Gospel of Wealth*, New York: Ford Foundation, 2019, p.14.
7. Stephanie Brobbey, 'Is it Time to Rethink Private Wealth?', Medium, 16 March 2021, https://stephanie-brobbey.medium.com/is-it-time-to-rethink-private-wealth-e0311296253f.
8. Iris Bohnet, Siri Chilazi, Anisha Asundi, Lili Gil Valletta, 'Be like an orchestra: how to eliminate gender bias in venture capital funding', King's College London News Centre, 29 October 2019, https://www.kcl.ac.uk/news/be-like-an-orchestra-how-to-eliminate-gender-bias-in-venture-capital-funding.

The wrong side of history

1. Angela Y. Davis, *Are Prisons Obsolete?*, New York: Seven Stories Press, 2011, p.107.
2. 'Small & Medium-sized charities after the crash: what happened & why it matters', Lloyds Bank Foundation, https://www.lloydsbankfoundation.org.uk/media/1fmb2eyp/small-charities-after-the-crash-summary.pdf, p.5.
3. ibid., p.1.
4. Karl Murray, 'Impact of COVID-19 on the BAME community and

voluntary sector: Final report of the research conducted between 19 March and 4 April 2020', Ubele, April 2020, https://static1.squarespace.com/static/58f9e592440243412051314a/t/5eaab6e972a49d5a320cf3af/1588246258540/REPORT+Impact+of+COVID-19+on+the+BAME+Community+and+voluntary+sector%2C+30+April+2020.pdf, p.7.

5. Priya Kantaria, '#CharitySoWhite campaign calls for "urgent action" to tackle racism in charities', Civil Society News, 20 August 2019, https://www.civilsociety.co.uk/news/charitysowhite-campaign-launches-to-highlight-racism-in-the-sector.html.

6. 'Racial Injustice in the COVID-19 Response', Charity So White, 2 April 2020, https://charitysowhite.org/press/putting-racial-justice-and-the-bame-communities-at-the-heart-of-the-response-to-COVID-19.

7. Derek Bardowell, 'COVID-19 and racial disparity: A time for urgent action', Association of Charitable Foundations, 15 July 2020, https://acf.org.uk/ACF/Blog/2020/July-20/Blog-COVID-19-and-racial-disparity-A-time-for-urgent-action-reflections-from-Derek-Bardowell.aspx?WebsiteKey=d0f7ae78-c224-4dd2-b51e-ee543629d1b2.

8. Fozia Irfan, 'In unprecedented crisis, funders aren't reaching BAME communities', *Alliance* magazine, 11 June 2020, https://www.alliancemagazine.org/blog/unprecedented-crisis-funders-arent-reaching-bame-communities/.

9. 'Interim Report on the Connections between Colonialism and Properties now in the Care of the National Trust, Including Links with Historic Slavery', National Trust, https://nt.global.ssl.fastly.net/documents/colionialism-and-historic-slavery-report.pdf.

10. 'White privilege – a guide for parents', Barnardo's, 30 October 2020, https://www.barnardos.org.uk/blog/white-privilege-guide-for-parents/.

11. Baroness Stowell, 'If you want to improve lives through charity, leave political fights out of it, writes Charity Commission chair', *Daily Mail*, 29 November 2020, https://www.dailymail.co.uk/debate/article-8996635/Charity-Commission-chair-BARONESS-STOWELL-Leave-political-fights-charity.html/.

Conclusion

1. Joel Gallen (dir.), *Chris Rock: Never Scared*, 2004, 47:21.

2. Arundhati Roy, *The End of Imagination*, Chicago: Haymarket Books, 2016, 'The NGO-ization of Resistance', extracted in Kana'an Online, 7 February 2018, https://kanaanonline.org/en/2018/02/07/the-ngo-ization-of-resistance-by-arundhati-roy/.

3. ibid., p.1.

4. Edgar Villanueva, 'On Redemption: Excerpt from "Decolonizing Wealth"', Medium, 15 May 2018, https://medium.com/@VillanuevaEdgar/on-redemption-excerpt-from-decolonizing-wealth-d6b1fa3f0366.

5. Brian Obara, 'Britain's new Foreign Secretary on Africa: "The problem is not that we were once in charge, but that we are not in charge any more"', This is Africa, 14 July 2016, https://thisisafrica.me/politics-and-society/britains-new-foreign-secretary-africa-problem-not-charge-not-charge/.

6. Rob Reich, *Just Giving: Why Philanthropy Is Failing Democracy and How It Can Do Better*, Princeton: Princeton University Press, 2018, p.168.

7. 'The Story of Our Times: shifting power, bridging divides, transforming society', Civil Society Futures, https://civilsocietyfutures.org/wp-content/

uploads/sites/6/2018/11/Civil-Society-Futures__The-Story-of-Our-Future.pdf, p.11.

8. Rob Reich, *Just Giving: Why philanthropy is failing democracy and how it can do better*, New Jersey: Princeton University Press, p.197.

Public enemy

1. Talia Soghomonian, 'How Public Enemy Became The Most Exciting Band On The Planet – A Classic NME Interview With Chuck D', *NME*, 31 July 2015, https://www.nme.com/features/how-public-enemy-became-the-most-exciting-band-on-the-planet-a-classic-nme-interview-with-chuck-d-756840.

2. Chuck D with Yusuf Jah, *Fight the Power: Rap, Race and Reality*, Edinburgh: Payback Press, 1997, p. 256.

3. Derek A. Bardowell, 'No more techno terror', *The Voice*, 27 September 1999.

The half that is never told

1. Derek A. Bardowell, 'The Half that Has Never Been Told', The Weeklings, 20 April 2013, https://theweeklings.com/dbardowell/2013/04/20/the-half-that-has-never-been-told/.

Ella Baker

1. Barbara Ransby, *Ella Baker & the Black Freedom Movement: A Radical Democratic Vision*, North Carolina: University of North Carolina, 205, p.261.

2. The Stuart Hall Project, BFI.

Conclusion

1. Bryan Stevenson, *Just Mercy: A Story of Justice and Redemption*, New York: Random House, 2014, p.18.

2. Stephen Martin, Joseph Marks, *8 Ways to Get Heard*, London: Random House Business, 2019, p.62.

Reparatory justice

1. Angela Davis in conversation with Jackie Kay, Manchester Literature Festival, 25 October 2020.

2. PISAB workshop.

3. 'Ron Chisom', Ashoka, https://www.ashoka.org/en/fellow/ron-chisom.

4. PISAB workshop.

5. HM Treasury response to Freedom of Information enquiry, 31 January 2018, https://assets.publishing.service.gov.uk/government/uploads/system/uploads/attachment_data/file/680456/FOI2018-00186_-_Slavery_Abolition_Act_1833_-_pdf_for_disclosure_log__003_.pdf.

6. Kimberly Latrice Jones, speech, https://www.rev.com/blog/transcripts/kimberly-latrice-jones-blm-video-speech-transcript.

7. Mary Pilon, 'The secret history of Monopoly: the capitalist board game's leftwing origins', *Guardian*, 11 April 2015, https://www.theguardian.com/lifeandstyle/2015/apr/11/secret-history-monopoly-capitalist-game-leftwing-origins.

8. Sebastian Ordoñez Muñoz, speech, Interdependence Festival, London, 22–23 November 2019.

9. Harpreet Kaur Paul, speech, Interdependence Festival, London, 22–23 November 2019.
10. 'ICTJ Program Report: Reparative Justice', ICTJ, 13 May 2013, https://www.ictj.org/news/ictj-program-report-reparative-justice#:~:text=Reparations%20in%20Chile%20and%20 Argentina,serious%20crimes%2C%20and%20reform%20institutions.
11. Stuart Hall, 1991, in Les Back and John Solomos (ed.), *Theories of Race and Racism: A Reader (second edition)*. Oxfordshire: Routledge, 2009, p.202.
12. Brian Gordon, 'As NC cities move toward reparations, will 'piecemeal' resolutions hinder federal support?', *Citizen Times*, 7 August 2021, https://eu.citizen-times.com/in-depth/news/2021/08/07/nc-cities-move-toward-reparations-they-hinder-federal-support/7956914002/.
13. William Darity Jr. and Darrick Hamilton, 'Make every child a trust fund baby', *News & Observer*, 18 January 2018, https://www.newsobserver.com/opinion/op-ed/article195470249.html.
14. Lynn Parramore, 'Baby Bonds: A Plan for Black/White Wealth Equality Conservatives Could Love?', Institute for New Economic Thinking, 25 October 2016, https://www.ineteconomics.org/perspectives/blog/baby-bonds-a-plan-for-black-white-wealth-equality-conservatives-could-love-1.
15. Annie Lowrey, 'A Cheap, Race-Neutral Way to Close the Racial Wealth Gap', *The Atlantic*, 29 June 2020, https://www.theatlantic.com/ideas/archive/2020/06/close-racial-wealth-gap-baby-bonds/613525/.
16. Farzana Khan and Rose Ziaei (eds.), *Voices that Shake!: Shake! The System Research Report – A Decade of Shaping Change 2010-2020*, London: Voices that Shake!, 2021, p.19.
17. Shakir Mohamed, Marie-Therese Png, William Isaac, 'Decolonial AI: Decolonial Theory and Sociotechnical Foresight in Artificial Intelligence', *Philosophy & Technology* (2020) 33:659–684, https://link.springer.com/content/pdf/10.1007/s13347-020-00405-8.pdf, p.664.
18. Anna Jones, 'How did New Zealand become COVID-19 free?', BBC News, 10 July 2020, https://www.bbc.co.uk/news/world-asia-53274085.

Knowledge equity

1. 'The Value of Lived Experience in Social Change', Clore Social Leadership, 3 August 2017 (updated 22 October 2020), https://cloresocialleadership.org.uk/blogpost/1885767/359205/The-value-of-lived-experience-in-social-change
2. Baljeet Sandhu, 'The Value of Lived Experience in Social Change: The Need for Organisational and Leadership Development in the Social Sector', Clore Social Leadership, 2017 https://knowledgeequity.org/publications/
3. Baljeet Sandhu, 'Lived Experience Leadership: Rebooting the DNA of Leadership', Clore Social Leadership (CLS) and the Knowledge Equity Initiative at the Tsai Center for Innovative Thinking at Yale (Tsai CITY), 2019, https://knowledgeequity.org/publications/
4. 'Violence Against Children in Kenya: Findings from a 2010 National Survey', https://evaw-global-database.unwomen.org/-/media/files/un%20women/vaw/full%20text/africa/kenya%20violence%20against%20children%20survey%20%202010.pdf?vs=1219.

Collective care

1. Anna Minton, 'The Price of Regeneration', *Places Journal*, September 2018, https://placesjournal.org/article/the-price-of-regeneration-in-london/?cn-reloaded=1; Owen Hatherley, 'Liverpool's rotting, shocking "housing renewal": how did it come to this?', *Guardian*, 27 March 2013, https://www.theguardian.com/commentisfree/2013/mar/27/liverpool-rotting-housing-renewal-pathfinder.
2. Claire Schwartz, 'When June Jordan and Buckminster Fuller Tried to Redesign Harlem', *New Yorker*, 22 August 2020, https://www.newyorker.com/culture/culture-desk/when-june-jordan-and-buckminster-fuller-tried-to-redesign-harlem.
3. June Meyer, 'Instant Slum Clearance', *Esquire*, 1 April 1965, https://classic.esquire.com/article/1965/4/1/instant-slum-clearance.
4. David Brooks, quoted at https://civicsquare.cc/2020/03/09/civic-square-2020-2030/.
5. Alastair Parvin, 'A New Land Contract', Medium, 21 June 2020, https://alastairparvin.medium.com/a-new-land-contract-684c3ba1f1b3.
6. Bardowell, 'They Just Don't Know', p.13.
7. Bob Herbert, 'Men and Jobs', *New York Times* Opinion, 30 September 1996, https://www.nytimes.com/1996/09/30/opinion/men-and-jobs.html.
8. 'Whatever It Takes: A White Paper on the Harlem Children's Zone', https://hcz.org/wp-content/uploads/2014/04/HCZ-White-Paper.pdf.
9. Sherri Geng, 'Meet HBS Leadership Fellows: Sherri Geng, Harlem Children's Zone', blog, Harvard Business School Social Enterprise, 8 May 2018, https://www.hbs.edu/socialenterprise/blog/post/sherri-geng-harlem-childrens-zone.
10. 'Healthy Harlem', Harlem Children's Zone, https://hcz.org/our-programs/healthy-harlem/.
11. 'Geoffrey Canada', Harlem Children's Zone, https://hcz.org/about-us/leadership/geoffrey-canada/.
12. Cheryl Greenberg, Review of *Hands on the Freedom Plow: Personal Accounts by Women in SNCC*, Urbana: University of Illinois Press, 2010. https://muse.jhu.edu/article/449048.

Radical solidarity

1. 'The Life & Death of Ken Saro-Wiwa: a history of the struggle for justice in the Niger Delta', Platform, http://remembersarowiwa.com/wp-content/uploads/life_death_ksw.pdf.
2. Jane Trowell 'White art for the few, extracted from the many', speech, Interdependence Festival, London, 23 November 2019.
3. 'The Life & Death of Ken Saro-Wiwa'.
4. 'Oil uprising: Two decades after Ken Saro-Wiwa's death, the Ogoni struggle is reigniting', War on Want, 12 March 2014,https://waronwant.org/news-analysis/oil-uprising-two-decades-after-ken-saro-wiwas-death-ogoni-struggle-reigniting.
5. 'NIGERIA: THE OGONI CRISIS: A Case-Study Of Military Repression In Southeastern Nigeria' Human Rights Watch, July 1995, https://www.hrw.org/reports/1995/Nigeria.htm.
6. 'The Life & Death of Ken Saro-Wiwa'.
7. ibid.

8. ibid.
9. Ben Amunwa, 2021, in Sai Murray, Farzana Khan, Tiff Webster and Rose Ziaei (ed.), *Voices That Shake! An Anthology of Creative Movements. Voices that Shake!* UK: Voices That Shake! p.234.
10. Derek A. Bardowell (host), *Just Cause*, podcast, Anchor, 2019–present, https://anchor.fm/derek-bardowell/episodes/Farzana-Khan--Sai-Murray-on-Voices-that-Shake--and-Environmental-Justice-e8arln.
11. Luke de Noronha, 'Dismantling immigration controls and the struggle for liveable futures', speech, Interdependence Festival, London, 22 November 2019.
12. Tessa Khan, 'Local and international strategies and solidarity', speech, Interdependence Festival, London, 22 November 2019.
13. Ed Pilkington, 'Shell pays out $15.5m over Saro-Wiwa killing, *Guardian*, 9 June 2009, https://www.theguardian.com/world/2009/jun/08/nigeria-usa.
14. Andy Rowell, 'Ogoni 9: 24 years after their execution, court told by key witness: "Yes, Shell bribed me."', Oil Change International, 11 October 2019, http://priceofoil.org/2019/10/11/ogoni-9-24-years-after-their-execution-court-told-by-key-witness-yes-shell-bribed-me/.
15. Harald Fuhr, 'The Global South's contribution to the climate crisis – and its potential solutions', OECD Development Matters, 20 June 2019, https://oecd-development-matters.org/2019/06/20/the-global-souths-contribution-to-the-climate-crisis-and-its-potential-solutions/.
16. de Noronha, 'Dismantling immigration controls and the struggle for liveable futures'.

Self determination

1. Joshua Bloom and Waldo E. Martin, *Black Against Empire: The History of the Black Panther Party*, Oakland: University of California Press, 2016, p.13.
2. Huey P. Newton, 'Functional Definition of Politics', *The Black Panther*, 17 January 1969, https://www.marxists.org/archive/newton/1969/01/17.htm.
3. 'The Black Panthers: Ten Point Program', http://www.blacklivesmattersyllabus.com/wp-content/uploads/2016/07/BPP_Ten_Point_Program.pdf.
4. ibid.
5. Stephen Shames and Bobby Seale, B, *Power To The People: The World of the Black Panthers*, New York: Abrams, 2016, p.24.
6. Kehinde Andrews, 'Fifty years since the Black Panthers formed, here's what Black Lives Matter can learn', *Guardian*, 14 October 2016, https://www.theguardian.com/commentisfree/2016/oct/14/fifty-years-black-panthers-formed-black-lives-matter-revolutionary.
7. Huey P. Newton, Toni Morrison (ed.), *To Die for the People: The Writings of Huey P. Newton*, San Francisco: City Lights Books, 2009, pp.100–101.
8. Mike Konczal, 'Mental Note: Link Black Panther Free Lunch Program, OWS Infrastructure', blog, 19 January 2012, https://rortybomb.wordpress.com/2012/01/19/mental-note-link-black-panther-free-lunch-program-ows-infrastructure/.
9. ibid.
10. Arielle Milkman, 'The Radical Origins of Free Breakfast for Children',

Eater, 16 February 2016, https://www.eater.com/2016/2/16/11002842/free-breakfast-schools-black-panthers.

11. Kelsey Engstrom, 'The Black Panther Party: Freedom Fighters or Radicalists?', Leiden Law Blog, 10 October 2019, https://leidenlawblog.nl/articles/freedom-fighters-or-radicalists-the-black-panther-party; Ruth Gebreyesus, '"One of the biggest, baddest things we did": Black Panthers' free breakfasts, 50 years on', Guardian, 18 October 2019, https://www.theguardian.com/us-news/2019/oct/17/black-panther-party-oakland-free-breakfast-50th-anniversary.

12. Joshua Bloom and Waldo E. Martin, Black Against Empire: The History of the Black Panther Party, Oakland: University of California Press, 2016, p.392.

13. Paul Field, Robin E. R. Bunce, Leila Hassan, Margaret Peacock, Here to Stay, Here to Fight, London: Pluto Press, 2019, p.237.

14. Zahra Dalilah, '5 British Black Panther women whose names you should know', Gal-Dem, 21 April 2017, https://gal-dem.com/5-female-british-black-panthers-whose-names-know/.

15. Hannah Richardson, 'Marcus Rashford welcomes school holiday support climbdown', BBC News, 8 November 2020, https://www.bbc.co.uk/news/education-54841316.

16. '"Sou-sou": Black immigrants bring savings club stateside', The Grio, 20 May 2011, https://thegrio.com/2011/05/20/sou-sou-black-immigrants-bring-savings-club-stateside/.

17. Anca Voinea, 'ABCUL marks the 50th anniversary of the first credit union in Britain', Co-op News, 26 March 2014, https://www.thenews.coop/66718/sector/credit-unions/abcul-marks-50th-anniversary-first-credit-union-britain/.

18. Eshe Kiama Zuri, '"We've been organising like this since day" – why we must remember the Black roots of mutual aid groups', Gal-Dem, 5 June 2020, https://gal-dem.com/weve-been-organising-like-this-since-day-why-we-must-remember-the-black-roots-of-mutual-aid-groups/.

19. ibid.

20. Michelle Alexander, The New Jim Crow, New York: The New Press, 2010, p.9.

21. ibid., p.6.

22. Greg Jobin-Leeds and AgitArte, When We Fight We Win, New York: The New Press, 2016. P.53.3.

23. Kehinde Andrews, 'Fifty years since the Black Panthers formed, here's what Black Lives Matter can learn', Guardian, 14 October 2016, https://www.theguardian.com/commentisfree/2016/oct/14/fifty-years-black-panthers-formed-black-lives-matter-revolutionary.

24. 'Abahlali baseMjondolo', Thousand Currents, https://thousandcurrents.org/abahlali-basemjondolo-abm/

Root cause

1. Darren Walker, From Generosity to Justice: A New Gospel of Wealth, New York: Ford Foundation, 2019, p.20.

2. Denise Valenti, 'Benjamin's "Race After Technology" speaks to a growing concern among many of tech bias', Princeton University, 15 May 2020, https://www.princeton.edu/news/2020/05/15/benjamins-race-after-technology-speaks-growing-concern-among-many-tech-bias.

3. 'Prevent', Liberty, https://www.libertyhumanrights.org.uk/fundamental/prevent/.
4. Associated Press in Orlando, 'Stand-your-ground gun laws benefit whites more than blacks, experts say', *Guardian*, 17 October 2014, https://www.theguardian.com/us-news/2014/oct/17/stand-your-ground-white-black-gun-law-harm-fear.
5. Ed Pilkington and Suzanne Goldenberg, 'ALEC facing funding crisis from donor exodus in wake of Trayvon Martin row', *Guardian*, 3 December 2013, https://www.theguardian.com/world/2013/dec/03/alec-funding-crisis-big-donors-trayvon-martin.
6. Susan Wilf Ditkoff, Abe Grindle, 'Audacious Philanthropy', *Harvard Business Review*, September 2017, https://hbr.org/2017/09/audacious-philanthropy.
7. Tim Gee, *Counterpower: Making Change Happen*, Oxford: New Internationalist Publications Ltd, 2011, p.18.
8. E. Yong, 'The Tipping Point When Minority Views Take Over,' *The Atlantic*, 7 June 2018, https://www.theatlantic.com/science/archive/2018/06/the-tipping-point-when-minority-views-take-over/562307/.
9. Rensselaer Polytechnic Institute, 'Minority rules: Scientists discover tipping point for the spread of ideas', *Science Daily*, 26 July 2011, https://www.sciencedaily.com/releases/2011/07/110725190044.htm
10. *Counterpower*, p.30.

Abundance

1. Steve Barrow, Peter Dalton, *The Rough Guide to Reggae* (third edition), London: Rough Guides, 2013, pp.16-17.
2. Kevin O'Brien Chang, Wayne Chen *Reggae Routes: The Story of Jamaican Music*, Kingston: Ian Randle Publishers, 1998. p.71.
3. Hg Helps, 'The bloody general election that changed Jamaica', *Jamaica Observer*, 30 October 2012, https://www.jamaicaobserver.com/news/The-bloody-general-election-that-changed-Jamaica.
4. Noel Cymore Walker, 'DJ Kool Herc Is Ready to Bring Hip-Hop Back to Its Roots With a Museum in Jamaica', *Billboard*, 24 February 2020, https://www.billboard.com/music/rb-hip-hop/dj-kool-herc-jamaica-hip-hop-museum-interview-8551728/.

Outsider within

1. Combahee River Collective, 'The Combahee River Collective Statement', 1977, available at https://www.blackpast.org/african-american-history/combahee-river-collective-statement-1977/.
2. ibid.
3. Katy Steinmetz, 'She Coined the Term "Intersectionality" Over 30 Years Ago. Here's What It Means to Her Today', *Time*, 20 February 2020, https://time.com/5786710/kimberle-crenshaw-intersectionality/#:~:text=Kimberl%C3%A9%20Crenshaw%2C%20the%20law,inequality%20is%20not%20created%20equal.
4. Maureen Douabou, 'The MWASI Collective Prove That a Safe Space for Black Femmes is Not "Reverse Racism"', Here You Are, 4 April 2019, https://www.hereyouare.com/paris/the-mwasi-collective-prove-that-a-safe-space-for-black-femmes-is-not-reverse-racism/.
5. 'Breonna Taylor: Police officer charged but not over death',

BBC News, 23 September 2020, https://www.bbc.co.uk/news/world-us-canada-54273317.

6. Hakima Abbas, Kellea Miller, Guest Contributors, 'The Dire State of Funding for Black Feminist Movements—and What Donors Can Do About It', *Inside Philanthropy*, 8 May 2021, https://www.insidephilanthropy.com/home/2021/8/5/the-dire-state-of-funding-for-black-feminist-movementsand-what-donors-can-do-about-it

7. 'Impact of COVID-19 on the BAME community and voluntary sector', p.7.

8. '#SayHerName', African American Policy Forum, https://www.aapf.org/sayhername.

9. Kimberlé Crenshaw, 'Breonna Taylor and Bearing Witness to Black Women's Expendability', Medium, 9 October 2020, https://level.medium.com/breonna-taylor-and-bearing-witness-to-black-womens-expendability-472abf5f6cee.

10. Christopher Metress, 'Let the World See', blog, OUPblog, 26 September 2017, https://blog.oup.com/2017/09/emmett-till-funeral-history/.

11. 'Wangari Maathai Planted 30 Million Trees, 2004 Nobel Peace Prize Laureate', The Community, https://thecommunity.com/project/2004-nobel-peace-prize-wangari-maathai-30-million-trees/.

12. The Green Belt Movement, http://www.greenbeltmovement.org/.

13. Tyrone McKinley Freeman, *Madam C. J. Walker's Gospel of Giving: Black Women's Philanthropy During Jim Crow*, Urbana: University of Illinois Press, 2020, p.1.

14. ibid., p.190.

15. ibid., p.193.

16. ibid., pp.190–194.

17. Black Feminist Fund, https://www.blackfeministfund.org/english.

Liberatory visions

1. Ruha Benjamin, quoted in https://www.ruhabenjamin.com/.

2. Eduardo Galeano, *Football in Sun and Shadow*, London: Penguin Classics, 2018, p. 141.

3. Jonathan Wilson, *Inverting the Pyramid: The History of Football Tactics*, London: Orion Books, 2008, p.228.

4. Simon Kuper, *Barça: The rise and fall of the club that built modern football*, London: Short Books, 2021, p.42.

5. David Winner, *Brilliant Orange: The Neurotic Genius of Dutch Football*, London: Bloomsbury, 2012, p.73.

6. *Inverting the Pyramid*, p.224.

7. Angela Davis in conversation with Jackie Kay, Manchester Literature Festival, 25 October 2020.

8. Subcomandante Marcos, 'The fourth world war has begun', *Le Monde*, September 1997, https://mondediplo.com/1997/09/marcos.

9. Dr Alex Khasnabish, *Zapatistas: Rebellion from the Grassroots to the Global (Rebels)* London: Zed Books, 2010, p.1.

10. ibid., p.4.

11. '1994: The Zapatista uprising', Libcom, 19 September 2006, https://libcom.org/history/1994-the-zapatista-uprising.

12. *Zapatistas*, p.9.

13. 'Landless Workers Movement', Grassroots International,

https://grassrootsonline.org/who-we-are/partner/
landless-workers-movement-mst/.
14. Baljeet Sandhu, interview for this book.

A common project

1. Wangari Maathai, Nobel Lecture, 2004, https://www.nobelprize.org/
prizes/peace/2004/maathai/26050-wangari-maathai-nobel-lecture-
2004/#:~:text=In%20the%20course%20of%20history,That%20time%20
is%20now.
2. Antonio Gramsci in Les Back and John Solomos (Ed.), *Theories of Race
and Racism: A Reader (Second edition)*, Oxfordshire: Routledge, 2009,
p.679.
3. Roger Harrabin, 'Climate change: Young people very worried –
survey', *BBC News*, 14 September 2021, https://www.bbc.co.uk/news/
world-58549373.
4. Leyla Acaroglu, 'Employees want climate-positive action from companies.
Here's how they can deliver', *Reuters*, 16 December 2020, https://www.
reutersevents.com/sustainability/employees-want-climate-positive-action-
companies-heres-how-they-can-deliver.

Bringing a book from manuscript to what you are reading is a team effort.

Dialogue Books would like to thank everyone at Little, Brown who helped to publish *Giving Back* in the UK:

Editorial
Sharmaine Lovegrove
Amy Mae Baxter
Adriano Noble

Contracts
Anniina Vuori

Sales
Caitriona Row
Lucy Howkins
Lucy Hine
Hannah Methuen
Dominic Smith
Toluwalope Ayo-Ajala

Publicity
Millie Seaward

Marketing
Emily Moran
Elke Desanghere

Design
Nico Taylor
Nick Evans

Production
Narges Nojoumi

Copy Editor
David Bamford

Proof Reader
Alison Griffiths

Operations
Kellie Barnfield
Millie Gibson
Sanjeev Braich

Finance
Andrew Smith
Ellie Barry